Praise for *Reading Witho*

"Insightful, detailed, original; *Reading Without Limits* is an outstanding guide for educators."

—Deborah Kenny, Ph.D., founder and
chief executive officer, Harlem Village Academies

"*Reading Without Limits* isn't just a tool for you to help get kids to pass a test. Maddie Witter gives teachers and leaders the tools to create lasting change in kids' lives."

—Wendy Kopp, founder and CEO, Teach For America

"Maddie Witter is a stunning teacher and leader and has given us all a tremendous gift in sharing her practice with us within the pages of this book. Teachers, school leaders, and anyone else interested in ensuring your students become only the strongest, most avid readers should devour this book, keep it near, and use it again and again."

—Susan E. Toth, director of Secondary Academics, KIPP DC, former
principal of Mercer Middle School with the Seattle Public Schools

"The developments have truly been remarkable. Maddie Witter's practical techniques have revolutionized literacy education within our setting. Our students now use a diverse skill set to build a deeper understanding. Further, Maddie's potent, yet simple strategies have allowed our students to develop an appetite for reading and created lasting change."

—Matthew Hyde, campus principal,
Parkville Juvenile Justice Precinct, Melbourne, Australia

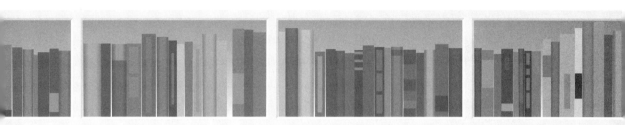

Reading Without Limits

Teaching Strategies to Build
Independent Reading for Life

Maddie Witter

Foreword by Dave Levin

JOSSEY-BASS
A Wiley Imprint
www.josseybass.com

Published by Jossey-Bass
A Wiley Imprint
One Montgomery Street, Suite 1200, San Francisco, CA 94104-4594 — www.josseybass.com

Jossey-Bass books and products are available through most bookstores. To contact Jossey-Bass directly call our Customer Care Department within the U.S. at 800-956-7739, outside the U.S. at 317-572-3986, or fax 317-572-4002.

Wiley also publishes its books in a variety of electronic formats and by print-on-demand. Some material included with standard print versions of this book may not be included in e-books or in print-on-demand. If the version of this book that you purchased references media such as CD or DVD that was not included in your purchase, you may download this material at http://booksupport .wiley.com. For more information about Wiley products, visit www.wiley.com.

Library of Congress Cataloging-in-Publication Data
Library of Congress Cataloging-in-Publication Data has been applied for and is on file with the Library of Congress.
ISBN 978-1-118-47215-6 (paper); ISBN 978-1-118-48373-2 (ebk.);
ISBN 978-1-118-48374-9 (ebk.); ISBN 978-1-118-48375-6 (ebk.)

Printed in the United States of America
FIRST EDITION
PB Printing   10 9 8 7 6 5 4 3 2 1

KIPP:
Educator Series

The key to KIPP's success is the remarkable team of teachers and principals who work at each KIPP school. We are excited to debut the KIPP Educator Series to share great ideas, practices, and proven strategies developed within KIPP schools. Each book in the series will feature work that has produced transformative results for students.

These books do not represent a single "official KIPP way." That's because at KIPP, we don't believe there is only one way to approach the teaching of any subject matter. In fact, great instruction often results from the synthesis of approaches previously considered diametric opposites and incompatible. Part of KIPP's credo is, "If there is a better way, we try to find it." As we find better ways, we will keep sharing them.

Rooted in a shared commitment to ensuring that all students will learn, KIPP teachers experiment and collaborate to maximize everyone's learning. KIPP encourages teachers to work together and share their practices in order to build off of each others' successes. And, when practices prove extraordinarily successful, as a team and a family we celebrate them. The KIPP Educator Series represents another way of sharing and celebrating these practices.

In this collection of books, educators will find practical examples, techniques, and approaches tried and tested in KIPP schools. We hope other educators will take these ideas and make them even better to help each and every student build a better tomorrow for themselves and us all.

To the students and families of KIPP Infinity Middle School

Contents

PART 3 **PUTTING THE POWER OF CHOICE, SHARED, AND GUIDED READING TO WORK IN YOUR CLASSROOM OR SCHOOL**

PART 4 **STEPS TO ENHANCE LIFELONG READERS**

PART 5 **PUTTING IT ALL TOGETHER**

Foreword

You've picked up a remarkable book written by a remarkable teacher, Maddie Witter. In *Reading Without Limits*, Maddie describes tried-and-true practices for teaching literacy and the research behind them in a simple and accessible manner. Maddie and countless other teachers have used these ideas to help thousands of kids transform their lives through reading—including the students at Maddie's former school, KIPP Infinity, which ranked number one out of New York City's 1,089 elementary and middle schools in 2008 and has since remained one of New York City's top-performing schools.

Reading, along with its companion skill, writing, is the gateway to deeper learning in the content areas, to higher education access, and to almost all career success. Since the earliest people populated this planet, reading has paved a path to knowledge and freedom.

Harriett Ball—one of the finest teachers in history, life-altering mentor to Mike Feinberg (KIPP's co-founder) and me, and one of the primary inspirations behind KIPP—enshrined reading's importance in this chant, popularized in KIPP schools nationwide:

"You got to read, baby, read. The more you read, the more you know. Knowledge is power and power is freedom and I want it!"

"I want it," is the wish, silent or stated, of every student who walks into every school in every city in the world. Sometimes they might not even know what "it" is yet. Nonetheless, they know they want "it"—let's call "it" the power to pursue their dreams. Reading is the key that opens almost all future opportunities.

Reading Without Limits starts by sharing some of the dispiriting statistics regarding literacy in the United States. Custom suggests that I do the same here. Instead, I'd prefer to share a small part of the story of one young boy and the life-altering difference a skilled teacher of literacy can make. That boy was me.

In 1979, my school informed my mom that I was reading several years below grade level. I was entering fourth grade. They told my mom that they weren't sure what was wrong with me or how to help me. Can you imagine that meeting? Scientific sounding words were used to describe the problem. You didn't need big words to describe my tears or my shame.

Leaving that meeting, my mom's resolve changed the course of my life. She refused to be discouraged. She found someone who could teach me—*really teach me.* Dr. Jeanette Jansky and I spent several hours a week together for nine years, until I graduated high school. Dr. Jansky taught me how to read, and that changed everything that followed. Learning to read transformed my shame into confidence. Learning to read opened the door for me to go to college, become a teacher, and help start KIPP. In short, learning to read unlocked my dreams.

Learning to read, however, shouldn't require a mom's extra commitment or the private services of a teacher as gifted as Dr. Jansky. Teaching reading should not be a mystery. But for too many kids and too many teachers, it is just that.

Reading instruction has always been fraught with ideological debates. In the 1990s it was whole language versus phonics. More recently, teacher-directed instruction has been contrasted to what's commonly known as a workshop-based approach. While well-meaning adults continue these intellectual debates with near religious zeal, our kids' literacy skills either fail to develop or atrophy after fourth grade. In Maddie's Introduction you'll find all the data you need—our kids aren't learning to read well and don't like reading.

Reading Without Limits defies categorization. It pulls great ideas from wherever they may be found—and that's exactly what kids need today. After all, anyone standing in front of kids every day knows this single fact: if it works, you use it.

Maddie unpacks the myriad of elements that make up effective reading instruction, including the triangle of shared reading, guided reading, and choice reading; vocabulary instruction; creating powerful reading assessments; and most important, how to make reading fun so that kids want to read for a lifetime. And she does this for all kids across all reading levels.

Thankfully, *Reading Without Limits* breaks each of these elements into easy to understand component parts. Maddie shows us how to start using these tools immediately "on Monday," as she says, and how to patiently develop the mastery that, to paraphrase K. Anders Ericsson, can only come from sustained deliberate practice.

As Maddie acknowledges gracefully throughout this book, *Reading Without Limits* "stands on the shoulders of giants," reflecting the collective insights of countless KIPP teachers. In 2005, KIPP Infinity was founded by Joe Negron who in his first year as principal hired five gifted educators—Maddie Witter, Michael Vea, Gerard Griffith, Dilcia Ceron, and Thomas Brunzell. Together, with Maddie leading their literacy efforts, they developed many of the ideas included in *Reading Without Limits*.

Each year since then, more remarkable teachers have joined both KIPP Infinity and the broader KIPP team. You'll meet many of them in these pages. I only wish you could meet them all. We are so fortunate that these amazing teachers used a combination of research and direct teaching experience to hone the elements of effective reading instruction. *Reading Without Limits* is the result of this work. And for this result we are extraordinarily grateful.

Dave Levin
New York City

Preface
Getting the Most out of This Book

You don't have to be a reading specialist to pick up this book. Anyone who wants to dramatically improve reading achievement will find helpful suggestions. You might be a third grade teacher whose students have mastered decoding, and you are ready to build their comprehension. Or you might be a high school English teacher whose students aren't yet reading on level with deep critical thinking. This book is for you. The primary audience for *Reading Without Limits* is teachers who want to raise reading achievement. The secondary audiences for this book are coaches, school leaders, and administrators who want to make programmatic changes. It doesn't matter whether you are a public, charter, private, or alternative education teacher. I've had the pleasure to work with teachers in all institutions, and the *Reading Without Limits* program works in each one.

THE PURPOSE OF *READING WITHOUT LIMITS*

Our entire literacy framework will be shared, including pitfalls that we discovered along the way. The book is designed to give a teacher, school, or district the guidebook and map to move their kids to the highest level of fervor, stamina, love of learning, and independent thinking. Not all teachers were as lucky as I to have had an incredible literacy coach beside me. The book is designed to accomplish what my coach, Jannett, accomplished for me: it will provide a framework, build confidence, offer perspective, and help do whatever it takes to get our kids to become lifelong, independently motivated learners.

I started teaching in 2002 in a low-income neighborhood in New York City after working as an elementary ELL guided reading teacher for several years. In 2002 I taught eighth grade special needs students, many emergent readers, most sixteen years old or older. Over the next ten years, I taught upper elementary through eighth grade reading, writing, and nonfiction studies for students at all ability levels. I also designed and supervised the literacy program at KIPP Infinity for six years, working with a team of dedicated, brilliant literacy teachers. Finally, I've had the pleasure to work with staffs across the United States and abroad to share strategies that boost literacy achievement.

Not every school looks like KIPP Infinity. Some teachers work in self-contained classrooms. Some alternative schools have class sizes of six. High school teachers can have nearly 200 students each. For the past seven years I've consulted with a range of educators. It's inspirational and extremely humbling. That's why I decided to write *Reading Without Limits*. The purpose of this book isn't about the particular literacy program at one individual KIPP school. Instead, it's to share all the *different ways* you can apply the strategies to make it work for your own community of scholars.

HOW TO USE THIS BOOK

What follows are chapters designed to get students reading without limits starting Monday. What sets the book apart from similar books is the practical approach it takes. I work with teachers who often are inspired by a great idea but don't know where to start in order to make their vision a reality. I also work with teachers who shoot for the stars for Monday's lesson, and are then tempted to give up on the stars when all they needed were some baby steps. This book will provide the baby steps necessary for teachers, coaches, and school leaders to make a change on Monday. It will also provide the tools to make a change for an entire school year, or even an entire literacy program, by providing the steps necessary to create the long-term love of learning, rigor, and stamina in each student. You might need the background research before applying practical strategies. That's why I made sure to couch everything in research. You might want to make tweaks to your class because your students are already doing well. Skim through the kid-friendly ideas and give one a try next week. Or you might want to make dramatic change to your school. In that case, apply the structural changes I suggest.

You will be able to mix and match how you want to implement suggestions from the book through the mild, medium, and spicy suggestions within each chapter. Each chapter is customizable for you and your kids, but no matter what combination you choose, you will be building *Reading Without Limits* learners.

Each chapter is divided into the following sections:

Kid-Friendly Teaching Ideas

Each chapter includes research based, ready-to-use, fun ideas. They can be implemented tomorrow with not a lot of set up. You don't need to include all to have a successful classroom. I hope that they will inspire more kid-friendly ideas of your own.

Keepin' It Real

Building a literacy program isn't easy. There will be times, many times, when all doesn't go as planned. Following each chapter are common pitfalls that many others have experienced along the way, so they won't happen to you.

Mild, Medium, Spicy

Sometimes we want to spend hours painting a mural in our class, other times the thought of spending five minutes stapling causes us to grimace because we are late getting home. Because teaching is not a nine-to-five job, we need time-efficient ways to make things happen in our classroom. Each chapter is divided into big ideas. The mild, medium, spicy table at the end of each chapter shows how to make those ideas happen based on time. Mild = less time. Spicy = more time. Mix and match to suit your needs.

For Coaches and School Leaders

Suggestions at the end of each chapter are included for how to make the chapter's big ideas a reality in your school. This section is specifically intended for administrators as a supplement to the chapter's content.

Additional Resources

Because we created so many strategies that work, we needed another forum to include more resources. We created www.reading-without-limits.com, which includes videos, interviews, webinars, podcasts, reproducibles, and lesson plans.

To Sum Up

We need review to remember, so the chapter ends with the biggest ideas.

Reading Without Limits Checklist

In the first pages you'll find the *Reading Without Limits* Checklist, which lists all of the kid-friendly teaching ideas in one place. Use it as a reminder, a self-assessment, or a bag of tricks.

Struggling Readers

This book is not for struggling readers. It is for all readers. However, most of the population of kids in schools where I've worked entered far below reading level. The principles of *Reading Without Limits* hold true for all readers, including disengaged readers. In order to raise struggling students' achievement, research suggests[1] to

- Model explicit direct instruction
- Create specific knowledge goals
- Provide frequent, specific feedback
- Create tasks that are challenging, but doable
- Link learning to real life
- Teach how to accurately self-assess
- Give students an abundance of interesting books that gives them some control and choice
- Encourage interactive learning

Text boxes throughout *Reading Without Limits* will show how chapters align to these learning principles, and how the principles directly impact struggling or disengaged learners. All of the *Reading Without Limits* strategies hold true for all of our readers, regardless of ability or interest in reading.

Nonfiction Studies

This book includes strategies that literacy teachers can use, regardless of grade level or genre. Content teachers who want to teach reading strategies should use strategies recommended in this book. Nonfiction needs to be thoroughly integrated into all aspects of the *Reading Without Limits* literacy program.

Make It Your Own

The *Reading Without Limits* program is not a one-size-fits-all program. Use this book as a guidebook and implement strategies that will work for your school, your classroom, and your kids.

MEET OUR STUDENTS

Throughout *Reading Without Limits*, I tell the true stories of students that I've worked with throughout the past 12 years. To protect the privacy of my students and their families, I've changed student names.

ON THE SHOULDERS OF GIANTS

This book was written on the shoulders of giants: dedicated educators who are committed to the relentless pursuit toward excellence in their classrooms. You will meet them throughout the pages of *Reading Without Limits*.

Lelac Almagor
> Lelac Almagor teaches literacy and coaches literacy teachers at KIPP DC AIM Academy in the Anacostia neighborhood of Washington, DC.

Adrian Antao
> Adrian is a high school English teacher and has made college readiness his mission for eight years. He has taught ninth through twelfth grade with a focus on honors curriculum.

Sarah Baumann
> Sarah is a fifth grade reading teacher at KIPP Academy. Joining KIPP as a former first grade teacher, she has taught fifth grade literacy for the past nine years.

Tamiko Forrest
> Tamiko is currently in her third year of teaching nonfiction research at KIPP Infinity Middle School. She has taught fourth through sixth grade in New York City.

Allison Willis Holley
> Allison Willis Holley was the founding sixth grade nonfiction studies teacher at KIPP Infinity Middle School and taught the class for four

years. After completing her master's degree in school leadership at Harvard Graduate School of Education, she returned to KIPP Infinity as an instructional coach and assumed the role of school leader in 2012.

Sheena Johnson

Sheena is a second grade teacher and Grade Team leader at KIPP Academy Elementary School in the Bronx. She is currently studying to receive her master's in education from Hunter College in New York City.

Amber Koppel

Amber is a reading teacher and dean of literacy at KIPP Infinity Middle School. She has taught sixth and eighth grade reading.

Lynn Liran

Lynn joined the New York City Teaching Fellows program in 2003, where she earned her master's degree in childhood education. She joined KIPP Infinity Middle School in 2006, and has served as a literacy and special education teacher for all four grades.

Annica Schroeder Lowek

Annica is an intervention specialist and special education coordinator at KIPP Infinity Middle School.

Theresa McCaffery

Theresa has held the positions of preschool teacher, third grade special education teacher, and fifth grade reading teacher at KIPP Infinity Middle School. She is currently on a hiatus from teaching while she raises her two children.

Joy Osborne

Joy is a founding member of the KIPP NYC College Prep High School staff. She has worked with students in middle and high school for eight years, the last four of which have been spent with KIPP NYC.

Elizabeth Raji-Greig

Liz is a dean of teaching and learning at KIPP AMP Academy in Brooklyn, New York. She has been involved in education for over eight years, teaching English language arts and coaching teachers across all subject areas.

Sayuri Stabrowski

Sayuri was a founding seventh grade reading and writing teacher at KIPP Infinity Middle School, where she continues to teach eighth grade reading. She serves as an instructional coach and curriculum writer for middle school literacy teachers throughout the KIPP NYC region.

Michael Witter

Michael was the founding sixth grade reading teacher at KIPP Infinity Middle School, and currently is the director of training and leadership for Teach for Australia. He is the proud recipient of the 2010 KIPP Excellence in Teaching award.

Dominique Young

Dominique taught English at KIPP DC for two years and is currently teaching seventh grade reading at KIPP Infinity Middle School. As a former KIPPster, she was a founding member of the KIPP Academy School in the Bronx, and is currently pursuing her master's degree in education at the RELAY School of Education.

Autumn Zangrilli

Autumn Zangrilli is the dean of teaching and learning at KIPP AMP in Brooklyn, New York. Autumn taught middle school reading and writing in Brooklyn and Rome, Italy, prior to joining the KIPP team and family.

ACKNOWLEDGMENTS

I am grateful to so many people for helping bring *Reading Without Limits* to readers. The support from KIPP has been extraordinary since I started my work with the Knowledge Is Power Program, or KIPP, in 2005. Dave Levin, co-founder of KIPP schools, brought vision, unending optimism, and support to each sentence of this book. Joe Negron, founding principal of KIPP Infinity, championed and cultivated KIPP Infinity's literacy program. I told Joe several years ago that one of my dreams was to write a book. At the time, I thought that dream was far-fetched: thank you Joe for making it a reality. KIPP Infinity was co-founded by a team of brilliant people: Tom Brunzell, Dilcia Ceron, Gerard Griffith, Joe Negron, and Michael Vea. They are truly the hardest working group and are doing whatever it takes to help lead a group of brilliant scholars to and through college. The staff of KIPP Infinity, from 2005 until now, are creative, hard-working, passionate visionaries. It was a privilege to work with them, and I miss having the opportunity to see them in action on a daily basis. I am forever grateful to the students and families of KIPP Infinity. In 2013, the founding class of KIPPsters are graduating high school. Does it get better than that? I can't wait to see them walk the stage.

For the past 10 years I have worked with schools and educators who are performing miracles. During my first year of teaching, my literacy coach,

Jannett Bailey, led me. She taught me that teaching isn't about figuring it out all on my own. She directed me to a community of educators: in books, workshops, and throughout the school. I followed her around like a puppy for three years, soaking up her wisdom. Jannett has been fighting to close the achievement gap for decades, and I am blessed to have started my career with her. I am also incredibly grateful to Harlem Village Academies, the Achievement First network, and RELAY School of Education in New York City for their commitment to New York City and the tri-state area's youth. Thank you to Teach for America, Teach for All, Teach for Australia, and KIPP Foundation for their pursuit toward excellence in teaching. In Melbourne, Australia, Brendan Murray is fighting to bring education equality to disengaged youth. I want to thank Brendan for his relentless commitment with an often-ignored population.

Several folks helped turn chicken scratches into something readable! Kate Gagnon from Jossey-Bass brought nothing but positivity from the moment we reached out with our idea. Paula Stacey, writer extraordinaire, patiently helped guide me into becoming a book writer, and thank you to Cathy Mallon and Suzanne Copenhagen for their help. Special thanks to Minnow Park who took beautiful photographs of our KIPPsters.

Finally, I want to thank my support team: Tom Brunzell, my dear friend who not only co-founded KIPP Infinity with me but also is now working miracles for disadvantaged children in Australia. I wouldn't have been able to make the move to Oz or write this book without him. Thanks to my family and friends who supported me through my first pregnancy while I moved abroad and wrote a book simultaneously. Thank you to my daughter Gigi for smiling in her fourth week and not stopping since, and to my husband Michael Witter. Michael is basically the best reading teacher I've ever seen, and it's his classroom and instruction that I aspire to emulate when I teach.

ABOUT THE AUTHOR

Maddie Witter presents nationally and internationally to help schools better their students' literacy and develop rigorous reading programs. She is a founding teacher of KIPP Infinity Charter School, one of the top-performing middle schools in New York City. At KIPP Infinity, Maddie taught literacy and was the school's founding director of instruction for six years, supervising teacher development and curriculum for the reading, writing, content, and nonfiction studies programs. In 2007, Maddie was honored to be one of ten teachers to receive a national KIPP Excellence in Teaching prize. Visit Maddie at www.reading-without-limits.com.

Introduction
What Is *Reading Without Limits?*

We opened KIPP Infinity in Harlem in 2005 to provide the best possible education we could to the kids and families in Harlem. The majority of our students were African American or Hispanic and almost all were also described as "low-income." According to the National Center for Educational Statistics (NAEP), in 2009 and 2011 African American and Hispanic students trailed their white and Asian American peers by more than 20 test points, or two grade levels, on the NAEP reading assessment in fourth and eighth grade. Students who are in poverty reading below grade level by the third grade are three times as likely to not graduate college compared to children who aren't poor. Many kids in central Harlem were performing below grade level, and some local students were sadly not getting world-class education options. When we opened KIPP Infinity our intention was to provide the best education we could to families and students in Harlem.

Data showed our incoming students would be struggling learners. In 2012, many students at KIPP Infinity entered far below grade level, 19% had

> Reading Without Limits *isn't*
> *about the future. It's about*
> *establishing lifelong learning today.*

learning disabilities and individu-alized education plans (IEPs), 11% were learning English as a second language, and 93% received free or reduced lunch. Most of our students enter far below grade level and therefore are statistically less likely to go to college. We face the same challenges that many teachers in the United States' education system face, including issues related to poverty. Some students suffered from truancy. Others were disengaged from school. Still some others experienced an unsafe school environment before coming to KIPP.

One challenge that we faced was that students particularly struggled in literacy, not unlike many communities in the United States. The literacy gap affects all of us. A 1998 report on reading difficulties in children and a 2005 report on college and career readiness from ACT reveal that the careers of 25 to 40% of Americans are in danger because they don't read well or quickly enough; 20% of American adults read at or below a fifth grade level; and 50% of American adults can't read an eighth grade level text. In fact, according to the ACT report, many students on track for college in grades eight through ten don't ultimately keep up. Compare that to Finland, top ranked on the PISA exams (an international assessment that evaluates education systems worldwide by assessing skills of 15-year-olds), where, according to a 2011 *New York Times* article by Jenny Anderson, the average resident checks out 17 books from the library each year. Indeed, as the article revealed, the United States ranks 15th in literacy according to the PISA results. Is it a surprise that 25% of Americans read zero books in 2011? If you've picked up this book, these numbers terrify you, and you are looking to do anything in your power to make a change.[2]

I joined KIPP because of one challenge I didn't have to face. We were starting from scratch. With a year of planning before our doors opened, we could create a dream program that aligned to research and experiences of what failed and worked. We first asked ourselves this question: Where would we send our own children? Our own children and all students deserve the best possible education.

For me, the best possible education is limitless. In answering what makes the best possible education, we didn't want to limit our kids to achieving high test scores. Getting our kids to advance 20 test points on the NAEP is finite and not very inspirational. Getting high test scores is a step in the right direction but it is not enough. So what does *Reading Without Limits* mean when developing a reading program? It means offering all students what we would want for our own children. I want students to not only go to and through college, but also to be confident, lifelong learners from tomorrow's lesson to when they join an adult continuing education class at age 80. Our students' potential is infinite in the same way that they should be infinitely learning. *Reading Without Limits* inspired our literacy program and the ultimate mission. The *Reading Without Limits* literacy mission is for all kids to be passionate, confident, lifelong learners who go to and through college. We believe that leads to a world-class education.

> The *Reading Without Limits* literacy mission: for all kids to be passionate, confident, lifelong learners who go to and through college.

The *Reading Without Limits* literacy program started with that mission. We aim to build confident, lifelong readers. If we want our children to become lifelong learners, what do lifelong readers do? They go to bookstores and grab piles of books and magazines. They read in a café for hours. They get excited when a favorite author publishes a new book, and they tell their friends about it. If that's what lifelong adult readers do, then our schools should teach those lifelong values to students starting on day one. That's the meaning behind the title *Reading Without Limits*. We want our kids to go beyond the basics. Beyond expectations. But *Reading Without Limits* isn't about the future. It's about establishing lifelong learning today. The ability to be a strong reader is one of the most powerful tools we can have. As Harriet Ball, KIPP co-founder Dave Levin's long time mentor, chanted with her students, *"The more you read, the more you know. Knowledge is power and power is freedom and I want it!"* The six co-founders of KIPP Infinity, Joe, Tom, Mike, Gerard, Dilcia, and I, committed to ensuring that our incoming fifth graders would go to and through college and meet our mission.

After establishing a mission, we made an end goal: we wanted all of our exiting eighth grade students, regardless of entering ability level, to read above grade level and be capable of competing in our nation's top high schools. You have to be pretty darn qualified to function well in those schools. We listed everything that a flourishing high school student would be able to do, and ensured that our eighth graders could do the same thing. For instance, successful high school students master class discussions, annotate high-level texts, and research independently. From there, we backward planned so that those skills would be taught within a scope of four years from the day our doors opened.

So are our students ready for the competitive careers and colleges they want? Our students entered our school door in July 2005. Upon publication of this book, they are graduating high school. Even though they entered the school behind their peers in literacy and numeracy, within two years 100% were at or above grade level in reading, writing, and math according to in-school, state, and national assessments. In 2008, they were ranked the number one school in Manhattan according to the NYC school report cards. Four years later, 100% passed their English Regents with 89% achieving the highest marks. How did we do it? We built a love for learning that transferred beyond the classroom to their young adult lives, and scaffolded a rigorous literacy program that addressed everything they would need to succeed in a top high school.

READING WITHOUT LIMITS OVERVIEW

When we founded KIPP Infinity, we made the intentional choice to not have a class called "English" and instead broke it up into its component parts: reading, nonfiction, and writing.

Based on those goals, we created research-based elements that would lead to high reading achievement. First, we decided to shape whole classes around reading, in addition to English classes, so that every day students had extended time for reading and nonfiction studies. We were determined to create a program that gave students extensive practice reading both in and outside their comfort zones so that they would stay motivated, learn to love reading, and also make progress and be challenged. As a result, the reading classes involve three types of reading: choice, shared, and guided reading, as depicted in Figure I.1. In order to determine students' individual needs and work toward higher levels of achievement, we continually assess

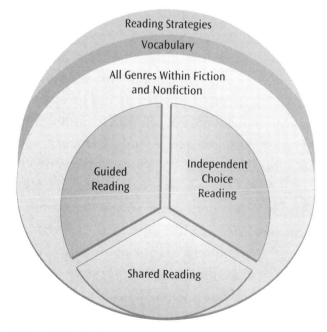

Figure I.1 *Reading Without Limits* Program Description

students, challenge students with questions that are increasingly difficult conceptually, link learning to real life, and make learning as interactive as possible through talk. Above all we instill a love of learning that empowers students to devote extended, rigorous time to their practice. The classes we created, though highly structured, allow for choice of learning. As you will soon see, the *Reading Without Limits* curriculum isn't too set in stone, but allows for freedom for adolescents to feel safe, supported, and individual. *Reading Without Limits* isn't a program that you must follow word for word in order to boost your readers. It's a collection of rigorous, researched best practices that will lead to high levels of academic achievement in reading.

In addition to more time for reading, we spotlighted nonfiction. According to the Alliance for Excellent Education, one in four secondary students cannot read and comprehend material in textbooks. Since most American content classes teach content (science, history, and geography) with textbooks and informational texts, students who struggle in reading therefore struggle in mastering content. Students who are poor or members of minority groups are disproportionately not showing a basic level of competence in content classes because of low reading levels. In fact, according to education researchers Catherine Snow, Susan Burns, and Peg Griffin, who researched struggling readers, "the educational careers of 25 to 40 percent of American children are imperiled because they do not read well enough, quickly enough, or easily enough to ensure comprehension in their content courses in middle and secondary school" (Snow and others, p. 98). Our kids' future lives are at stake because they don't understand the content they read! Kids who struggle with literacy are also struggling in their content classes. This is a crisis that we must overcome.[3]

In 2005, when we opened KIPP Infinity, we made nonfiction a priority. Six years later, the Common Core Standards backed up this belief. The Common Core, aware that students lack proficiency in reading nonfiction texts, pushes schools to integrate nonfiction, about 50%, into what students read in order to prepare them for college and career readiness. The Common Core argues that there is too much emphasis on narrative texts in schools, and students need to read more informational texts. This will build their ability to read in content classes and later to achieve greater success in their careers. We are fully aware of the need to build nonfiction skills. Therefore, we made nonfiction studies a serious part of our reading program in two ways. First, we embedded nonfiction into choice, guided, and shared reading. But that wasn't enough. Our second approach is unusual. Because we knew that nonfiction might take a back seat to fiction, we strongly felt that we needed a second reading class: nonfiction studies. This class exclusively teaches nonfiction narrative and expository texts. That way, we knew that students were getting still more time to independently read and that would be sacred time devoted to nonfiction texts. While *Reading Without Limits* doesn't specifically address the structure of our nonfiction studies class, this book shows how to intentionally weave nonfiction into choice, guided, and shared reading.

This program is working for charter schools, but is it applicable to others? I am convinced it is. My conviction isn't just based on enthusiasm for the program I helped create. It is based on experience. Recently I began consultancy work with a school of high school aged, incarcerated youth from rural and urban backgrounds in a justice center. A common criticism is that the students of KIPP Infinity were successful because we were able to build a program from the ground up. I took what we did at KIPP Infinity and applied it to the justice center. Despite being an alternative education program for a different demographic and age range, the students are demonstrating an equal level of success. The purpose of this book is to show you how you can apply all the aspects of *Reading Without Limits* for your students, regardless of the type of school, location, or age range of students. If your students aren't reading on level, then this book is for you.

CHOICE READING

The big goal of *Reading Without Limits* is to nurture lifelong readers. What do lifelong readers do? They read books. I always tell my students that nothing would make me happier than seeing them years after graduation on the subway reading. They can be reading a trashy magazine, the latest novel, or browsing *Wikipedia*. I'd be thrilled simply to see them reading because it shows me they are one step closer to becoming lifelong readers. If we want to help create lifelong readers, we need to create a program that gives kids the opportunity to read a ton in school. Though in 2005 we knew we were facing a big challenge, that same challenge holds true today and probably always will. Not only do many students dislike reading, some also don't have a culture of literacy at home, and many are far below grade level. In order to nurture lifelong readers, students must find independent reading pleasurable.

In order to establish love of reading, I considered what worked and what didn't in launching lifelong readers. Before coming to KIPP, I tried many approaches that didn't work. What turned kids off from reading was filling in worksheets, reading from textbooks, and answering multiple-choice questions. When I chat with kids in other schools, from public to private to alternative, I get the same feedback. So we considered everything that lifelong readers authentically do. Lifelong readers chat with their friends about books. They get excited about a favorite author, find informational texts that support a topic of interest, and above all, they read a ton. They read books they choose comfortably. What are they not doing? Filling in worksheets. Therefore, we decided to create a classroom environment that simulated what successful readers do in their adult lives. Above all, successful readers make time to read. We built a lot of time in our day so kids would have time to independently read books that they could comfortably read.

Even though some may question the value of choice because of its lack of rigor, something I address in more detail in Chapter 3, if done correctly it is not only motivating but also the best way to encourage kids to read for long periods. Research supports more time for reading. Yi-Chen Wu and S. Jay Samuels from the University of Minnesota created a study in response to the National Reading Panel's (NRP) statement that there was no experimental study yet showing how the amount of time reading raised achievement. Comparing students who read 15 minutes a day to those reading 40 minutes a day, they found that students who read 40 minutes regardless of reading level made much higher gains in their reading than students who read 15 minutes. Barbara Taylor and Barbara Frye, also in response to the lack of research noted by the NRP, studied the relationship between independent reading and academic achievement. They concluded that independent reading was the best predictor of reading achievement, and greater time spent reading leads to greater achievement. Reading researcher Thomas Gunning, in response to ways schools can increase achievement after No Child Left Behind, concluded that nothing is better in building higher-order thinking skills than independent reading. Stephen Krashen studied independent reading over the past 40 years in *The Power of Reading*. His research concluded that there is no other literacy activity that you can do that will raise achievement in comprehension, vocabulary, spelling, and writing more than independent reading. The research speaks for itself. In order to build lifelong learners and boost achievement, we knew that the first place to start was to build lifelong *independent readers:* readers who CHOOSE to read. This is true regardless of grade level or type of school environment. Lifelong readers choose books to read, and then read them. It sounds simple![4]

James Patterson, author of many thrilling adult and young adult books, said it beautifully in a CNN article in September 2011: "The best way to get kids reading more is to give them books they'll gobble up—and that will make them ask for another. Yes, it's that simple: 1+1=2. It just does. Kids say the number one reason they don't read more is that they can't find books they like. Freedom of choice is a key to getting them motivated and excited. Vampire sagas, comics, mangas, books of sports statistics—terrific! As long as kids are reading."[5] You have to love learning if you are going to become a lifelong learner. Otherwise, wouldn't reading be a drag?

We knew how important reading for pleasure is in order to drive student achievement. We also knew that managing a group of students independently reading who all have different needs is really hard: some students might fake read, get easily distracted and disruptive, spend too long reading a book, or read books that are too difficult or too easy. As most educators know, it can be difficult to make independent reading happen in a serious way. In fact, many have tried and given up. Faced with such a challenge we developed an approach that insisted that no one opt out, that devoted at least 30 minutes a day to independent comfort reading in all grades, and that allowed students choice based on our knowledge of their reading levels. This book will give you strategies to launch, or relaunch, a choice reading program.

SHARED READING

Independent comfort reading mimics what lifelong readers do: they read a ton of books for pleasure. But you can be a voracious reader and not necessarily demonstrate a high degree of success in a top-quality high school or college or in the competitive world beyond. When I worked in New York, I rode the train to work every morning with students from Riverdale High School, a top private school in New York City. They were annotating Shakespeare, *The Odyssey*, and historical theory. Independent reading isn't going to teach those skills, because there's another dimension of reading that successful readers do. They are able to closely pick apart a text on an analytic level. Typically, when adults read comfortably, they aren't doing extensive annotations in the text's margins. Nor are they picking up a text that's too hard to read for pleasure.

Shared reading does just that. During shared reading, students closely analyze a difficult text together with the teacher, going from literal to inferential interpretations with a high degree of accountability to the text. I wanted my students to be able to do what top students do, so we built in a second block to our program.

In shared reading, together the whole class and teacher look at a text that is on grade level or slightly beyond. This is unlike independent reading, where students are reading texts comfortably on their individual levels. Also, students don't pick this text—the teacher does. Shared reading is an interactive reading experience in which readers engage with an expert reader, the teacher. In shared reading, the teacher prompts students to use literacy strategies, and students apply those strategies to a shared text that is difficult. It allows for a shared conversation—all students have read the same text, and therefore it's as if the characters from that text have joined your class's family. Students do close analysis of the text and back up their analysis with textual proof.

In 2005, we realized the importance of integrating above-grade-level texts into our curriculum. The Common Core Standards also push for students to read complex texts because "the clear, alarming picture that emerges from the evidence is that while the reading demands of college, workforce training programs, and citizenship have held steady or risen over the past 50 years, K–12 texts have, if anything, become less demanding. This finding is the impetus behind the Common Core's strong emphasis on increasing text complexity as a key requirement in reading" (2010).[6] Just as those formulating the Common Core Standards did, we looked to what kids needed in their future, and then backward planned to integrate those skills into our school.

Shared reading means reading an at grade or above grade—level text that may be difficult to read. Shared texts can be any genre or length. It's essential to weave short and long nonfiction texts into shared reading. Within shared reading there are several components that help make it a success.

Close Reading

During close reading, the teacher heavily guides students to pick apart a small piece of text. This can be a stand-alone short text such as a poem, a short story or informational article, or an excerpt from a longer text. The purpose of close reading is to build your students' ability to deeply construct text. Close reading is not done with the entire text, just parts.

Assigned Independent Reading

During shared reading, all students are reading the same text. After a close reading, the teacher may ask kids to independently read part of the text that she assigns. This should happen in class, as well as outside of class for homework. The purpose of assigned reading is two-fold. First, it builds students' independent skills so they can do difficult tasks on their own. Second, it builds in more time for students to independently read, which, as mentioned above, is essential in building achievement.

Classroom Discussion

Classroom discussion is structured around a shared piece of text that builds students' ability to analyze a text using talk. It's ideal for a shared text, as everyone has read the same material. Research from the *American Education Research Journal* concluded that incorporating rigorously demanding classroom discussion in a reading program allows students to internalize the strategies necessary for them to do difficult reading on their own.[7] It's for this reason that incorporating classroom discussion is necessary in a shared reading block.

Shared reading is the second part of the *Reading Without Limits* program that will lift your students to high levels of mastery in literacy. Incorporating shared reading into your schedule is an excellent way to align your program to the values of the Common Core Standards.

GUIDED READING

There is still one element missing from the ideal reading program that neither choice reading nor shared reading adequately addresses if we want to build lifelong readers. Many readers enter class below or significantly below grade level in reading ability. While choice reading and shared reading increase achievement, each reader has his or her own unique needs that can't be addressed in a whole class. If Antonio is reading on a first grade level and is still working on matching sounds to print, and Aiko is an insatiable reader but doesn't get beyond literal meanings, then they have to have their needs addressed individually. Therefore, we decided to build guided reading into all students' schedules until they were above grade level in reading.

Students with similar abilities or who need to acquire similar reading skills are placed in groups of eight or fewer. Unlike shared reading, these texts are not necessarily difficult. They are a little bit beyond a student's ability. It's like their "comfort plus" level. They aren't on that level *yet*, but they will be soon. You use texts that are a little bit beyond a student's reach, and over time those texts eventually become just right for choice reading. Guided reading is the stepping-stone between choice and shared reading. It's the bridge that will lift your students' ability. Over time, students' reading levels will advance and the books that they choose for choice reading will become increasingly complex. You explicitly teach students strategies that will allow them to comprehend texts that are a little bit beyond their ability. Then you give them time to practice reading those texts with your support. Over time, you lift your support, as they will be able to read those texts on their own.

First introduced in New Zealand and Australia in the 1980s, guided reading became popular in the United States based on the work of Gay Su Pinnell and Irene Fountas. As they note, "We can see that children who achieved at the 98th percentile read 4,358,000 words in books over the twenty-six weeks, and children at the 90th percentile read 2,357,000 words. But children at the 10th percentile read only 8,000 words" (Pinnell and Fountas, p. 7).[8] As an additional plus, guided reading gives kids even more time to read, thus raising achievement even further. Guided reading is the final piece in the *Reading Without Limits* program that will get your kids toward the 98th percentile that you know they can achieve. Not only does guided reading allow for more time reading, it also allows you to develop literacy skills in small groups. That means more time checking for understanding and working with individual kids.

READING WITHOUT LIMITS' VALUES

Reading Without Limits' Literacy Values

- Stamina
- Joy
- Rigor
- High expectations
- More time

An ideal literacy program should be based not only on research and sound practice, but also on several values that inform your teaching. I suggest incorporating the following values into your teaching for several reasons. First, we want students to not only become life-long learners but also to have skills that will lead them to success in the nation's most competitive high schools and colleges. Therefore, we researched what habits are essential for successful people. Then we translated those habits as values. The second reason is consistency. In many schools, there isn't consistency as kids rise from grade to grade. One teacher might spend several months on folktales. Another teacher might devote most of her class to making book reports. Still another might spend copious time showing movies. Instilling values that are inherent to your literacy program establishes a consistency regardless of the grade level or class in addition to the structural consistency you will establish with choice, guided, and shared reading. If you visit a KIPP school, you should see a consistency in what teachers value. In my work with other schools, those same values translate regardless of the educational setting, from private to alternative programs.

The following briefly describes values inherent to the *Reading Without Limits* program.

Stamina

Many students have never experienced reading for extended periods of time. It's essential that our students have stamina to not only sit through classes or an extended school day, but also to read for an extended period. Therefore, a major *Reading Without Limits* value is to develop reading stamina in our students during choice, guided, and shared reading. We know that perseverance is a trait that the highly successful embody,[9] and building perseverance through reading and research is a college, career readiness, and lifelong skill. Whether that's reading 50 books, tackling a research project, or critically analyzing a dense text, it all takes grit and we model daily how to build grit for our kids. Those who can persevere through a task for an extended time demonstrate high levels of success, so we build our students' stamina starting day one.

What does that look like in a classroom? First, we start small. We'd rather a student was able to do on-task, rigorous work really well for short periods than for long periods in a mediocre fashion. But the ultimate goal is extended time. We create stamina checklists showing kids exactly what they should look like when on task. We model what on and off task looks like. Finally, we give students multiple ways to establish and set their own goals, so that their stamina increases at their own rates and is self-monitored. Building stamina ultimately prepares our students for college and beyond.

Joy and Rigor

Something that characterizes KIPP is the balance of joy and rigor. It's essential that our kids look forward to coming to our classrooms. They should be laughing during daily lessons. At KIPP Infinity, teachers high five kids in the hall, the principal is known to belt out songs during assemblies, and we visit the home of every student to welcome each one to our team and family. Joy is essential to our practice. More than anything, we want our students to love school. Coupled with joy must come a rigorous education full of inquiry, critical thinking, and high expectations. *Reading Without Limits* shows that rigor doesn't mean boring instruction. For instance, students in nonfiction studies class each year choose a topic of inquiry to study. They create an independent research paper, PowerPoint presentation, and display board depicting their findings. They joyfully find answers to their questions, stencil awesome titles on their board, and dress up in costumes to present information while doing high school level inquiry.

While joy and rigor could be considered yin and yang, I will show that they can bring Oneness to your instruction. We do not advocate for joyous activities just to get kids smiling. In fact, those fluffy extensions that teachers like to do (like book reports) are fun but will not make a difference in student achievement. When writing *Reading Without Limits*, I only included kid-friendly, rigorous ideas that are aligned to pushing your readers to their highest abilities that you can immediately apply in your classroom.

High Expectations

KIPP began in 1994. Teachers Dave Levin and Mike Feinberg completed their Teach for America commitment and launched a program for fifth graders in inner city Houston. Although only half of the students passed their fourth grade tests before enrolling in KIPP, more than 90% passed the Texas fifth grade exams in English and mathematics after one year at KIPP. In 1995, Mike's KIPP Academy Houston became a charter school, and Dave established KIPP Academy New York in the South Bronx. As of Fall 2012, there are 125 KIPP schools in 20 states and the District of Columbia serving over 40,000 students.

I truly believe that all students will rise to a teacher's high expectations. A sign hung above my blackboard each day, inspired by the same sign that hung above Dave Levin's class in his first year teaching: *all of us will learn*. There is no other option. Levin was fired after his second year teaching despite winning teacher of the year in his school. His Houston school district had strict quotas on racial percentage passing standardized tests. If more than 75% of students in an ethnic group failed the test, the school would be labeled unsatisfactory. Levin's principal asked Levin to push for his Latino students to opt out of the state test, asking parents to sign a form saying they weren't proficient enough in English to pass. His principal's fear drove low expectations. Levin refused, got fired, and over 90% of his Latino students passed. Levin's high expectations inspire the work I am doing in 2012. The current picture is dismal for the incarcerated youth with whom I work. Over 90% of the students were dropouts before being incarcerated, and over 90% later go on to jail. Naysayers have countless reasons for why this population of kids won't succeed. But guess what — they will. You can count on it. How do I know? Because they will rise to the level of our expectations. Raise your expectations, and your kids will follow. Sadiq, a boy who proclaimed he hadn't read a book in his life, is already on his ninth book this term. The judge, impressed by his tenacity, shortened his sentence. Our high expectations rubbed off on Sadiq, the judge, and Sadiq's community. Sadiq is now on the pathway for online college.

Not all examples of high expectations are as extreme as Levin's or Sadiq's, and the difference between high and low expectations can be quite subtle. Yet it's that same relentless optimism that drives great teachers around the world. For instance, we are extremely intentional in the questions that we ask to ensure that they are cognitively challenging. We don't just celebrate good behavior. We aim to celebrate hard work and innovative thinking. When you see a teacher praising students, she is not only praising their thinking, but also pushing them to take it to another level by expanding on their thoughts. Our high expectations aren't just happening in the classroom. Field trips are a great opportunity to reinforce your literacy goals. For example, we took our seventh grade students to tour top New England colleges, stay in dorms, attend lectures, and reflect on collegiate life. Not only do we have high expectations, but we also have a plan for how we communicate those expectations, and we enforce them.

More Time

KIPP believes there are no shortcuts when it comes to success in life. According to psychologist K. Anders Ericsson, one contributing factor to highly successful people, whether in sports, music, academics, or other activity, is that they spend a ton of time deliberately practicing something that is a little bit outside their ability.[10] If you want your students to make incredible academic gains in literacy, then more time has to be spent in literacy.

For this reason, try to incorporate

❑ *At least* 30 minutes of independent choice reading four times a week
❑ *At least* 30 minutes of shared reading four times a week
❑ *At least* 30 minutes of guided reading two times a week

Deliberate Practice

More time learning only equates to greater achievement if we are giving students as many opportunities to deliberately *practice* the reading skills that we teach. The *Reading Without Limits* model does just that. Students spend extended time deliberately practicing what you teach.

This book is based on the work that so many awesome teachers have done over the past seven years in the relentless pursuit of boosting our kids' reading achievement. But even though there have been many successes, we are also learning new ways daily to nurture our lifelong readers. This book is part of that journey. Thanks for joining us.

READING WITHOUT LIMITS TEACHER CHECKLIST

From photocopying to checking in with parents, there's a lot to remember as teachers. The following is a checklist that encompasses every *Reading Without Limits* teaching tip. Use it as a bag of tricks or to self-assess.

Part One: Launching Lifelong Readers

Finding Students' Reading Levels

- ❑ Figure out students' comfort reading levels using running records.
- ❑ Do group inventories when you need to save time.
- ❑ Match students to books based on their reading level during choice and guided reading.
- ❑ Create an environment where peers support each others' differences.

Part Two: Steps to Creating Lifelong Readers

Kids Need to Understand What They Read

- ❑ Use the read-aloud/think-aloud to introduce strategies.
- ❑ Check for understanding throughout the think-aloud and allow time for students to try the strategy on their own.
- ❑ Avoid common think-aloud pitfalls.
- ❑ Choose the just-right text for a think-aloud.
- ❑ Prioritize figuring it out and paraphrasing strategies.
- ❑ Teach strategies that build lifelong readers.

Incorporate Choice Reading So Kids Read More

- ❑ Explicitly teach stamina then build it.
- ❑ Help students make good book choices.
- ❑ Build the state of flow in your classroom.
- ❑ Harness student engagement.
- ❑ Apply strategic reading to choice reading.
- ❑ Hold students accountable to their thinking.

Shared Reading to Teach, Reinforce, and Challenge
❑ Create a schedule that allows for 30 minutes of shared reading four times a week.
❑ Choose the right text.
❑ Guide students through the text by doing close reading.
❑ Be strategic when assigning shared texts for independent reading.
❑ Scaffold shared reading for struggling readers.

Guided Reading to Move Students Along Their Continuum
❑ Follow the same predictable structure of before-reading strategies, read-aloud, independent practice, and after-reading strategies.
❑ Group students homogenously and teach one grade level above their comfort level.
❑ Give kids tons of time to read aloud and at the same time conference for grow goals.
❑ Be proactive to have successful guided reading classroom management.
❑ Reassess every six to eight weeks.

Part Three: Putting the Power of Choice, Shared, and Guided Reading to Work in Your Classroom or School

Make It Visible
❑ Set up comfortable reading spots.
❑ Be intentional with what you put on your walls.
❑ Intentionally set up your library and desks.

Muscle Memory Routines
❑ Figure out all of the details of the routine before you teach it.
❑ Teach the routine by using examples and non-examples.
❑ Incorporate something bizarre or creative so it sticks in students' memories.
❑ Use the remind-and-reinforce strategy as you keep the routine alive throughout the year.

What to Do When Choice, Shared, or Guided Reading Isn't Working
- ❏ Use growth mindset when thinking about students.
- ❏ Utilize whole class and one-on-one (O3) management tricks.
- ❏ Tweak your teaching to address common pitfalls.

Part Four: Steps to Enhance Lifelong Readers

Reading Conferences, Our Aha *Moments*
- ❏ Start with halftime and racetrack conferences.
- ❏ Create a grow goal for each student for one-on-one conferences.
- ❏ Take notes to track student growth.
- ❏ Hold students accountable to their goals.

Teaching Vocabulary
- ❏ Devote lots of time to reading to boost vocabulary.
- ❏ Speak with high-level vocabulary.
- ❏ Choose the right words to teach.
- ❏ Explicitly teach new words, and create an organized review and application schedule that extends to homework.
- ❏ Assess weekly.

Class Discussion
- ❏ Before the discussion, create great discussion questions.
- ❏ Before the discussion, give students time to prepare their thinking in advance.
- ❏ During the discussion, hold kids accountable with formative, summative, and self-assessments.
- ❏ Explicitly teach excellent communication skills.
- ❏ After the discussion, summarize and reflect.

Standardized Tests
- ❏ Teach standardized tests just like you teach reading strategies.
- ❏ Build test-taking stamina.

❑ Recognize leveled reading.
❑ Design intervention groups.
❑ Include standardized tests weekly and spiral in daily do-nows.

Testing 1, 2, 3 . . . Testing
❑ Test this week's strategies with shared passage.
❑ Test this week's strategies with a passage they've never seen before.
❑ Spiral review content from the past month.
❑ Spiral review content from the past year.
❑ Incorporate standardized testing.
❑ Evaluate weekly vocabulary.
❑ End with a survey and self-assessment.
❑ Keep assessments kid-friendly.
❑ Don't let assessment logistics keep you from doing weekly assessments.

Part Five: Putting It All Together

Planning a Lesson
❑ Determine explicit criteria based on the aim.
❑ Follow the same predictable structure each day.
❑ Introduce the lesson by activating prior knowledge, sharing the purpose, and connecting to what kids did yesterday.
❑ Teach doing a read-aloud/think-aloud or close reading.
❑ Check for understanding throughout.
❑ Allow extended time for independent practice and reading (once it has been built).
❑ Don't forget to close out your lesson.

Building the Reading Without Limits *Program*
❑ Start with the essentials and create predictable routines.
❑ Build when your class is ready.
❑ Spiral.

PART 1

Launching Lifelong Readers

1

Finding Students' Reading Levels
Why Trying to Bench Press 150 Pounds Doesn't Make Me Stronger

This chapter will show that by incorporating the following into your classroom, you will have established the groundwork necessary to start building lifelong readers:

- ❏ Figure out students' comfort reading levels using running records
- ❏ Do group inventories when you need to save time
- ❏ Match students to books based on their reading level during choice and guided reading
- ❏ Create an environment where peers support each others' differences

I want to introduce you to one of my past students, Sofia. Sofia was 13-years-old entering the fifth grade. An English language learner with special needs, she struggled in literacy and was retained in her previous

Rigor isn't throwing students in the deep end of the pool and hoping they don't drown. Rigor is leading the development of each student so that they become incrementally stronger and stronger.

school three times. As the U.S. Department of Education reported in 2003, 8 million students in grades 4 through 12 are struggling readers, so Sofia wasn't alone. In 2007, Sofia received a reading assessment to determine what texts she could read comfortably. Sofia read aloud a couple paragraphs from *A Wrinkle in Time*, a text frequently recommended for 13-year-olds. She miscued, stumbled, or made up over 85% of the words. After 30 seconds, her voice started to shake. After 40 seconds, 100% of the words were invented. Her read-aloud made me want to reach out in empathy. Have you ever done something so frustrating that it seemed at the time impossible? It's like watching me try to do a pull up. However, *A Wrinkle in Time* is a text deemed appropriate for Sofia's age level, and students like Sofia reading below grade level are being asked to read it when they cannot, yet.

The key word is *yet*.

This chapter will show why *A Wrinkle in Time* wasn't right for Sofia at that moment. This book will show how to boost readers like Sofia so *A Wrinkle in Time* becomes a comfortable text.

Impossible will become possible for your readers. Reading is just like weightlifting. If I tried to bench press 150 pounds today, I couldn't. I wouldn't get stronger and I would leave with some broken bones because 150 pounds is beyond my ability. But if I did what I could do, 30 pounds comfortably, and tried 40 pounds a few times this week, I would slowly become stronger. Eventually, 40 pounds would become no problem, and then I could try 50.

A good approach to reading follows the same philosophy. We figure out what kids can read comfortably, and encourage them to read a ton of books with a similar difficulty level. In addition we develop their skills by guiding them with harder texts (akin to 40 pound weights) until those texts become easier. Then, voilà! Kids are able to do those harder texts with ease, becoming *Reading Without Limits* readers. That's what rigor is. Rigor isn't throwing students in the deep end of the pool and hoping they don't drown. Rigor is leading the development of each student so that they become incrementally stronger and stronger.

How do you start matching texts to kids accurately? What is appropriate for Sofia to read? We follow the same

Figure 1.1 Getting Comfortable During Choice Reading

principles that a physical trainer follows. Don't start with their age. Don't start with their grade-level. A trainer doesn't just look at your age when you walk into the gym. She diagnoses your ability by asking you to press weights. Then she gradually adds more until she determines what you cannot do. This chapter will show that to determine your students' reading levels, you give them different leveled texts on a developmental continuum that become increasingly difficult until you determine what they cannot do. Then you can match them to texts that they can read comfortably with excellent fluency, guide them with texts that are a little too hard, and push their reading ability with shared reading. That is why leveled reading is the basis for the *Reading Without Limits* program. We need to first identify our students' comfort zones for choice reading, then push them with guided reading on their comfort plus level, and finally practice high-level rigor with shared texts.

2/3 (AVERAGE AGE OF STUDENTS) = THE READING SPAN

For most classrooms, readers are on a range of reading abilities, in many cases a span of six years, according to the thorough reading researcher Thomas Gunning. The range of reading levels in a class is usually two-thirds

Figure 1.2 Students Reading on Different Levels
During Choice Reading

the average age of students. The average age of fifth graders is 10. Two-thirds of 10 is 6.3. That means on average you may have a range of second to eighth grade reading levels in a fifth grade classroom. The span only increases as students get older. With such a span, we need to differentiate the reading material.[11] Figure 1.2 shows Alex reading *The Kite Runner* and Theo reading *Time Warp Trio*. That's a span of over six years in reading ability. The class runs smoothly because each seventh grader is matched to the appropriate level text in his or her comfort zone.

For teachers who studied education in school, you might have heard of a theorist named Lev Vygotsky who championed developmental learning. Vygotsky believed that we are each on our own developmental continuum and therefore we have our own individual needs. This is why Sofia shouldn't be reading *A Wrinkle in Time*, yet. Parents know that first hand. Just because your child is 12 months old that doesn't mean she is walking. Lev Vygotsky makes the case for differentiated instruction and describes three zones of learning.[12]

The Zone of Actual Development is where a learner can do the task independently without help. This is what I have been referring to as the *comfort zone*. Weight lifters who do many reps are in their comfort zone. Choice reading should take place in this zone.

The Frustration Zone is where work is too difficult, even with the teacher's support, the zone that Sofia demonstrated. For the most part, we shouldn't be giving any work to kids in the frustration zone. Kids aren't going to become better readers if you give them frustration zone work; in fact, they are going to become more disengaged from school. That doesn't mean that you can't give them difficult work, just stay away from the frustration zone. If learners are working in their frustration zones, it must be carefully planned, clearly communicated with empathy, and be limited to short periods.

The Zone of Proximal Development is where learners can accomplish the task with the help of their teacher. That's the ideal zone for shared and guided reading.

Go to www.reading-without-limits.com for a list of commercial reading inventories if your school doesn't already have one. Here is a list of some of my favorites:

- *Teachers College Running Records:* This inventory is my favorite because it is quick to use, free, and includes authentic texts. You typically can pinpoint a reading level in 10 minutes.
- *QRI-5:* This is a great choice if you want a more comprehensive assessment. It includes word lists and listening passages.
- *Comprehensive Reading Inventory:* If you have Spanish-speaking students, this assessment includes Spanish assessments so you can determine students' English and Spanish reading levels.
- *Make It Yourself:* If you have a leveled classroom library, you can ask kids to read 100 words straight out of the book with follow-up comprehension questions. You can also supplement a purchased reading inventory with your own leveled texts to add more authentic passages to your assessment kit.

If you don't already have one in your school, choose a reading inventory, make lots of copies, and create a schedule that allows you to meet with each student.

The implications are clear: We need to assess reading levels in order to make sure kids are working in a zone where they can learn. Thus, the first step in developing a strong reading program, and the first step we take in *Reading Without Limits*, is to find our students' levels. This step applies to all teachers, whether you are teaching struggling readers in high school or students ranging from emergent to fluent in elementary school. It is also extremely relevant if you aren't a reading teacher. What if you are giving students material, from word problems to work in textbooks, in their frustration zone? This chapter will show you how to find an answer to that question.

I will show practical ways to assess reading levels, both for teachers with more time and teachers with very little time, in all grades. If your school already has an assessment in place that determines reading levels, this chapter shows kid-friendly ways to supplement your program. Mix and match the suggestions to best suit the needs of your students, classroom, and school. Once you determine what your students can read comfortably, then choice reading, guided reading, and shared reading will all fall into place.

DETERMINE A STUDENT'S READING LEVEL BY USING A RUNNING RECORD

There are many different ways to assess student reading levels, ranging from commercially developed inventories to teacher-developed approaches unique to each classroom. No matter which method you choose, we have found at minimum it should be able to do the following:

- Determine a student's comfort reading level
- Be scaled so that it measures progress
- Assess students' reading fluency, ability to decode, reading comprehension, and ability to retell

In order to do all of the above, we administer one-on-one reading assessments. My favorite is running records, developed by New Zealand reading researcher Marie Clay.[13] Running records ask students to read a passage out loud so we can assess fluency and decoding. Halfway through the reading, students read on in their heads. After the reading, students answer comprehension questions and retell.

There are many commercial running record inventories available, many for free, that produce running records as a system. These reading assessment systems provide a range of texts on different levels of difficulty. Using the texts and the questions provided, you match students to the texts that they can read comfortably. Running records require meeting with a student one-on-one. I know one-on-one assessments may not be realistic for every teacher. Some high school teachers teach upward of 200 students a day. Therefore, in the section that follows I suggest alternatives for teachers who aren't able to do one-on-one inventories. But I recommend one-on-one assessments above all others.

Here is an example of a running record. It is divided into three parts.

1. Students read 100 words aloud so you can assess fluency and decoding
2. Students read on in their heads
3. Students answer comprehension questions and retell the passage

As a student is reading aloud, the teacher takes notes. Determine if a student makes an error as she reads aloud (a miscue) or self-corrects herself (not a miscue). Basically, you are looking for your student's percentage accuracy with a passage. If the passage is just right, the student will read with 96% or better accuracy. I will explain why 96% is an important number in the next section. That's why running records stop oral reading at 100 words. It's simple math!

Alex Rodriguez

Imagine you are about to graduate high school. One of the most famous baseball teams gives you a call. They want you to play for them! This is exactly what happened to Alex Rodriguez.

At eighteen years old, Alex Rodriguez played his first major league game. He started with the Seattle Mariners. Rodriguez, or A-Rod, is now famous for playing for the New York Yankees.

Rodriguez was picked first out of every player to play when he was just eighteen years old. This happened in 1993. It took A-Rod three years to start leading the pack. After three years playing

---

1. The section above the line includes 100 words. Ask the student to read it out loud. Track how many words the student accurately is able to read or decode. Each time they make a mistake, write down what they said. Note their fluency: Is it smooth?

with the Mariners, he had the best batting average in the league. He also hit 36 home runs. In 1998, he became the third player in all of history to hit 40 home runs and steal 40 bases in one season. He was definitely "out of the park"!

2. Students read the rest of the passage in their heads.

After a couple of trades, A-Rod started playing for the New York Yankees. This was great for Rodriguez, because he got to also play with his best friend. Wouldn't you want to be on the same team as your best friend? Together, they also made it to the World Series!

Comprehension Questions:

(Retell) Can you tell me what the passage was about?

3. Then, students answer multiple comprehension questions that range in difficulty. In addition, they retell the passage in their own words.

1. (Identify detail) How old was Alex Rodriguez when he first played for the Major Leagues?

2. (Interpret multiple details) When did Rodriguez start demonstrating that he was a baseball star?

3. (Make inference) What does the following mean? "It took A-Rod three years to start leading the pack." Why?

Record Miscues with a Running Record

In order to determine a student's comfort level, you need to record percentage accuracy as they read. As the student is reading, record miscues: mispronunciations, insertions, omissions, and any words that you shared because the student asked for help. Miscues subtract from percentage accuracy. If a student makes five miscues out of 100 words, then they read the passage with 95% accuracy. For instance, if a student says "sweet" instead of "sweat," leaves off the "s" on the end of a word, or adds a word like "the" to the sentence, these are all errors that count against percentage accuracy.

The Difference Between Self-Corrections and Miscues

In addition, record self-corrections: hesitations, corrections, or repetitions. If a student miscues a word and fixes it later, do not count it as an error. Self-corrections do not take off from percentage accuracy. Table 1.1 shows what distinguishes miscues from self-corrections.

Running records also include comprehension questions and time to retell. Start with the retell. Proceed level by level until you find texts that students read with 96% or better fluency and decoding and 90% or better comprehension. That means you found their comfort level. Table 1.2 shows how to determine whether or not a text is at a students' comfort, guided, or frustration level.

Evaluate Comprehension with Tiered Questions and a Retell

When evaluating the retell, consider if students incorporated any miscomprehension as part of the accuracy score for comprehension. However, if you

Table 1.1 The Difference Between Miscues and Self-Corrections

Miscues (count off accuracy)	Corrections (do not count off accuracy)
Mispronunciation	Hesitations
Insertion (sound or word)	Corrections
Omission (partial or whole words)	Repetitions

Table 1.2 How to Calculate a Student's Comfort Level

	Word Accuracy	Comprehension Accuracy
Comfort Level for Choice Reading	96% +	90% +
Guided Reading Level for Guided and Shared Reading	76–95%	75% +
Frustration Level	75% or below	50% or below

haven't taught students how to retell yet, then don't count an incomplete retell as part of their comprehension accuracy score yet. Some commercial running records come with retell rubrics. Try to find the passage that a student can retell comfortably with few or no errors for the comprehension questions: that's their comfort level.

Where to Start?

I highly recommend choosing a running record inventory that has been prepared for you. My favorite inventory is the Teachers College Running Records, which are available for free on the Teachers College website. This inventory comes with everything you will need, including running record student and teacher passages. I typically start about two years below a student's grade (not age) level when beginning a running record as a baseline. If they rock it, I jump up a couple years. Otherwise, I continue administering running records moving up the continuum until I find where they hit about 96% accuracy and good comprehension. It's just like weightlifting . . . find the spot right before their arms start to quiver.

Visit www.reading-without-limits.com to see reading assessments in action for a range of levels, as well as the notes teachers took for each assessment.

Kid-Friendly Way to Start the Assessment

Students may become stressed when they get an individual reading assessment. It can almost feel like a pop quiz. If you purchased an inventory, it might include a script for how to start the assessment. I find that many kits' scripts are too formal and potentially scary—especially for a struggling or disengaged learner. Here's what I say, regardless of the inventory, to keep it kid-friendly to ease comfort. We used this script with great success with the incarcerated youth who are wary of one-on-one meetings.

- **Establish Purpose:** We are about to do a reading assessment so I can figure out what books to recommend to you.
- **Determine Personal Habits:** What does reading look like in your day? What was the last book that you read? Has a teacher ever given you a reading level before? What did the teacher say?
- **Explain Process:** (If the test asks students to read aloud) You are going to start by reading aloud. Then, halfway through, I'm going to stop you and ask you to keep reading on your own. If you make a mistake as you read aloud, it's OK to go back and fix it. I want you to do your best. At the end of the passage I'm going to ask you a few questions about the passage. You can go back as often as you like to find the answers, if that's easier for you. Have you ever done something like this before?
- **Check-in:** How are you feeling? Do you have any questions?
- **Address Common Concern:** You may notice that I'm taking some notes. Don't worry about it; they just help me remember!

Testing Frequency

The ideal frequency is to administer a new running record, or whatever assessment you may be using, every six to eight weeks until students are on grade level. We do this because we found that most students move up comfort levels every six to eight weeks. For students on grade level, we administer assessments every term. I recommend frequent assessments because it pushes kids to their fullest potential.

Find Time

One of the biggest pitfalls is finding time to administer running records. Therefore, plan to set aside time to meet with each student individually.

With our schedules, this is really hard to do. In our first year at KIPP Infinity, Michael Vea, the nonfiction studies teacher, and I met each student at their local library to administer the reading inventory before the school year started. Now when students come to the school to register, we have half a dozen teachers on hand to administer the reading assessment over the course of a few hours. That system is much more sustainable! Your school might already have a schedule in place for you to administer the inventory. But some schools do not. If you find yourself in the latter category, as I did in my previous schools, my best advice is to try to administer the inventory as quickly as possible. Make a schedule and stick to it. Or find colleagues to help. For secondary teachers, try using lunchtime and time before or after school. For elementary or self-contained teachers, create centers activities that allow you to do running records while the rest of the class is busy doing something different. The sooner you know your students' reading levels, the sooner you can start choice, guided, and shared reading.

Sabrina,

I'd love to spend time getting to know you a little better as a reader.

You have an appointment with me this Wednesday at 12:30. Please meet me in the classroom and bring your lunch. You don't need anything else. It should take about 15 minutes.

See you then!

Mrs. Witter

IF YOU DON'T HAVE TIME FOR ONE-ON-ONE RUNNING RECORDS DO GROUP INVENTORIES

If administering one-on-one assessments isn't practically possible, here are some other ideas for ways to determine a student's comfort reading level.

Five-Finger Test

Teach students the five-finger test. Students read a page aloud to themselves. If they don't know the meaning of five words on one page, the book is too hard. If they don't know the meaning of one word or fewer, the book is too easy. To find their comfort level, students should be aiming for not knowing about three words a page. Teach students to do a spot check at the beginning and middle of the book. The five-finger test is great for elementary students.

Self-Evaluation

In class, give students a selection of texts to read, but don't put them in leveled order. Ask students to read through the materials and answer comprehension questions for each. Then ask students to self-identify the text that they felt most comfortable with. This will give you at least a ballpark of what texts your student should be reading. It's also a great indication of how well students self-assess. Then, once you set up reading conferences in your class, you can ask kids to read the text level that they identified aloud to see if it falls within 96–99% accuracy. Self-evaluation is a great tool to use for secondary students.

Group Inventories

In my first couple years of teaching, I used group inventories because my class periods were very short and I didn't have the opportunity to give inventories to students outside of class. The QRI-5 provides a group administration option for grades three and above. In a group inventory, students are given grade-level passages to read independently. For students who do well, give a harder passage the next day. For students who struggle, give an easier passage. You can assign this for homework. Then assess students who don't do well comprehensively to get more information. Group inventories do not allow you to hear students read aloud, but they are practical if you are running low on time and provide a starting point. They work well in any grade. Many are available online, such as the Measures of Academic Progress (MAP) assessment, if you have computers in your classroom.

MATCH STUDENTS TO BOOKS BASED ON THEIR COMFORT LEVEL

Now it's time to match kids to texts. All of the different reading inventories use different scales: some use letters, lexiles, or numbers. Table 1.3 shows the most common developmental reading scales and how they correlate to grade level.

Most approaches to scaling books look at vocabulary, sentence structure, and the overall structure of the text. It's actually really cool! Books on the lower developmental end start off simply: typically with one plot in fiction or one main idea in nonfiction. But as books become more difficult, their structures become more complex. If you want to see how these formulas calculate levels, check out the Fry graph readability formula on www.reading-without-limits.com.

Table 1.3 How Different Reading Levels Correlate

Grade	Fountas and Pinnell Letter	Lexile	DRA
K	A-E	200–400	A-1 through 3
1	D-I		4–16
2	J-M	300–600	18–30
3	N-P	500–800	30–38
4	Q, R	600–900	40–42
5	S-U	700–800	44
6	V-X	700–1050	
7	Y	850–1100	
8	Z	900–1150	
8+	Z +	1000–1200	

Which books students read and how they are matched will depend upon what kind of reading they are doing. Next I give some guidelines for matching students to choice, shared, and guided reading texts. Now that you've identified your students' comfort zones, it's time to match them to texts to read during choice, guided, and shared reading.

Texts for Choice Reading

Match students to texts where they are able to decode 96% or more words and have at least 90% comprehension of the texts. These are texts that students can read comfortably. Give students the opportunity to choose their books, and allow tons of time for students to read those books. If your library for choice reading is leveled, you can show kids where to go to find their comfort level.

Texts for Guided Reading

Texts that fall a grade level above comfort level are a student's guided reading level or comfort-plus level. These texts are teacher-chosen and usually shorter than a text a student would choose for choice reading. Teachers group students according to their guided reading level, and they might have half a dozen groups at once in their classroom. Avoid matching students to guided reading texts where students decode less than 75% of the words or where their comprehension falls below 75%.

Texts for Shared Reading

The teacher chooses shared reading texts and everyone in the class reads the same text. These texts are more difficult than guided reading texts. If decoding or comprehension falls below 75% for a student, the teacher should scaffold the text for those individual students.

Not sure how to level a text? Try http://www.arbookfind.com or http://www.lexile.com. Enter the name of the book and the Web site will give you its reading level.

CREATE AN ENVIRONMENT WHERE PEERS SUPPORT EACH OTHER'S DIFFERENCES

Kids love videogames because they advance levels and moving up to the next level, while not easy, isn't impossible. The level of difficulty is just right to push kids to want to achieve more, in the same way that leveled reading gives students a myriad of texts at a harder level awaiting them. With students working with different reading levels, it's a reality that you will have students who might either feel self-conscious that their level is lower than others, or you might have students who tease kids who have a lower level than they do.

Here are some ways to anticipate those pitfalls and keep leveled reading fun.

Post Growth

Encourage growth mindset, a theory established by Stanford psychologist Carol Dweck. Growth mindset suggests that people develop their abilities through dedication and hard work. It also suggests that achievement is limited by encouraging fixed mindset. Fixed mindset is when people believe that skills are innate and not able to change.[14] Show leveled growth without posting original levels. Each time students grow a level they color in the chart. Or, to make it more of a team effort, save time for the class to track their progress by coloring in each of their teammate's progress whenever growth is achieved. During morning announcements, principals can celebrate growth and effort. *Juan advanced a reading level today. Let's give him five snaps!* A secondary school leader could say, *Agnieszka continues to try to learn as much as possible. She has embraced her challenges and has been especially receptive to critical feedback regarding how to improve her reading. I want to praise her for her continued love of learning in English class.*

Build a Differentiated Community

From the beginning of class, show that you are celebrating growth, not achievement. Lelac, a fifth and sixth grade reading teacher in Washington, DC, does an activity similar to the following. She posts the developmental leveled continuum (she uses the A–Z scale) in a circle around the room. She asks Shamar to stand under level L. As this activity is a simulation, it doesn't represent his real level. Lelac then tells the class that Shamar came in on level L, but he worked really hard during class. He started zooming up levels. By January he was level N (Shamar moves to that level). By June, he was level P (Shamar moves). Shamar ended up making a ton of growth. Then she does a different simulation with Shamar. She asks Shamar to stand under O. Shamar, who started class as a strong reader, didn't push himself. He kept reading similar books, and didn't want to read harder texts during shared or guided reading. By the end of the year, he only moved up to P (Shamar moved). Lelac then asks her class, "Which student ended up ahead?" With the class, she discusses that the first, hard-working student's habits would enable him to continue growing even after this year. As Lelac recounted, "It is crucial for students to understand that they are in fact in a position of infinite power and potential, that they should feel inferior to nobody and be ashamed of nothing. If they work hard, they can and will come out on top."

Start with an Easy Book Unit

If you haven't had the opportunity to determine reading levels, start the year with an "easy book unit" in elementary or middle school classrooms. Urge students to identify books that they think would be quick reads. For the first few weeks of school, students read upward of a dozen books. This helps build library routines because kids are moving at an accelerated pace. When the playing field becomes equalized during an easy book unit, there is less stigma attached to reading levels later on, once you have the opportunity to administer reading inventories. I find this strategy effective for all grade levels, and it helps give you a little more time to administer reading inventories.

Use Texts from All Levels

During instruction, avoid using texts that are exclusively on grade level. There are rich resources within texts at all gradients. For instance, in the first grade book *Henry and Mudge,* the first page's text reads "Henry and Mudge, a boy and his dog, are meant to be together. Most often they are, but not always." What a great text to teach understanding appositives! *Who's Henry? Who's Mudge? How do you know? Has anyone read this book before? Isn't it awesome?* Books at all levels are rich with teaching opportunities. If you are a secondary teacher, don't knock elementary texts and vice versa.

Once you figure out your students' reading levels, you are well on your way toward meeting the needs of all of your kids, including the Sofias in your classroom. Guess who just started high school, and who can read *A Wrinkle in Time,* no problem? Sofia advanced from level G to Z, a difference of seven grade levels, in three years and is well on her way to and through college.

ADDITIONAL RESOURCES

1. Sample inventories with several students reading on a range of levels and the notes that the teacher took
2. Fry Graph for Estimating Readability
3. Suggestions for how to set up a leveled library

MILD, MEDIUM, SPICY NEXT-STEP SUGGESTIONS

	Mild	**Medium**	**Spicy**
Assessing Readers	Administer a whole group inventory to determine which students are not able to answer on grade level passages. Then pull identified students for additional inventory assessments.	Get your friends to help! Show a couple running record videos and teach your friends the basics. Later, match five kids per friend. You just finished a class!	Ask students to do a think aloud as they independently read to show you the thinking that is happening in their head as part of their reading inventory. Tell students, "*I want to hear the thinking in your head. Each time you do a reading strategy, say it out loud.*" Then evaluate which strategies they are using.
Peer Support	Nothing works better than keepin' it real. Share with students your concerns about teasing from the offset, and what you do and don't want to see.	Celebrate texts within all gradients of difficulty. As you keep a chart of books you are reading, make sure to throw in books at all levels and sell the heck out of them. Allow students at higher levels periodically to check out a high-interest lower-level text.	Create progress growth charts rather than level growth charts. At the beginning of the year, give each student an end of year grow goal two or more grade levels above where they entered, and chart progress.

SUGGESTED FURTHER READING FOR LEVELED READING

1. *Guiding Readers and Writers* by Irene Fountas and Gay Su Pinnell
2. *Differentiated Reading Instruction* by Laura Robb
3. *Running Records for Classroom Teachers* by Marie M. Clay
4. *Qualitative Reading Inventory-5* by Lauren Leslie

KEEPIN' IT REAL

Here are some problems that we faced when assessing students' reading levels. Address the pitfalls in advance and I hope they won't happen to you!

Sneaking Harder Books

Some teachers require students to read exclusively within their comfort level during choice reading. I wasn't that teacher, because if a kid was begging for a book, I let them read it. But, and this is a big but, monitor carefully. What you don't want is reluctant or struggling readers choosing a book on their frustration level and then getting stuck, discouraged, or starting the bad habit of fake reading. Continually check in and if it's not working out suggest a level-appropriate book with a similar theme. Another idea is to give kids some leeway by allowing students to read any level that they want once a month. Marie Clay says, ". . . there must be the opportunity for the child . . . to pull himself up by his bootstraps: texts which allow him to practice and develop the full range of strategies which he does control, and by problem-solving new challenges, reach out beyond that present control" (Clay, p. 215).[15] Therefore, don't be too strict in regards to kids "sneaking" harder books.

Teacher Language Around Levels

Be mindful of your language when referencing levels in the classroom. Avoid language like, *Don't read this book because it's too hard for you* or *Is this book above your level? Put it down and get a book on your level.* Try more kid-friendly, growth-mindset language like, *I think that the books in the green baskets are going to make you feel like a strong reader. Find one that you are interested in.* Or, *Is this book a little confusing? See if you can find a book in the _____ basket with a similar theme.*

Order Lots of Lower Reading Level Books

Middle and high schools must order first and second grade level books. Many adolescents are reading in that range. Kids who read books within that range read a lot more books than kids who read books in higher book bands because the books are shorter with larger font. I am currently working with high school boys who are sixteen to eighteen years old, and of those boys, 20% are reading below a second grade level. I find myself doubling the number of books in the first and second grade range each year when I purchase books for libraries. Kids can read upward of two a day.

"Baby Books" + Big Kids

Although I've never experienced this first hand, some teachers who work with high school students notice disengagement when older readers are assessed using lower-level passages that have juvenile topics. If that's the case, consider supplementing your books with high-interest, lower-level books that are produced by literacy companies targeting that market. For instance, companies produce short texts that are on a first grade level with topics that interest upper middle and high school students. Capstone Press produces nonfiction readers on a similar readability range that should interest students through high school. Or consider writing a grant for e-readers. Then download a range of books onto each tablet. E-readers provide anonymity if students are self-conscious of their levels.

FOR COACHES AND SCHOOL LEADERS

Time for Assessments

Provide time for teachers so that they can assess reading levels. Consider changing the schedule so secondary teachers have the day "off" to pull kids to assess. Or cover your teachers' classes for the day for the same purpose.

In elementary school, consider bringing in community volunteers for a day. Share leveling resources with them. The more folks on board, the faster you will be able to determine levels.

Organize

Whether it's an administrator or reading specialist who does the task, someone needs to be "in charge of" keeping the inventory records so you can track student progress as they advance in grade levels. A simple excel spreadsheet does the trick. I recommend that a non–classroom teacher performs this job so one person for all students in the school keeps the records.

TO SUM UP

- Determine the reading level of each student, ideally one-on-one using a running record.
- Do group inventories when you need to save time assessing.
- Do not match a book to a student's grade or age; match it to his or her reading level.
- Create a "reading level" free community that doesn't get hung up on peer reading levels, but instead supports stamina, love of reading, and strategic growth.

PART 2

Steps to Creating Lifelong Readers

2

Teaching Students to Understand What They Read
Why Videogames Beat Candyland

In order to ensure that students *really understand* what they are reading, follow these steps as outlined in this chapter:

- ❏ Use the read-aloud/think-aloud to introduce strategies
- ❏ Check for understanding throughout the think-aloud and allow time for students to try the strategy on their own
- ❏ Avoid common think-aloud pitfalls
- ❏ Choose the just-right text for a think-aloud
- ❏ Prioritize figuring it out and paraphrasing strategies
- ❏ Teach strategies that build lifelong readers

Our KIPPsters play board games at lunch when it's raining. Games range from decks of cards to Candyland. At first, Candyland had retro appeal. Do you remember the rules? It's a simple racing game. There are 134 spaces in six different colors. Players take turns drawing a card from a stack, and jump to the next color. The player who gets around first wins. As I stood with the seventh graders, Candyland glee went to "Candyland is wack." Kids got bored quickly. That's because Candyland involves zero strategic thinking. In this chapter, I show why our seventh graders were right, "Candyland is wack," and if there's one thing our classrooms should mirror, it's videogames.

There are many benefits to videogames that can be applied to a literacy classroom. Not only are videogames leveled, and therefore follow a developmental continuum, but individual strategy plays a big part in videogame fun. Kids are *thinking* while they play videogames. They love videogames because they are in control of the outcome. Using skills that they collect through trial and error, manuals, and friends, videogamers figure out ways to win. As James Gee, a researcher who studied the links between videogames and literacy, argues, people like videogames because they become co-producers of the story, in the same way that readers should be co-producers of the text. It's essential that we create constantly thinking readers who have a unique experience as they read. Great readers are strategic: they are impressed by amazing sentences, immerse themselves in the plot to fall in love with characters, and scrutinize terrible books. Teaching students to apply many of the same strategies that they already access when playing videogames will make them rigorous, critically thinking, active readers. I recognize the problem with using videogames as a metaphor. There is a debate about whether or not videogames, particularly violent ones, are harmful to teens. The purpose of this chapter is not to advocate that kids should play videogames. Instead,

> *We really believe that practice makes kids better readers. The number one priority is making sure kids are reading books that they thoroughly understand. I teach around it over and over and over. Kids who say they hate reading, what they really hate is reading books they don't understand. It makes sense that you hated reading up until this point. It's my point to help you find a book that you will love.*
>
> —Lelac, 5th and 6th grade English teacher

it's to analyze what makes videogames so motivating and engaging for kids. I then share how to lift that criteria and apply it in your classroom.[16]

When students are reading books, it's vital that they really understand the text: kids should be able to recall meaning, paraphrase meaning, uncover implied meaning, and make new meaning. That's why we match them to their comfort level, because they are more likely to comprehend texts on their comfort level. However, even after you match kids to the right level, that doesn't mean they'll *really* understand. They might understand the page they're on and forget everything before it. They might misinterpret parts of the book because of an incorrect inference. Now that kids are matched to their comfort levels, the next step is to teach them how to really understand their texts both on a literal and inferential level, because matching students to their comfort level isn't enough.

> *Kids need to really understand the text: recall meaning, uncover implied meaning, and make new meaning. However, even after you match kids to the right level, that doesn't mean they'll really understand.*

This chapter will show that the principles behind playing videogames are what will make your readers stronger. Ultimately, our goal is for our readers to *really understand* what they are reading. That happens through strategic reading.

STRATEGIC READING: WHAT INDEPENDENT READERS DO

Strategic reading means giving students a strategy that they can apply to lots of texts, not just one. Does it get more rigorous than that? As Susan Zimmerman eloquently states in *Bring the Joy Back to Reading*, "The human enterprise is to think. Why else would we have these amazing brains? When children are thinking, when they are challenged, when they are engaged—they own their learning. They do it because it is theirs and they are getting something of value from the process. There is a strong commitment to inquiry, to embarking on the quest for new information, and to learning how to learn . . . The thinking strategies are not an end in themselves. They are a means to an end. The end is avid reading and good thinking" (Zimmerman, p. 38).[17] Unfortunately, too many of our students are not thinking as they read. Therefore, they aren't applying strategies to their lifelong reading habits.

Why is strategic reading important? Consider the following example. Let's start with an exercise. As you read through the following excerpt from "Fine Structure of Synaptogenesis in the Vertebrate Central Nervous System," try to fully comprehend the paragraph. Feel free to jot notes in the margin if it helps!

> The brain appears to be especially sensitive to gaze direction in process-ing features of the face. Behavioral and functional magnetic resonance imaging (fMRI) studies have found that direction of eye gaze provokes an automatic, reflexive orienting of covert spatial attention, and affects responses in brain structures such as the amygdala and ventral striatum, involved in processing emotional signals such as threat or reward, during the observation of expressive faces. One early fMRI study revealed the importance of temporal regions in processing shifts of eye gaze, and a related study established that activity in these areas is sensitive to context and the perceived intentions of others [Davies and others, p. 2].[18]

I chose a text that was probably a little bit outside your comfort zone, unless you are a neuroscientist. What did you do to try to understand it? Reread? Use what you understood to pick apart confusing parts? Connected to what you already knew? As readers, we employ many strategies in order to pick apart and comprehend difficult texts. Therefore, we want our students to do the same thing. Stephanie Harvey and Harvey Daniels powerfully compare it to driving:

> It's important to realize that since we are veteran readers, we take these cognitive steps mostly automatically and unaware. We have relegated most of the brainwork of reading to the unconscious level, just like

driving a car. But when we encounter some really difficult text . . . just as when the car in front of us comes to a screeching halt, we suddenly become acutely aware of our thinking (or driving!).The cognitive strategies at our disposal are now explicit, right out in the open. We can literally hear our strategic thinking at work as we say, "Hit the brakes!" or "Whoops, I better go back and reread this." [Harvey and Daniels, p. 21][19]

Dependent readers are like drivers driving through stoplights. They aren't aware of their reading, and often rely heavily on teachers, fake read, "hate" to read, or don't remember what they read. Many dependent readers work at decoding words rather than making sense of the text. When confronted with a text a little bit outside their comfort zone, they don't try to figure it out because they don't have an arsenal of strategies to use. So we need to give them an arsenal. On the other hand, independent readers are strategic, as shown in Figure 2.1.

In 2005, when KIPP Infinity's door's opened, the majority of our students were significantly below grade level, many as much as two to three years or more. Most were dependent readers. This picture isn't unique, and

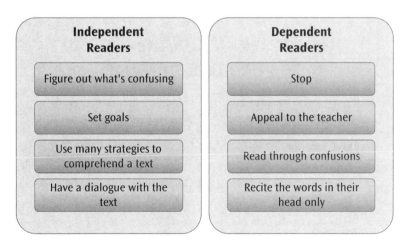

Figure 2.1 The Difference Between Independent and Dependent Readers

Derived from Kylene Beers's *When Kids Can't Read*.

is similar to the situation in many of our classrooms. By giving our students strategies that independent readers do subconsciously, we lifted them to become independent readers who are then able to read above grade level.

How do we help readers make the move from dependence to independence? It's important to show your students the strategies that you use subconsciously. As readers, we do our best to try to understand what the author is trying to communicate. Unfortunately, dependent readers aren't actively involved with the text. Reading researcher and teacher Jeffrey Wilhelm likens it to "sitting on a bench during the big game, completely bored, without even realizing they hadn't participated in the action" (Wilhelm, p. 119).[20] Athletes are co-producers just like gamers. It's why videogames are more fun than Candyland. Remember Sofia? Sofia can be an independent thriving reader when she's matched to the appropriate text level and taught strategies that independent readers use. Before coming to KIPP, Sofia was driving through stoplights, completely unaware of her reading.

Next up: guidelines for how to lift your dependent readers to strategic, independent readers so that they stop driving through stoplights and start becoming co-producers of the text.

USE THE READ-ALOUD/THINK-ALOUD
TO INTRODUCE STRATEGIES

In order to ensure that students aren't dependent readers, I've found that the best way to give students an insight as to what expert readers do is to model, or demonstrate, my thinking before asking kids to try it on their own. When teaching a new strategy, I do a read-aloud/think-aloud. The read-aloud/think aloud is an excellent way to teach a strategy to dependent readers. Model expert reading with a text. This whole process should take about 15 minutes.

In a read-aloud/think-aloud, read a small portion of a text aloud to students and stop three times to demonstrate the thinking going on in your head. If you want to, you can also stop to ask students questions along the way. The thinking is the strategy that you want students to be able to do. Think-alouds are one of the best ways to demonstrate strategic reading. Think-alouds are an essential part of shared reading, particularly during close reading.

Figure 2.2 Be Expressive During a Read-Aloud/ Think-Aloud

One of the foundational reading strategies we want to model during think-alouds is paraphrasing. In order for students to understand the text, they need to be able to say what happened. In order to paraphrase what happened, they have to figure out what happened. So it's almost like the two strategies are dancing together: telling yourself what's happening in your head (paraphrasing) and constantly figuring out what's happening in the text. You can't have one without the other. It's important to teach and re-teach this strategy many times to all grade levels through a think-aloud.

Example of a Read-Aloud/Think-Aloud

Next is an example of a read-aloud/think-aloud using *Twilight* by Stephenie Meyer. I share one think-aloud, then in a read-aloud/think-aloud continue doing the same process *three* times. The purpose of this think-aloud is to model paraphrasing and figure it out by asking questions. This is a lesson I teach many, many times. Dependent readers would just read the words on the page and not remember any of the details. The following strategy—asking questions in order to paraphrase—helps students become co-producers of the text.

Preview for Students the Strategy That You Will Be Modeling
Class, today we are going to read the beginning of one of my favorite stories, *Twilight*. During the exposition of a story, readers sometimes get confused because they don't really know the characters or the setting or what's happening. Good readers try to figure out what's happening so they can start paraphrasing to themselves. In order to figure out what's happening, I'm going to ask myself three questions:

1. Who is in the scene?
2. What are they doing?
3. Where are they?

Then I'm going to answer those questions so I can paraphrase what's happening. If I can't answer one of those questions, I will reread or read on to figure out the answer. Let me show you as I start reading aloud from *Twilight*.

> I didn't sleep well that night, even after I was done crying. The constant whooshing of the rain and wind across the roof wouldn't fade into the background. I pulled the faded old quilt over my head, and later added the pillow, too. But I couldn't fall asleep until after midnight, when the rain finally settled into a quieter drizzle.

Think-Aloud 1
- I'm going to pause my reading for the first time in order to apply this strategy. Who is "I"? Not sure yet.
- Where is this taking place? It mentions a quilt and a pillow and falling asleep so it must be the narrator's bedroom.
- What's happening? The narrator is trying to sleep but can't.

> Breakfast with Charlie was a quiet event. He wished me good luck at school. I thanked him, knowing his hope was wasted. Good luck tended to avoid me.

Check for Understanding

Class, now I'm going to ask you some questions to check your understanding.

- Has the scene changed? How do you know?
- Who's in the scene?
- What's happening?

Notice how I

- Stopped to model my thinking
- Modeled one strategy
- Checked for understanding along the way to see if kids were with me
- Used a short piece of text (in total, I recommend no more than a couple pages)

Continue the same process, stopping no more than three times.

MOVING FROM CHECKS FOR UNDERSTANDING TO GUIDED PRACTICE

In order for our students to eventually master the strategies that we model on their own, we need to gradually release responsibility so that they can give it a try. Allow students to try the strategies a little while you are doing a think-aloud, a little more right after the think-aloud, and then even more during independent reading. This is the critical cycle of choice, guided, and shared reading.

Check for Understanding During the Read-Aloud

During the read-aloud, stop a couple times to check for understanding. Do this by asking a couple preplanned questions. In the model of a think-aloud just discussed, you'll notice that I preplanned times to check for understanding. It's that little opportunity for kids to try it on their own. Avoid reading a text aloud and exclusively modeling your thinking. Be sure to check for understanding along the way.

Try to avoid passive learning, like watching or listening, for more than a few minutes. In a research study, Dr. Ethna Reid aimed to identify what vital behaviors top-performing teachers did regardless of content, geography, or age group that led to their students' success. Of the three vital behaviors, top teachers rapidly go back and forth between teaching and questioning. They make corrections as needed. Poor performers drone on too much.[21] Consider the following when checking for understanding during a read-aloud/think-aloud.

Dipstick Strategies

- Nod your head if you are with me.
- Give students a green paper and a red paper. When they don't understand, they turn over the red paper.
- Thumbs up, to the side, or down if you get it.
- Pause halfway through the lesson and give a one question quiz.
- Use white boards.
- Rank your understanding on a scale of 1–5.

Dip Sticking

One way to check for understanding during a read-aloud is to incorporate what Madeline Hunter calls "dip sticking."[22] Dip sticking is when you do a quick check to see if kids get it, in the same way that you dip an oil stick into an engine to see how much oil is in the tank.

Incorporate Wait Time

Have you ever noticed that some of your students raise their hands immediately while some students rarely raise their hands? First off, provide think time before students share. It doesn't have to be a ton of time, but students must think about their answers first before answering. Not only will it increase the quality of the answers, but also it will encourage more participation and engagement. Research varies on the most effective amount of time to wait, but it ranges between three and five seconds. I literally count three Mississippi's in my head every time I ask a question. Researcher Mary Budd Rowe found that the average teacher waits 1.5 seconds between questioning and calling on a student. When increased to at least three seconds, the following occurs:[23]

- Accuracy increases
- Students responses are longer
- "I don't know" decreases
- More students participate
- Achievement on tests increase

Beyond waiting, here are some ways to make wait time more kid-friendly so that you get more student hands up.

Stop and Jot

Give students a few minutes to consider the answer to the question, and allow them to jot their answers down. Then open it up to the class.

Signal

After asking a question, prompt students to make eye contact with you once they are ready to share. Students like it because it's a secret. Some students are fearful that their peers will judge them if they take longer to consider an answer, but if you ask the class to make eye contact with you, their peers won't know who is taking longer. Waiting awhile? Just prompt your class by saying, "I'm waiting on a couple eyes" and you will get the last kids.

Figure 2.3 Encourage Active Participation

Right Is Right

Doug Lemov, author of *Teach Like a Champion* and one of the leaders of the Uncommon School Network, coined the term "right is right."[24] Right is right means pushing for answers that are precise. Too often teachers praise students for attempting to answer a question, when the answer is wrong or partially incorrect. Teachers will say "good" or "thank you" then say, "anyone have a different answer?" Unfortunately, this celebrates inaccurate answers and while nice, will not boost engagement. Instead, push students to clarify or expand on their answer. Or, if necessary, re-scaffold the question until students get the answer right. Then celebrate their accurate answer. This process shows students that they can, with revision, have precise answers, which ultimately leads to a sense of accomplishment.

Allow Students to Try the Strategy Together Before Trying on Their Own

After the read-aloud/think-aloud and checks for understanding, give students more of a try before launching them into independent reading. Guided practice fluidly becomes the next part of the lesson after a read-aloud/think-aloud. Here are some ways to do guided practice. I recommend that you choose one, and mix it up for each lesson! Guided practice usually takes anywhere between two and ten minutes.

The Classic Whole Group

The classic guided practice allows students to try what you did, in exactly the same way that you modeled during the mini lesson. If you modeled thinking aloud questions in *The Giver*, ask the class to create questions about *The Giver*. Then, call on a few students to share.

The Classic Partnerships

This is just like the Classic Whole Group except that students try the strategy in partnerships. The strength of doing partnerships is that all students get to participate.

Whiteboards

Give each student a whiteboard and a dry erase marker as a response card.[25] Let students try the skill and ask them to write their answers on their whiteboard. For example, continue reading on in *The Giver*. Pause. Ask students to write their question on their whiteboard, then ask students to hold up the boards. This is a great way to get a temperature check from all students.

Musical Chairs

Preplan four check-for-understanding questions that you really want to ask. Students get a chance to think about the questions by writing down their answers. Then, like musical chairs, play music as students mingle. When the music stops, that's their partner. They share their answer to number one. Music starts up again, stop, switch partner. Repeat four times.

> ## For Struggling Readers: Encourage Interactive Learning and Provide Frequent, Specific Feedback
>
> *Avoid lessons where you teach and students passively watch. Instead, make it interactive from start to finish. Check for understanding constantly throughout. Avoid giving vague feedback like "good job." Instead, try "Joel, you found a theme that shows what the author thinks about the world. Now I want you to find the best textual evidence. Everyone, turn and talk to your neighbor and see what you come up with. Joel, we're coming back to you."*

The Envelope, Please

Students upon entering are given an envelope with a question. Throughout the class the teacher draws a question to ask.[26]

Guided Practice Strategies That Push Rigor and Critical Thinking

All of the above guided practice strategies are rigorous. That's because reading and using reading strategies is cognitively demanding. But the ones below are even more rigorous. Give them a try!

Figure 2.4 Give Lots of Opportunity for Talk in Your Classroom

Force Rank

Give students the opportunity to generate multiple examples of the skill that you are teaching. For instance, write four questions about *The Giver*. Then kids must force rank the examples that they believe are the most masterful. Finally they share why.

Non-Examples

Rather than asking students to create an exemplary example of the aim, ask kids to create a non-example. This is a great way to highlight the criteria that shows what to avoid.

Criteria Check

During the mini lesson, forget to do one of the criteria. Ask students which criteria you demonstrated, and which one you forgot to do.

Rotten Tomatoes

After a think-aloud, share a few more models on paper in a range of quality. Ask students to give the models a critic score, just like on the website Rotten Tomatoes. On the website, critics give new movies a score out of 100%. For example, at the time I am writing this, the final Harry Potter movie has a score of 97%. That's a fresh tomato! Whereas *Bad Teacher*, starring Cameron Diaz, has a rotten score of 44%. Students draw a picture of a fresh tomato or a rotten tomato to go with their score. After coming up with their scores, they need to defend their answers aloud with their partners. By asking students to rank your think-alouds, students are active participants in their learning rather than watching you do all of the heavy lifting. This way, your direct instruction is "I/We Do" rather than "I Do."

Figure 2.5 Check in with Students with the Thumbs Up Strategy

Your-Life Questions

These questions take what students already comprehend about the strategy you taught, and then ask them to apply that knowledge to their outside lives. For instance, if you were teaching students to analyze character decisions, you could ask:

> Think about something in your life where you made a decision that you wish you hadn't made. Now think of ways you could change that decision. What could you say or do that would make the biggest change? What would happen if you weren't able to say or do anything? Now let's go back to the text. Can you think of a moment where X may want to change a decision he made? Do you think X should change? What could X do to make that change? How would the situation be different if X made the change?

I try to incorporate at least one your-life question per class. Applying new knowledge to what you find meaningful in your outside life boosts retention. Researcher Gillian Cohen, who coined the Baker/baker paradox wonderfully, illustrates the importance of attaching meaning from your life to memory.[27] Researchers showed two groups of people the same face. For the first group, the researcher described the face as a person whose profession was a baker. For the second group, the researcher said that the man's last name was Baker. Two days later, the researcher showed the groups the face and asked them for the word. It turns out that if you are told a person's profession, you are much more likely to remember the word than if you were told a person's last name — even though they are the same word with the same photograph. The reason you are apt to remember the profession is because all of the associations that you make inside your complex neural network with the concept "baker." For instance, "baker" may make you think of the lemon bars your grandmother bakes. This is why your-life questions emotionally and conceptually encode your students' learning and help cement content into memory. The Common Core Standards emphasize what can be unpacked in the text, and not outside of the text. Remember, your-life questions should be used to enhance textual understanding.[28]

Just like a polo shirt won't go out of style for awhile, neither will the classic whole group guided practice. That's why I use this type of guided practice at least 50% of the time. However, in order to mix things up, I sprinkle in the other kid-friendly guided practices. Keep it fun to help engagement and retention. If you have time in your lesson (make sure to save an extended block for independent practice!), you can incorporate a couple different types of guided practice.

COMMON THINK-ALOUD PITFALLS

Avoid Teachable Moments

Refrain from "teachable moments" in a read-aloud/think-aloud when you want to think-aloud other awesome parts of the text, new vocabulary, or explain something complicated. Stick to one strategy when you model it and do a think-aloud three times. I know how hard it can be to stick only to the skill you are teaching, especially if you are teaching rich, amazing literature; but if you think-aloud about lots of different things, you run the risk of demonstrating *less* mastery for your aim. That doesn't mean that you shouldn't spiral strategies that you've taught before. There is a place for teachable moments during shared reading, which I will describe in the chapter on shared reading, Chapter 4.

Keep Think-Alouds Short

Typically, we keep read-aloud/think-alouds to less than 15 minutes in order to save time for checks for understanding, independent reading, and all the other fun stuff that happens in a class period (see Chapter 14 for how to put together a lesson plan).

Plan a Think-Aloud in Advance

When planning a think-aloud, plan where you are going to stop in advance by writing it into your lesson plan, onto the book, or on stickies. Gradually release responsibility as you do a think-aloud. Do the first two yourself, and then bring in the class to help you with the third. Don't start without a plan. I find that this is the most common pitfall as some teachers, due to all of our time commitments, take shortcuts and don't plan think-alouds. Then the lesson falls apart. Take the extra few minutes and preplan where you want to stop to demonstrate your thinking.

Get Your Drama On

In a read-aloud/think-aloud, really show your love of the book with a melodious reading. Get into it with character voices, expressive gestures, and emotion. The better your read-aloud, the more likely kids will love the book.

CHOOSING A THINK-ALOUD TEXT

Here are some options when choosing a text for a read-aloud/think-aloud listed below.

The Shared Reading Text

In the shared reading block, the teacher and students spend 30 minutes analyzing a shared text. This text is not necessarily a novel—it can be a poem, speech, narrative nonfiction, or article. You can use the same shared text during a read-aloud/think-aloud. That way, students get to spend more time with the text, which they've probably grown very attached to.

A Picture Book

Picture books are great for read-aloud/think-alouds, not only because so many have rich stories, but also because they follow an entire plot that you can read aloud in one sitting.

Adult Book

If you want to show students that you are an expert independent reader, choose an excerpt from a book that you are reading at home (that's engaging) and model the strategy. Remember to model with nonfiction as well.

Short Excerpts

Anything from a poem to an advertisement is great for a read-aloud/think-aloud. Don't just use novels! Use all different texts and make sure that you use lots of nonfiction documents. It's essential that students are transferring their strategic thinking to *all* text structures and genres. For example, my husband and I were thinking about getting a used car. We found an article in a car magazine that discussed small cars. I had a lot of questions while reading the article. I thought this was an excellent teaching opportunity for my students, so I did a read-aloud/think-aloud showing that good readers ask questions as they read nonfiction by relating questions to their own lives. I brought in the car magazine and shared my own authentic questions.

- The article said that the Mazda 2 won an award in 2008. I asked, "Should we get that car because it won an award?"
- The article mentioned the Civic as budget focused. I asked, "Does budget mean that it isn't good quality? Do we need a good quality car?"
- The article had a table showing how cars depreciate over time. I asked, "Should we get an older car? They are cheaper, but are they safe?"
- When I started checking for understanding, I asked, "How were my questions personal to me? How did they use the information in the article?"

WHERE TO BEGIN: A SEQUENCE OF STRATEGIES FOR READING COMPREHENSION

In working with struggling, dependent, and reluctant readers for the past decade, I'm indebted to the reading research on strategic thinking. Adopting from the work of reading experts, trial and error, and student feedback, I compiled the following sequence of strategies to teach *Reading Without Limits*, which is aligned to the Common Core Standards. The sequence I recommend is adapted from the work of *I Read It, But I Don't Get It* by Cris Tovani, *When Kids Can't Read* by Kylene Beers, *You Gotta BE the Book* by Jeffrey Wilhelm, *Mosaic of Thought* by Ellin Oliver Keene and Susan Zimmerman, *Developing Critical Awareness at the Middle Level* by Holly Johnson and Lauren Freedman, *Shades of Meaning* by Donna Santman, and *The Common Core State Standards* of the National Governors Association for Best Practices and the Council and Chief State of School Officers. Through the last 10 years, I've found that the sequence presented in the following sections not only lifts dependent readers, but also takes kids far beyond grade level in their reading abilities.

As mentioned, start with the foundational skills. We want our kids to really understand what they are reading while they read. Start with the foundational skills even with choice books because many kids aren't able to paraphrase accurately when they read. Just because you matched your students to their comfort level doesn't mean that they really understand. Start with paraphrasing and figuring it out, and take as long as you need until your dependent readers start doing it independently. Note that foundational skills do not equate to low-level skills. The ability to figure it out while paraphrasing is very sophisticated and extremely rigorous. All strategies below are skills your students will use up to and through college. During guided and shared reading, as students are working with harder texts, still teach paraphrasing and figuring it out, because we want students to really understand difficult texts, too. Those strategies are the "magic beans" of strategies.

Each strategy isn't meant just for one day of teaching. Continually reteach until students demonstrate mastery. Use the shared reading and guided reading blocks to reteach and model the same strategy with a harder text. We need repetition to remember.

Most strategies are relevant for any grade level. Differentiation occurs due to complexity of text. The strategy tracking dialogue by identifying which character is speaking is developmentally appropriate for upper elementary using *Matilda* and high school using Faulkner. However, while each strategy discussed below can be taught at most age levels, some are more appropriate for secondary students. Strategies unique to nonfiction or fiction are marked NF or F.

I hope Table 2.1 is helpful in breaking down how you want to structure your read-aloud/think-aloud into one bite-sized strategy. If your kids can ultimately do all the strategies, they will become masterful readers.

"BEFORE-READING" STRATEGIES

Start with these strategies because they are habits good readers should have before choosing a book. I like to start with these strategies during the first couple weeks of school.

Table 2.1 Before-Reading Strategies

Upper Elementary	Upper Middle and High School
• Choose just-right book • Build stamina by setting goals • Preview text, analyzing cover, title, and back, and make predictions based on the preview	(see all upper elementary strategies) • Set a purpose for reading • Connect to personal experience in order to build excitement about the text • Connect to other similar types of books, and compare to current book

Teach each category sequentially

STRATEGIES FOR THE BEGINNING OF A TEXT

These strategies are ideal to teach next (see Table 2.2). Many readers become disengaged with the text during the exposition, since they don't have a relationship yet with the text. The strategies are about building a relationship with a text so you are motivated to continue reading it. Since kids don't choose the text during shared reading, these strategies are excellent for the shared reading block.

STRATEGIES TO DETERMINE LITERAL MEANING

Paraphrasing and Figuring It Out

Before kids can start doing reading strategies where they "add on" to the text, they first need to figure out what the text is saying. These strategies help

Table 2.2 Beginning of the Text Strategies

Upper Elementary	Upper Middle and High School
• Determine if first few pages met your expectations • Determine who is in the scene, what is happening, and what they are doing in order to paraphrase • Ask questions as you read • Make predictions about what will happen next • Evaluate your own personal engagement • Abandon a book only when appropriate • All stamina strategies (stamina strategies should be taught ongoing and not just at the beginning of a text)	(see all upper elementary strategies) • Highlight what the author wants you to notice in the beginning • Connect to schema in order to understand and what you need to know • Figure out how events in the exposition arose (F)

Table 2.3 Paraphrasing and Figuring-It-Out Strategies

Upper Elementary, Middle, and High School

Paraphrasing
- Pay attention to verb tenses to say when events happened
- Summarize the events of a story or text in chronological order
- Describe a character, person, event, or setting in depth
- Retell the story by highlighting important events
- Retell the story following plot elements (exposition, rising action, climax, falling action, resolution)
- Keep a running paraphrase dialogue in your head
- Revise your initial paraphrases if new information contradicts your paraphrase
- Use nonfiction text features in order to paraphrase (NF)
- Avoid using technical vocabulary in your paraphrase unless you can rephrase in your own words (NF)

Figuring It Out

- Be aware of the three reading voices (off task, reciting, and conversation) and turn on conversation voice
- Use clarifying questions when you don't understand something. "What does ___ mean?" Use predictive questions if you think you know what's going to happen next. "Does this mean that ___ will happen?"
- Ask yourself, who is in the scene, where are they, and what are they doing?
- Reread to fix wandering mind or lack of recall
- Adjust reading rate
- Answer questions as you read
- Track characters or people to remember which one is which
- Track dialogue by identifying which character is speaking using text cues
- Track time including flash forwards and flashbacks
- Reflect on what it feels like to be in the "flow" of reading

Reading to Get Information from Nonfiction

- Read with a question in mind (NF)
- Skim and scan to find an answer (NF)
- Read to get the gist (NF)
- Use the table of contents and index to find answers to your questions (NF)
- Read with a purpose (to answer your question) (NF)
- Study diagrams and pictures to get information (NF)
- Analyze text features like subheadings, titles, and italics (NF)
- Use the glossary to figure out unknown words (NF)

Table 2.4 Visualizing Strategies

Upper Elementary	Upper Middle and High School
• Create a mental movie for extended period of text • Be aware of when the mental movie is off • Identify what parts in the text help you see a picture • Follow the scene by seeing it from different vantage points • Use nonfiction text features to aid visualization (NF)	(see all upper elementary strategies) • Cut through descriptive or figurative text to create an accurate image of what the author is literally describing • As with monitoring and fixing, teach all of the visualizing strategies from upper elementary school in upper middle and high school. Students who don't visualize are most often my most struggling, dependent, or reluctant readers.

them get a literal understanding of the text. Figuring it out and paraphrasing are so important that I devote a ton of teaching time during the year to ensure kids have mastered them (see Table 2.3).

Visualizing

Visualizing is a type of figuring it out strategy. I isolated it as its own category because it is so important. Visualizing will help students be able to have literal understanding of the text (see Table 2.4).

IMPLIED MEANING STRATEGIES

Analyzing Characters in Fiction or People in Nonfiction Texts

I like to start with analyzing characters as a reading strategy that uncovers implied meaning (see Table 2.5). This is the first jump past literal understanding.

Table 2.5 Analyzing Characters Strategies

Upper Elementary	Upper Middle and High School
• Create expectations about characters "I hope she will . . ." • Identify clue words that show the character's personality • Connect to personal experiences that help you better understand character decisions/motives/actions • Feel emotive with or toward characters "I'm excited/nervous/for __" • Use facts and details from story to support character's physical and personality traits • Identify obstacles and challenges that characters or people face and infer what's inside their character that will help them meet those obstacles • Judge character actions and decisions • Put yourself in the character's shoes through empathy • Question how you would do things similarly/differently if you were the character	(see all upper elementary strategies) • Figure out the most important supporting character • Identify foreshadowing, and use foreshadowing to make predictions • Analyze complex characters • Evaluate reliability of the narrator

Inferring

Students are already making a ton of inferences when they analyze characters. Now they will be able to make different types of inferences (see Table 2.6).

Determine Importance and Synthesize

Once students are able to analyze literal and implied meanings of individual parts of the text, they are ready to analyze implied meanings of the entire text (see Table 2.7).

Table 2.6 Making Inferences Strategies

Upper Elementary	Upper Middle and High School
• Use basic plot structure to generate predictions (F) • Analyze basic cause-and-effect structure to generate predictions • Use knowledge of genre or other books written by the same writer to make predictions • Question why you are particularly turned off by different scenes • Be aware that sometimes we misinterpret the text without realizing it, and read on to make sure you are developing ideas that have textual support • Argue what was left out of the story that you wish was included • Figure out inferences that make sense of what's really happening in the story. Make inferences elaborate on the text. • Figure out the intonation of character or person's words • Make more of what the characters or people do, say, and think by analyzing their personalities, motivations, and internal conflicts • Know the difference between an inference that has textual evidence and an opinion	(see all upper elementary strategies) • Examine significance of events in the text that seem on the surface to be insignificant and analyze why the author chose to include those events • Judge fairness of different moments of the text (F) • Determine which episodes or information the author left out and how to fill in that information • Question if an event hadn't happened and how that would impact the story • Use the text to defend theories about the writer's values and beliefs • Determine what values or assumptions are beneath the text • Question whose voices are missing from the text and how that affects the text • Infer what additional information the author would have provided if the point of view would have been third person and not first person (F)

Analyze Literary Elements

Literary elements are another type of implied meaning analysis (see Table 2.8).

Table 2.7 Determining Importance and Synthesis Strategies

Upper Elementary	Upper Middle and High School
• Determine which parts of the story you liked the most/the least • Determine and support with text evidence possible themes/messages/morals • Assimilate new information into the theme while reading and revise thinking when necessary • Pay attention to character's or people's thoughts, feelings, and words and how they relate to the theme • Explain how a series of chapters, scenes, or stanzas fit together to provide the overall structure • Distinguish between fun facts and most important facts (NF)	(see all upper elementary strategies) • Determine what the author is saying about the theme • Question what the author might believe • Compare texts with the same theme (F) • Analyze causal relationships • Describe different aspects of major and minor characters or people, and explain how those characteristics influence interactions and plot elements • Identify and describe the setting and analyze connections between the setting and other story elements • Analyze how a particular excerpt contributes to the development of the theme, setting, plot, or sequence of events • Determine the message the author is conveying through the use of different characters

MAKING NEW MEANING STRATEGIES

Once your students are able to understand the text on a literal and implied level, and once they are able to look at the text as a whole, they will then be able to see themselves as co-producers of the text (see Table 2.9). As co-producers, they can start creating their own justifiable interpretations of the text. Once they can do this, they are on track to becoming successful English majors in college!

Teach your students reading strategies that will not only make them lifelong readers, but also confident readers who gain new insights out of everything that they read. Each of the strategies above is its own separate lesson. Teach the strategies by doing a read-aloud/think-aloud. Don't forget to continually reteach the strategy because students need repetition to

Table 2.8 Analyzing Literary Elements Strategies

Upper Elementary	Upper Middle and High School
• Identify and describe different plot elements (F) • Distinguish between different points of view • Analyze which part of the (plot, action, climax . . .) is your favorite/least favorite (F) • Explain the author's use of humor • Explain major differences between different structures (prose, drama, poetry) and genres • Identify and interpret different types of figurative language	(see all upper elementary strategies) • Determine the significance of a first person point of view story (F) • Identify and interpret symbolism • Compare themes and plots by the same author across a variety of texts (F) • Determine how literary devices show the author's intent • Explain how different events move the story forward

Table 2.9 Making New Meaning Strategies

Upper Elementary	Upper Middle and High School
• Distinguish your point of view from that of the main character or narrator • Explain why/why not you'd like to get to know the author • Determine why your reading rate varied • Explain whether or not you'd read the text again • Discuss what you'd do differently next time you read	(see all upper elementary strategies) • Identify, analyze, and evaluate the historical and biographical influences of the text and how it impacted the text • Analyze social, ethnic, gender, and cultural contexts and other characteristics of the time period • Compare and contrast social power dynamics in text and analyze how it connects to our own lives • Consider the background and qualifications of the writer • Identify techniques the author uses to persuade • Criticize the author's use of certain techniques and their affect on the reader • Describe how a narrator's or speaker's point of view influences how events are described • Analyze how an author's choices create surprise, tension, excitement, sadness, etc.

remember. Try reteaching the strategy using different genres. Ultimately you are turning on the thinking voice in your readers' heads.

ADDITIONAL RESOURCES

1. Teachers modeling read-aloud/think-alouds on video
2. Lesson plans that build strategic thinking
3. Professional development includes narrated PowerPoint explaining how to do a read-aloud/think-aloud

MILD, MEDIUM, SPICY NEXT-STEP SUGGESTIONS

	Mild	Medium	Spicy
Model What You Want Students to Do	Do read-aloud/think-alouds in which you stop three times as you read to model the thinking in your head. Make sure that during the three times you stop you are modeling the same strategy.	Bring in nonfiction material from home with your thinking jotted in the margins. Show students how great readers constantly are reading and thinking as they read by sharing your thinking with the adult text. It's essential that you preplan check-for-understanding questions to ensure that it isn't a passive experience for your students.	Read the entire book before reading it aloud to the class. Ideally, preplan all of your think-alouds as well. You want to choose chapters that best illustrate the strategy you are going to teach.

	Mild	Medium	Spicy
Scaffolds for Struggling Readers	When doing a read-aloud/think-aloud, make a copy of the text so students have it in front of them.	If you can't get material on students' instructional reading level, then copy gloss notes, described in Chapter 4, and give your assisted notes to struggling readers.	Try a predictable story: Give students 15–20 important words from the chapter. Ask them to make predictions based on the chapter's content.

FAQ

Q: If students have questions about the text, do I ignore them because they are "teachable moments"? I don't want to shut down a student's voice.

A: It becomes negotiation for time. If there are only a few questions, answer them. If the questions are taking away from timing, then ask the student if it's OK if you talk to them during independent reading. Or, try a "Parking Lot," a popular strategy during business meetings. Post up a paper in your classroom of questions, and save time during a later class to answer them.

Q: Should I stick with one text during a read-aloud over the course of a few weeks or mix it up with different texts?

A: For read-alouds, you can use one text over time or mix it up with short texts. The same holds true for shared reading. Remember to mix up genres as well.

KEEPIN' IT REAL

Here are some problems that we faced when introducing strategic reading. Address the pitfalls in advance and I hope they won't happen to you!

Teachable Moments

It can be appealing to stop more than three times during a think-aloud to explain or discuss other parts of the text. But if you do, it detracts from the lesson's objective. Instead, save teachable moments for shared reading. Using the same text, go back and do a close reading.

FOR COACHES AND SCHOOL LEADERS

Professional Development

Narrated PowerPoints are available on www.reading-without-limits.com that show how to do a read-aloud/think-aloud.

SUGGESTED FURTHER READING FOR TEACHING STRATEGIC READING

1. *When Kids Can't Read* by Kylene Beers
2. *Teaching Reading in Social Studies, Science, and Math* by Laura Robb
3. *Strategic Reading* by Jeffrey D. Wilhelm

TO SUM UP

- Aim to show kids that good readers think as they read. They don't merely recite the text.
- Model strategies by reading and thinking aloud to build dependent readers' toolkits.
- Check for understanding throughout the think-aloud and allow time for students to try the strategy on their own while you give feedback.
- Avoid the most common think-aloud pitfalls.
- Prioritize teaching students how to simultaneously figure out what the text is saying in order to paraphrase in their heads. Then move down the suggested strategy sequence.

Choice Reading to Encourage a Ton of Reading
Reading in Istanbul

In order to set up a rigorous choice reading component to your literacy program, incorporate the following:

- ❏ Explicitly teach stamina then build it.
- ❏ Help students make good book choices.
- ❏ Build the state of flow in your classroom.
- ❏ Harness student engagement.
- ❏ Apply strategic reading to choice reading.
- ❏ Hold students accountable to their thinking.

My friend Hannah and I recently went to Turkey. We each brought a series of books to read. How do you plan your vacation reading? Are you psyched to grab a trashy magazine at the airport, or do you grab a stack of books that you've been dying to read? Our tastes were really different. Hannah's collection consisted entirely of medical memoirs that she picked up from the library. I filled my e-reader with books exclusively by one author. While our reading plans were different, there were two things that they shared: we had a plan and we chose what we loved. While in Istanbul, I carved away time to read. Wouldn't it be cool if instead of waiting until vacation, your students got to do vacation reading all the time? That's the goal when building choice reading in your classroom.

WHAT CHOICE TIME LOOKS LIKE

For classroom teachers, I recommend that students read without many interruptions for at least 30 minutes straight as it most closely mimics what lifelong readers do. But 30 minutes isn't enough. If your school can build in even more time, incorporate an additional block where students get more time for independent comfort reading. KIPP Infinity used to build in 30 extra minutes halfway through the school day, since they knew the more students read, the more they will achieve. Reading researcher Stephen Krashen concluded that independent reading is the leading indicator in achievement for comprehension, vocabulary, spelling, and writing.[29] The more kids read, the more they will grow.

There is a common misconception that choice reading isn't rigorous. Rigor means doing something cognitively demanding, not boring. The keys to leveraging the power and potential of choice reading are

1. Ensuring that students are employing a myriad of high-level thinking strategies as they read, such as those listed in Chapter 2
2. Making sure students are choosing books that fall into their comfort zone, as described in Chapter 1

When structured correctly, choice reading allows students to determine where and how they will apply these important strategies, in the same way that a videogamer often chooses her game. But that doesn't make moving to the next level less difficult. If you include choice reading as part of your reading program, you will be incorporating a ton of high-level critical thinking in your classroom.

TEACH STUDENTS HOW TO BUILD THEIR STAMINA

Building independent reading stamina is critical to the *Reading Without Limits* program.

Explicitly Teach Stamina

During choice reading, start by building reading stamina. We must deliberately practice reading for long periods in order to get really good at it. In fact, to be an expert at something, in our case reading, you need to do it well for at least 10,000 hours.[30] If you break down the math, and assume students start reading in kindergarten, in order for them to reach mastery, they would have to read (while deliberately practicing their strategies) for just over 2 hours a day, 365 days a year, for 13 years. Perfect timing for college.

In the first few weeks of school, prioritize explicitly teaching how to build stamina. In this chapter, stamina will mean reading many books and reading for a long time. In order to build reading stamina, help your kids create a plan individualized to their tastes as if they were about to go on a long vacation, and hold them accountable to that plan.

Don't assume that your students will have the stamina to read independently for 30 minutes without getting distracted on day one. And even if individuals have that stamina, the class as a whole will not. It's for this reason that many teachers give up on choice reading in their classroom, because it becomes hard to manage. You must break down what great reading stamina looks and feels like in order to get a class to read well for an extended period. Figure 3.1 shows the criteria for teaching stamina to your students. Follow

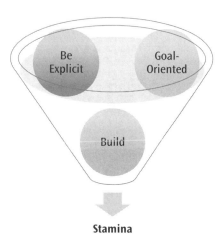

Figure 3.1 Criteria for Building Stamina

the steps and your students will be deeply immersed in their reading for long periods. Remember the metaphor to driving a car? Dependent readers don't see stop signs, and drive right through. Awareness of stamina, and building stamina, is one more strategy that independent readers use to become co-producers with the text.

EXPLICITLY TEACH STAMINA

Here are specific guidelines for how to explicitly teach stamina.

Stamina Checklist

In your dream world, what would a class of readers who are really into their books look like? List all of those characteristics below:

What Does Great Stamina Look Like?

1. _____
2. _____
3. _____
4. _____
5. _____

Put together a checklist of those characteristics. The stamina checklist shows what my dream class looks like. Share your stamina checklist with your students. Halfway through independent reading, pause your readers. Ask students to self-assess by checking off the criteria that they did well. Then ask them to create one goal for the latter half of independent reading based on what they can do better. Remember, teaching self-assessment helps build motivation for struggling or disengaged learners. And if your readers can accurately self-assess, research shows they will make tremendous gains in achievement.[31] Customize a stamina checklist to suit your own personal preferences.

Stamina Checklist

I . . .

Read without looking up for as long as I could

Read for 25 minutes without looking up

Read comfortably with my head up

Kept the reading class silent during independent reading because I didn't tap my pencil or foot

Wasn't distracted by the teacher or other students moving around the room

Met my daily stamina goal

Laughed, smiled, or grimaced because I was really into my book

Was only in the library for 2–3 minutes because if I'm there longer, I take away from my reading time

---

Abandoning a Book or Sticking It Out

There are times when books bore me half to death. But I do not teach students to abandon all books they don't like. Instead, I teach how to be mindful about choosing and abandoning. For instance, model that since you don't yet know the characters and setting, you won't be ready to abandon until you've read at least 50 pages. If after 50 pages the book isn't working, do one of two things: either read a different book and then plod on with the original book, or abandon the book for a just-right book.

Stamina is key to building a reader; in addition to absolutely loving what they read, they have to be able to read for a lengthy amount of time—for all of their classes: reading, history, and science. It's a skill they will use through college and beyond. As a result, we do spend a lot of time especially at the beginning of the year on stamina. But it's something that we continue throughout the year.

—Sayuri, 7th and 8th grade reading teacher

PROACTIVELY BUILD STAMINA

After explicitly teaching what stamina looks like, incrementally build stamina so students get stronger.

Incremental Time

You need to build stamina. Start by reading for a small amount of time, like eight minutes; as the entire group gets stronger, build the number of minutes the whole class reads until you get to thirty minutes. It's like doing 10 perfect push-ups as opposed to 30 sloppy ones. Eventually, build up to your ideal amount of independent reading. If your group is reading seven minutes by the end of month one and fifteen minutes by the end of month two, that's so much better than pushing them to read for thirty minutes in the beginning, then abandoning choice reading when it falls apart.

Make It Visible

As an adult, visible accountability helps push my stamina. When I returned from Turkey, I joined www.goodreads.com, and used the website as a book tracker. My account screamed out "I did a ton of reading over vacation!" Part of my gym's program is posting a bar graph online showing how many times I went to the gym over the course of a week. The bar graphs slowly grew month by month. I wish I could say that I wasn't obsessed with that bar graph. I needed accountability to get to the gym. While exercising has become a norm in my life, I still check out the bar graph. Visible accountability is critical in building stamina. Sticker or grow charts are great for making stamina visible in the classroom. Add to the class's bar graph every time the whole class adds two minutes to their independent reading stamina.

Remind and Reinforce

The Morning Meeting Book by Roxann Kriete[32] shares classroom management strategies that can be converted to stamina strategies.

Remind

Remind to elicit from your kids the criteria that you already taught from previous lessons. For example, before starting independent reading say,

- Who can remind me how quickly we take out our books?
- What does good reading stamina look like? Tell me one strategy.
- Remind me, what's our reading stamina goal for today?

Reinforce

Reinforce when you notice a student improving, demonstrating effort, or achieving excellent stamina. For instance,

- Sharisha, I noticed that you were really into your book the last 10 minutes. You are building your own stamina.
- Reggie, I noticed you checking in on your stamina goals. Are they helping?
- I see so many students got their books out right away.

Use the remind and reinforce strategy *all year* in order to build and maintain stamina.

Whole-Class Time Goal

Ask the class to set their own stamina goals. "Do you think we can read seven exceptional minutes today? Does that number sound right? What number would you suggest? I'll stop us halfway through and check-in."

Total Books Goal

Identify a goal for your students. Is it 50 books? Tracking is pretty straight-forward if you choose a set number of books. However, some kids read longer books than others. In that case, identify a number of pages read that you want each student to achieve. Accelerated Reader is a program that helps schools track numbers of books or pages read through a series of online quizzes. For many schools, Accelerated Reader saves teachers a lot of time. Make sure to make the big goal visible and hold students accountable to it. Some kids will try to race through books to hit the goal. Prioritize understanding books well rather than finishing a ton of books. It's for this reason that I can be wary of suggesting total books, as some kids may value hitting a quota over comprehension. Make sure to praise comprehension over speed-reading.

Goal Setting with a Reading Calendar

Model how to plan out how many pages you will read each night until a book's completion using a calendar as shown in Figure 3.2. We aim for our kids to finish books every four to seven days. Teach students to consider after-school commitments as they plan their calendar. Still plan a little bit of reading even if you have after-school commitments. Plan out how many pages you want to read each night so that you are able to meet your goal of

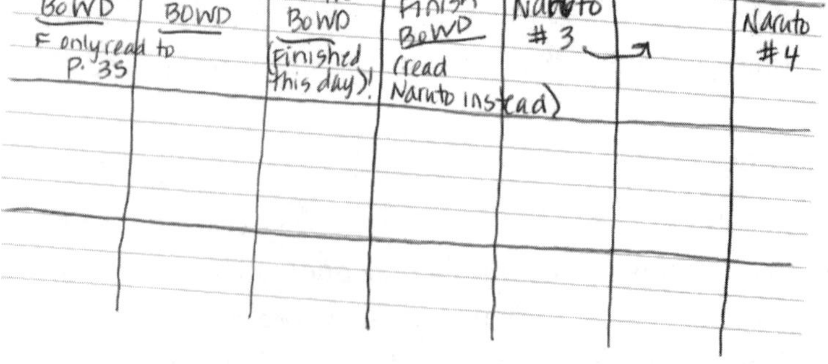

Figure 3.2 Reading Calendar for Boosting Stamina

finishing the book by the end of the week. This is a routine that I strongly suggest that you have your students do frequently, if not each time they start a new book. Notice how in Figure 3.2 the student also made notes to herself when she met or exceeded goals.

Goal Setting with Book Marks and Sticky Notes

For most readers, reading calendars work. Other readers need something more tactile. Here are two ideas from Lucy Calkins's *The Art of Teaching Reading*. Before starting independent reading, give each student a bookmark and ask kids to put the bookmark on the page they want to reach by the end of the class.[33] Halfway through the period interrupt the class and ask, "How many of you are on track toward reaching the bookmark? Has anyone made it to the bookmark?" Here's another idea that helps kids goal-set. Give kids seven sticky notes. Each sticky note represents a different day of the week. After writing "Monday" on one of the sticky notes, students stick it on the page they want to read to on Monday. Do this for each day of the week. Sticky notes are great tools for special needs students. Halfway through the week, teach kids how to revise their reading goals by rearranging the sticky notes in order to still meet the penultimate goal of finishing the book by the end of the week. Bookmarks also offer an excellent way to self-assess or show praise, as Figure 3.3 shows.

Figure 3.3 Bookmark That Encourages Growth Mindset

Make Genre Goals

Brigitte Madrian, a Harvard economics professor, gave the following advice to folks looking to save money. We all have different saving goals, perhaps saving for a house, college for our children, and an awesome Hawaiian vacation. When you save $100, you think you've saved $100 for Hawaii, Little Billy, and Dream House almost as if you saved $300. But, you didn't . . . you saved $100. Rather than save in one account, Madrian recommends earmarking your money in different accounts, like a house fund and a 529 plan for college.[34] Let's use Madrian's advice for our classrooms! Rather than read 10,000 pages, instead set up goals by genre. This works well for high school students who may have to do much of their independent reading outside of class. For instance, a high school student could plan to read all books by Maya Angelou, three romantic classics like *Pride and Prejudice*, and two plays by Tennessee Williams.

Celebrate Growth

Some schools set a quota for number of books read. For instance, reading 50 books. And what if a kid doesn't? Do I punish the kid? Nope. Because if students read 12 books for instance, that is not only more than what the average American adult reads in a year (which is only four books!), it's an accomplishment. In fact, 25% of American adults read zero books a year. We wonder why there's a literacy crisis. When I do a reading conferences with students who are behind in their goals, I follow the principles of growth mindset established by psychologist Carol Dweck. Instead of pushing for achievement-based learning, celebrate growth. I remember teaching fifth grade and some kids came in having read no books the year before. I ask, "How many books did you read last year? You've read 10 more than you did last year! How did you accomplish that?" Then we establish goals together to keep reading following the goal calendar. Please don't create a program about meeting quotas. *Please!* That's not the point of reading. Demonstrate empathy and celebrate growth.[35]

HELP STUDENTS MAKE GOOD CHOICES

By allowing students to have some choice in what books they read, thus giving them control, which is especially important for adolescents, students will start reading for longer and longer. Indeed, there is research that supports the importance of choice in increasing motivation. Jeffrey Wilhelm and Michael Smith, authors of many important books on literacy, embarked on a study of young men and their literacy habits in *Reading Don't Fix No Chevys*. The authors concluded that the freedom to pursue interests and choice is pervasive in building engagement and achievement.[36] Allow students to pick what books they want to read, even if you yourself wouldn't read it. Sadly, I heard a principal tell me that he banned *Goosebumps* in his school because they were "trash." Trash to a thirty-year-old is gold to a nine-year-old. Allow students some choice in what they read for independent reading.

But don't overwhelm students with choice. Barry Schwartz, author of *The Paradox of Choice*, says, "we become overloaded. Choice no longer liberates, it debilitates. It might even be said to tyrannize" (Schwartz, p. 2). Less is more in choice, as a study on taste tests shows. Columbia professor Sheena Iyengar, in *When Choice Is Demotivating*, ran a test in a grocery store. She set up a table with 24 jams. Though 60% of the customers stopped to taste, only 3% actually bought a jam. Then she set up a table with six jams: 40% of customers stopped to taste and 30% purchased a jam. This study shows that while choice is important, narrowing a field of choice increased purchase power. In-clude choice, but narrow the field. Instead of putting every young adult book in your library, cultivate it by choosing high-leverage books (high interest, readability, excellent writing), order lots of copies of those books, and allow students to choose within your edited library. Every term, rotate in new books.[37]

Figure 3.4 Choice Reading Is a Lot of Fun

During choice reading, it's essential to steer students toward books within their comfort zone while not decreasing motivation. This can be a delicate process with some students, as they might want to read books in their beyond-comfort or frustration zones due to the content. It's your job to help students make good choices, and part of the criteria is choosing a book within their comfort zone. Instead of language like, *That book is too hard for you*, try instead, *I think you will have a better reading experience with books from this bin. See if there's one you are interested in.* Or provide students with a couple choices that you hand select from the appropriate reading level.

I've just described our thinking about choice during independent reading. Next I offer specific guidelines for incorporating choice in your classroom.

Use Break Books

Break books are shorter texts that stimulate stamina. They are engaging and allow students to engage quickly in a short amount of time. Break books include comic books, magazines, graphic novels, newspapers, and how-to guides. Spread break books out in different areas of the room so that magazines are in a different area from comic books. This way, eyes can wander and see love-of-reading materials throughout your space. Allow students to read break books in between each longer book that they read. During a video game, gamers can play for hours. One way they do so is pausing the game that they are playing and doing "side games." In *Mario Cart*, there's the main racetrack and little interval games one can play. In the same way that videogames provide breaks, break books still stimulate critical thinking but allow the brain respite.

Have an Up-to-Date Library

Make sure your library includes some of the hottest titles, like *The Vampire Diaries, DK Eyewitness*, or *The Vladimir Tod Series*. Ask a student to help choose books while you peruse a book catalog so that the library has student picks. Each year I ask students to write down three books they want me to order, and I make sure to get all of the titles in a grant. Students have unusual requests!

Make Use of the School or Public Library

Donalyn Miller, author of *The Book Whisperer*, treats visits to the school library like field trips, despite already having an amazing classroom library. She announces the visit a couple days in advance on her bulletin board because she wants kids to think that visits to the library are "events to anticipate." The key is making the trip super joyful. She excitedly browses through books, making her own list of books that she wants to read, and recommends books along the way. Then kids get to sit back, relax, and read for the rest of the period. What a nice treat![38]

What are other simple ways to build choice during choice reading?

- Allow kids to choose books within their comfort level. Create a robust classroom library that kids will drool over that is still organized by level so students can choose the appropriate text.
- Give kids the opportunity to read in their heads or aloud. If out-loud reading distracts nearby readers, invest in some Toobaloos. Toobaloos look like toy phones and amplify whisper voices so kids can read to themselves quietly. These are great in elementary school classes.
- Allow kids to decide if they want to read with or without a partner. Partner reading is very engaging, is a great way to elicit peer pressure, and develops critical thinking as it gives students an opportunity to develop insights with someone else. Partner reading is awesome in all grade levels, including high school.
- Create comfortable seating in your classroom. Give kids the choice as to where they want to do their comfort reading. For more on how to build cozy spaces, see Chapter 6, Make It Visible.
- If students in high school are assigned a summer book list, let them choose five of the books instead of all. Or allow them to choose which order they will read the books.

HELP STUDENTS GET LOST IN THE FLOW OF READING

During choice reading, we want our students reading in a state of flow. *Flow* refers to being completely immersed in an activity, according to psychologist Mihaly Csikszentmihalyi. Whether that's when you have time to work on a painting, develop a creative project for your boss, or playing an amazing game of tennis, it's flow. Research says flow leads to a ton of happiness.[39] Have you ever been so caught up in something that when you checked the clock you were shocked as to how much time went by? There are seven criteria according to Csikszentmihalyi that lead to flow:

1. Be completely involved in what you are doing
2. Feel as if you are outside reality
3. Know what needs to be done and how well you are doing
4. Believe that the task is doable
5. Avoid worries
6. Experience timelessness
7. Develop intrinsic motivation—whatever produces flow is its own reward

Figure 3.5 Routines Help Students Read in the Flow

If you analyze these criteria, you can see how video gamers get into the flow. Certainly we can get in the flow when reading. It's when you have the insatiable desire to turn to the next chapter despite other obligations. It happened to me while reading Michael Ondaatje's book *Cat's Table*. I couldn't put it down. Ideally, get your students in the flow every single day. Being in the state of flow is one of the most cognitively rigorous activities one can experience. With a ton of time for choice reading, students will get in the flow. Keep in mind that independent reading time doesn't have to be 100% silent. You can be in the flow and have a chat with a friend about what you're reading. Here are some specific kid-friendly strategies for encouraging flow during choice reading.

Figure 3.6 Collaborative Learning Is Essential During Independent Reading

Have Lots of Series Books Available

If you have *The Hunger Games, Diary of a Wimpy Kid*, or *The Lightning Thief* in your classroom, you know that kids love series books. Series books are instrumental in nurturing flow, as they create a longing for what happens next. Books with resolution cliffhangers are excellent, as kids will want to grab the next book in the series. Series books are particularly helpful for disengaged, reluctant, or struggling readers. Any teacher who found *Twilight* a few years ago knows that a series can turn a nonreader into a lifelong reader. With series, you build a connection with characters, and don't have to "start over" with each book. Beyond building love of reading, series books are phenomenal for tracking multiple plot lines, analyzing a character over time (think about how Harry Potter changed over seven books!), and even questioning how an author's craft got better. I recommend spending an entire month devoted to a series unit. Ask students to find a series. Over the course of the month, students use that collection of texts as they do in-depth analysis. I was recently talking to Mitchell, a 16-year-old

Sample Playlist for *Hunger Games*—great for upper grade high school

1. (movie) *Running Man*
2. (short story) "All Summer in One Day" by Ray Bradbury
3. (novel) *The Road* by Cormac McCarthy
4. (short story) "The Lottery" by Shirley Jackson
5. (movie) *The Truman Show*
6. (nonfiction) *Collapse* by Jared Diamond
7. (painting) "Four Horsemen of the Apocolypse" by Albrecht Durer
8. (series) Margaret Peterson Haddix's "Among" series
9. (novel) *The Long Walk* by Stephen King
10. (novel) *Lord of the Flies* by William Golding
11. (novel) *Fahrenheit 451* by Ray Bradbury
12. (short story) "The Most Dangerous Game" by Richard Connell

boy who dropped out of school when he was 14. According to Mitchell, he hadn't ever read a book straight through. But in a short span of two weeks after being taught some stamina strategies, he finished the entire *Diary of a Wimpy Kid* series. Series are safe, predictable, and excellent for reluctant readers.

Create Playlists

Text sets, or what we call playlists, are a bundle of books, movies, or any other relevant media that are grouped by an idea.[40] Playlists are an excellent way to build love of reading, boost stamina, and integrate a ton of strategic thinking skills. For instance, if a student really loved *Hunger Games*, a dystopian post-Apocalyptic story and movie,

they could build a bundle in a small basket of other books about dystopia or the Apocalypse. It's really fun to conference with kids as they build their playlist. Here's how it plays out:

MRS. WITTER: Hey, I noticed you were reading *Hunger Games*. How do you like it?

AARON: Rue just died. This book is so insane.

MRS. WITTER: One thing that I love about *Hunger Games* is that it's all about a world that was created after a society collapsed.

AARON: They created the arena so people wouldn't uprise.

MRS. WITTER: Exactly. Have you seen the movie *Blade Runner?*

AARON: No.

MRS. WITTER: I think you are going to love it. It is similar in that it's a messed up society after everything in our future goes downhill. Do you think you could rent it?

AARON: I'm with my dad this weekend. We could pick it up.

MR. WITTER: I can't wait to hear what you think about it. Put it in your playlist and let me know if it reminds you of *Hunger Games.*

Playlists are super-duper kid-friendly and one of my favorite units in secondary classes. The reason I prefer them in upper grades is because older students appreciate critically unpacking movies, art, and nonfiction in relation to their favorite texts. Playlists develop critical thinking, encourage choice, and motivate stamina.

Create Reading Partnerships

If Oprah likes a book, chances are we like it, too. Book clubs are fun because we get to talk about our book, and knowing that someone else is reading the same book will push you even deeper into your flow. One thing that I suggest establishing as soon as possible is reading partnerships. Adolescents love talking to their peers.

Create a partner book library. Rubber band the books together or keep them in a baggy so they stay together.

This year I found I had to very explicitly teach stamina. We did a lot of lessons on what stamina looks like and sounds like in different situations. It has made them more aware. I notice students who tap their pencil, look at it, and put it down whereas they would have kept on tapping before. I've noticed students keeping their eyes on the book instead of looking up when someone walks around.

—Amber 6th grade reading teacher

- Divide students into partnerships. Group students with similar interests or needs, or match students based on their strengths and weaknesses. For instance, if Kimberly is very verbal but loses track of the story, match her with Tracy who, while less communicative, holds on to the main idea.
- Partners meet, choose a book, and create a goal for when they want to finish the book.
- Students take turns being the "coach" and the "player." The player reads aloud for five minutes, demonstrating her thinking. The coach pushes her partner's thinking and corrects any oral miscues.[41]
- Partners hold each other accountable to daily classwork.

HARNESS STUDENT ENGAGEMENT

Reading for pleasure should be fun ... right? Therefore, be intentional by making choice reading fun, without taking away from the purpose of choice reading.

Reading Warnings

Sometimes kids get stuck at the tricky parts in books and then zone out. I know I do! Teach kids to write in warnings on stickies as they read, such as "Watch out: Time jumps backwards!" or "Caution ... lots of character names." Then, when the next person reads the book, he has a friend guiding him along.[42] This is a fun way to build interactive learning, which is an excellent motivator for struggling readers.

Read-a-thons

I was inspired by dance-a-thons, where couples dance until they drop. I thought, I wonder if we could do something similar with reading? I wanted the read-a-thon to be super joyful and not a drag. So we were intentional: posters went up and prizes that included gift certificates for books, arm wrestling with our principal, or putting a cream pie in a teacher's face were announced. Suddenly, our daily stamina building lessons were given a powerful new focus. Students had a week to choose all the titles that they thought would encourage them to read the longest. They could rotate from their favorite series books to break books such as magazines and comic books. They could also bring food if that helped sustain them. There are only a couple rules to read-a-thons: look at the book, read the entire time, and stay awake! After the first few hours rolled by, we were amazed because we had a hard time tapping students out. Was this going to be an all-nighter? Our band teacher came in and loudly blew his trumpet. That got one student to look up. Our principal came in and made weird noises. That got another student to look up. Over time, as the hours rolled by, one by one kids either looked sleepy, zoned out a little, or looked up when we did something silly. You can have as few or as many winners as you want. But one thing is certain: kids love read-a-thons. When setting up your read-a-thon, let students come in their pajamas. Bring in blankets or stuffed animals. Collect beanbags, couches, and pillows from around your school. Make sure that students get to choose their reading material, that they have a plan for their reading material, and read on!

Sell Your Students on Reading

Has a student ever told you that she hates to read? Did your stomach fall like mine? In order to be lifelong, confident readers, first and foremost kids must love to read. Therefore, daily, we need to sell reading. The ideas that follow are ways to sprinkle in your "pitch" as you teach. Try a different idea each week to mix it up.

Songs

Yesterday, I was in the car and Usher's "You Make Me Wanna" came on the radio. It's been 15 years since I've heard the song, and somewhere deep within my hippocampus the words came out. It's why learning the ABCs is so effective and why I can't get the Oscar Meyer bologna song out of my head. Songs are easy to remember.[43] KIPP math teachers capitalized on that and created a series of math rap chants to help students learn basic math skills. Take a popular song and rewrite it to capture a theme or a skill that you want to teach. There are two provided in Chapter 7 on routines. It's great for elementary students. For secondary students, use songs in a different way. Students will love analyzing a song during a close reading, interpreting words and phrases as they relate to the bigger meaning of the song. Then together belt out the song aloud.

Connect to Life Interests

Last year Davina came up to me in the hallway, completely unprompted, and told me that she hated reading. Davina was a disengaged seventh grader dealing with severe home hardships. While it doesn't happen frequently, I would be lying if I said this was the first time I heard a student say this. I stopped what I was doing and asked, "Why do you hate reading?" I knew the problem instantly: like many reluctant readers, Davina read books that failed to connect with her own interests. I knew that Davina loved fashion, so I angled a pitch to her around her interest:

MRS. WITTER: Why do you hate reading?

DAVINA: It's so boring.

MRS. WITTER: Everything that you've ever read?

DAVINA: Yes. It's so boring.

MRS. WITTER: I notice your headband is really unique today.

DAVINA: (smiles) I got it at that shop on 125th street where they are all handmade.

MRS. WITTER: Have you seen any of the New York Spring fashions from *Fashion Week* yet?

DAVINA: No . . . what's that?

MRS. WITTER: That's when all of the designers send their models down the runway showing their new lines. I think you'd really like *Vogue* magazine because they interview the designers who are up and coming. But you don't like reading so I probably shouldn't bring in the last few issues.

DAVINA: But that's a magazine. It's different!

MRS. WITTER: Or the Met just did this insane exhibit on Alexander McQueen. He is a fashion designer who pushed boundaries. He recently died and the fashion world was devastated. I have the museum's book in the library. But, it's a book, so ...

DAVINA: Mrs. Witter!

MRS. WITTER: You might think that the book you are reading right now is boring, but just think of the infinite books you haven't read yet. I'll bring in the *Vogues* tomorrow and we can see which designers you are most interested in. Would you be interested?

DAVINA: Sure!

If a student says that they hate to read, do a similar conference with them, tweaking it so it fits the student's interests.

Set Up Recommendation Shelves

Tap into positive peer pressure by choosing a few students each month to create their own recommendation shelves. Recommendation shelves are a great way to make love of reading visible. Be strategic with who you choose. Davina would be top on my list for creating a recommendation shelf for her peers.

Choose Passages from Your Own Books

Did you ever see your teacher at the grocery store when you were young

> **For Struggling Leaders: Link Learning to Real Life**
>
> As often as possible, push students to evaluate how what you are doing in class links to learning they would do in real life. This is possible within every genre of books; students can connect to emotions, themes, and decisions even if the book doesn't exactly mirror their own lives.

and hide in another aisle? I sure did. That's because my teachers didn't seem like they had outside lives, so when I saw them outside of school hours with their families, it was weird. Break down that barrier by bringing your home life to the classroom. Your reading life! When designing read-alouds, bring in passages from a book that you are currently reading. Use them to teach any skill or standard. If you teach older students, when appropriate allow kids to read them once you are done. Kids love it when they can read my adult books. It makes them feel confident, and then we become reading partners because we can talk about the book. By choosing books from your own reading life, you are selling reading as a lifelong habit.

Get to Know Your Students to Harness Student Engagement
How well do you know your students? Could you identify which ones are obsessed with Hello Kitty? Justin Bieber? UFC? Take a moment and consider a student in your classroom. As you picture your student, see how many of the following questions you can answer:

Student: _____

- What does the student do immediately after coming home?
- What's the hardest part for that student about being a teenager?
- What is the student's biggest fear?
- Who's the student's best friend? What makes the friend so special?
- If the student could be great at anything, what would it be?

> *Extra credit:* During lunch tomorrow, find that student. See what his or her answers are. Did you get any right?

In order to build love of reading during choice reading, identify what drives students, what worries them, and what makes them special. With this knowledge, you will be able to build a love of reading based on their individual interests, as I did with Davina.

Use Surveys
I know how hard it is to get to the nitty-gritty with each of your students, especially when you have large classes. Having the time to meet with

each student one-on-one to chat isn't always feasible. Consider giving a reading survey as homework that questions reading and general interests. In addition, ask off-the-wall questions such as

- If you could ask me any question, what would it be?
- What do you want your college roommate to be like?
- Would you rather fly, be invisible, or read people's minds?

Can you think of any other fun survey questions?

Once you have a glimpse into what makes your student tick, then start recommending books that are unique for them.

> **Say**: I noticed that what you really like about your best friend is that he sticks up for you, yet calls you out when you are annoying him. That reminds me of these two characters in *The Tiger Rising*. The main character Rob is going through some major stuff in his life, and he meets a girl named Sistine. She's pretty tough: she's rude and intense. But she does just what your best friend does. You should check it out.

Try a few recommendation conferences next week. It may go without saying, but if you are recommending young adult (YA) books to your students, you need to read YA books. I try to read at least one a month; most are quick reads.

APPLY STRATEGIC READING TO CHOICE READING

Now that students are building their reading stamina, they will start zooming through their books. That's a big step in building *Reading Without Limits* readers. However, if students aren't understanding their books, they won't become stronger readers. The next step is teaching students how to apply strategic thinking to their books.

It's important to transform dependent readers to independent readers. During choice reading, students must apply reading strategies to their books.

How do you do that during the choice reading block? Try the following. Use a short passage and model one strategy with a read-aloud/think-aloud. You can use any text: a picture book, an excerpt from your own book, or a passage from the shared reading text. Then move onto guided practice. Give students the opportunity to try the strategy on their own or in partnerships, along with a ton of checks for understanding. At this point you are still heavily guiding. Finally, launch students off to their choice book. They apply the strategy as they read. During that time you check their notes (more on that later) to ensure that they are justifying their thinking with details from the text. What's important is that they are independently reading for a long time, trying out the strategy on their own. Kids get to then be co-producers, read in the flow, build love of reading, build stamina, and have tons of time for deliberate practice. Win, win, win, win, win.

I suggest the following structure during choice reading, as shown in Figure 3.7:

- **Direct Instruction**: (I Do/We Do) Teacher models how to do the strategy with a read-aloud/think-aloud
- **Guided Practice**: (We Do) Students practice the strategy and the teacher gives feedback
- **Independent Practice**: (You Do) Students apply the strategy to their choice book and teacher assesses

Figure 3.7 How to Go from Direct Instruction to Independent Practice

Follow the sequence of strategies that I suggested when teaching students how to build strategic thinking in Chapter 2. Remember, the strategy with the "magic beans" is the combination strategy of paraphrasing and fixing it. It's essential that students understand what they read before they start unpacking implied meaning. The goals are to read a ton of books during choice reading, to really understand those books, and then to build deep interpretations.

HOLD STUDENTS ACCOUNTABLE TO THEIR THINKING

As kids are reading, ensure that your students can do the strategy you modeled. How? Presumably many students are reading different books, and you may not have read all of them. But you need to know whether or not your students can do what you taught them. I suggest mixing and matching any of the following ways to assess whether or not students are applying the strategy to their choice books.

Figure 3.8 You Can Read Comfortably and Still Be Accountable to Your Reading

i-Think Journal

i-Think journals are a tool for students to record their thinking. They're also a very organized journal for teachers to grade in order to get inside their readers' heads. i-Think journals are set up in three columns. Any thinking can go in an i-Think journal. For instance, Table 3.1 shows an example of Ashley's i-Think journal. Once the routine is built, students can record several i-Think notations per class.

Table 3.1 Sample i-Think Journal

Symbol	My Thinking	Page #
T	In *The Chocolate War*, Jerry posts "Do I dare disturb the universe?" in his locker, showing that he wants to stand up against the "norm" (The Vigils) in his school. This shows the theme Individual vs. Society.	105

In this class, the teacher wanted students to include a direct citation, explanation of that citation, and how that linked to a theme. She showed students how to do it and gave them guided practice time. Then Ashley went off to independent reading and produced the thinking shown in Table 3.1 in her i-Think journal. As you can see on a video in which Sayuri launches the i-Think journal in her class, on www.reading-without-limits.com, every page of the i-Think journals is numbered. When teaching a lesson on theme, she asks kids to turn to page 21 of their i-Think journals. The class creates an exemplar notation together, which they all put in their i-Think journals. Then during independent practice, all students generate two to three examples in their journals. For homework, they do the same thing, on page 22 of their journals. Then, Sayuri collects the journals to see whether or not they have mastered the skill.

It's essential that students justify their interpretations with text evidence. i-Think journals are not a free-for-all or diary. They are an academic tool where students demonstrate their text-based thinking.

Reading Symbols

The first column in the i-Think journal is a symbol for thinking. There are several ways to do reading symbols in your classroom. You can just write the skill, for instance THEME. Or come up with simple letter for the skill. Want to take it up a notch? Try a symbol. Golden Arches? McDonalds. White Apple? Mac. A symbol for theme could be a spool of thread to represent the central idea that holds the book together. Whatever your style, I recommend

Table 3.2 Reading Symbols That Align with the Common Core Standards

Skill	Symbol
(Standard 1) Inference	Magnifying glass
(Standard 2a) Theme	Spool of thread
(Standard 2b) Summarize	Upside down pyramid
(Standard 3) Plot analysis—you may want to divide this into different skills	Book
(Standard 4) Interpreting words or phrases	Molecules
(Standard 5) Analyze the structure of the text	Skyscraper
(Standard 6) Author's purpose	Microphone
(Standard 7) Evaluating an idea in multiple texts	Jigsaw pieces
(Standard 8) Evaluate the argument	Scale
(Standard 9) Comparing different texts' themes	Venn Diagram

determining the symbols from the onset and to have fewer, not more. With lots of symbols, your students aren't going to be able to keep them straight. With our country moving toward Common Core Standards, consider using the standards in Table 3.2 as your limited list.

Double-Entry Journals

Create a two-column document. On the left side, type the passage that you are modeling. Leave the right column blank. Model your thinking by writing it in the right column, and mark up the text underlining your evidence in the left column. Then ask students to do the same thing for guided practice. It's time consuming to type up passages but excellent for visual learners. Elmos, Smartboards, and overhead projectors are great tools to demonstrate double-entry journals. Figure 3.9 is an example using a passage from John Marsden's *Tomorrow, When the War Began*. The teacher is modeling visualizing. Teachers model their thinking in the right column opposite the text.

The dogs were dead. <u>That was my first thought.</u> They didn't jump around and bark when we drove in or moan with joy when I ran over to them, like they always had done. They <u>lay beside their little galvanized iron humpies,</u> <u>flies all over them,</u> oblivious to the last warmth of the sun. <u>Their eyes were red</u> and desperate and their <u>snouts were covered with dried froth.</u> I was used to them stretching their chains to the limits- they did that in their manic dancing whenever they saw me coming, but now their <u>chains were stretched and still.</u>

Lots of visual imagery— I can really see the dead dogs. It's disgusting.

The author is comparing the dogs to how they used to be.

Used to:
Jump around and bark
Moan with joy
Stretching chains
Manic dancing

I am visualizing the two images: before and after.

Figure 3.9 Sample Double Entry Journal

Blog

For homework, set up a class blog in which students enter their i-Think notes. Give students questions to analyze or ask them to generate thinking based on a skill. There are a couple really awesome things that result from class blogs. First, a blog is incredibly sustainable. Rather than going through ninety journals once a week, you can evaluate on your laptop at home. Since the blog will be online forever, you have plenty of time to grade! Also, students read each response, and their thinking gets better because they want to show their peers that they have cool thinking. Knowing that the whole class will be reading their response is an incentive to make it awesome. Check out www.stabookski.wordpress.com to see a class blog from KIPP Infinity. Figures 3.10 and 3.11 show examples of how you can use blogs for both choice and shared reading. Do your students love Facebook? You can do the same thing as the blog but use Facebook as your platform.

TaniaS2016
May 26, 2011 at 10:12 pm

I'd like to discuss question three about how citizens can break through racial barriers. I think that one big way to break through these barriers is to stick to what yo believe in despite what the stereotype might be or what other people are pressured think. The only real way to change anyhing is to have a unique opinion and stay true to it. Even if there is no one thing that you believe in, at the very least, have respect and equality for everyone because at the end of the day, the only real difference between any of us is the color of our skin. I can tell that Harper Lee is trying to communicate this through the father and lawyer in ther book, Atticus. He is accepting this case to fight for a "nigger" against another of his own kind. Beacuse of this, his role of once being the most respected and honored man in the neighborhood, has changed to being a man of betrayal against white people. He knows that taking his case could wrisk his reputation and relationship with a lot of his friends, but he is true to his morals and believes so he put his all into this case.

Reply

Figure 3.10 Sample Shared Reading Blog Entry

I Love Reading Pages

I Love Reading pages were created in response to something that wasn't working in our reading program. Our students were doing a wonderful job tracking their thinking as they read, and demonstrating in many cases a pretty intense level of critical thinking in their i-Think reading journals. But the students were in a rut and becoming uninspired quickly. After attending a workshop at Teachers College on reading journals, we were inspired to launch I Love Reading pages. I Love Reading pages are an artistic or three-dimensional representation of student thinking and push creative thinking. After reading a newspaper article about the trapped Chilean miners, Aryani, a seventh grader, took a piece of black construction paper and cut out a flap that represented a door. Opening the door led to another piece of black construction paper with a flap, and then another, and other. Getting deeper

aliciar2016
July 14, 2011 at 12:18 am

1) I read My Sister's Keeper by Jodi Picoult

2) I read 104 pages

3) If I were Anna I would be heartbroken and furious. Her family only made her to save Kate. They don't notice her or care about her like they do Kate. It's so unfair because if it weren't for her Kate would have died a long time ago and they are so ungrateful to have Anna.

4) If I was Sara I would not neglect Anna or Jesse like she does. She doesn't show at all that she cares about them. I can understand that Kate needs extra attention because of her leukemia but she doesn't have to completely neglect her other kids. Jesse is caught up in drugs and drinking and Anna dealing with a her parents not really caring about her or at least not showing it. Anna has every right to sue her family and get emancipation for her medical decisions. She won't listen to her or try to talk to her about it.

5) Kate was diagnosed with APL and has been fighting it since she was 2 years old. Anna was born to save her sister and donate bone marrow and blood cells -anything Kate needs. But she has filed for medical emancipation and doesn't want to give Kate a kidney although the reason is not completely clear.

Reply

Figure 3.11 Sample Choice Reading Blog Entry

through the tunnel of doors led finally to a collection of thought bubbles, written very small, embodying what she inferred were the thoughts of the miners. How cool is that? I Love Reading Pages can take any format: from video to models.

I Love Reading pages are a creative way to represent student thinking. I suggest mixing it up. Once a week do I Love Reading pages instead of i-Think pages. You can either teach students to all do the same format, elicit from the class different ideas that could represent the skill that you are teaching, or make it a free-for-all and see what they come up with. I Love Reading pages also are a great homework assignment. Examples include tracking a character's emotions using a line graph and

Table 3.3 So What? Graphic Organizer

Fact Paraphrase facts Include confusing words	So what? Write your thinking about the fact Try to clarify what's confusing you
The Earth revolves around the Sun.	Does that mean that I'm spinning around in circles right now? Am I moving?

determining importance in a nonfiction article by making a pop-up picture book.

So What?

Create a double-entry note-taking system for nonfiction texts where students record facts on the left and "so what" on the right in order to assess student thinking as shown in Table 3.3. Starting with the text, students use their reading strategies to determine importance with nonfiction texts.[44]

During choice reading, your goal is to build a classroom of readers who read books of choice for long periods. In addition, inspire your students by connecting to their interests and making choice reading fun. Finally, make sure your students understand what they read. Model strategic thinking, and then assess whether or not students are applying that strategy to their choice book. That's choice reading in a nutshell.

ADDITIONAL RESOURCES

1. A list of routines to track stamina goals
2. Free read-a-thon prizes
3. There were too many ideas to fit inside one chapter, so we included eight more kid-friendly ideas for how to build stamina in your reading classroom
4. Videos of teachers reflecting on stamina

MILD, MEDIUM, SPICY NEXT-STEP SUGGESTIONS

	Mild	Medium	Spicy
Build Stamina	Start with eight minutes of independent reading during your first day of class. Add one minute each day.	Halfway through each independent reading block, ask the class to set a stamina goal together for the last half of the block. For example, we will not look up as the teacher moves across the room.	Write a grant for timer bookmarks. Have students key in their individual goal time, and praise if they are able to read without getting distracted the entire time before the buzzer buzzes.
Individu-alized Goal-Setting	Teach students to create individual goals for how many books, or pages, they want to read for the entire year. Check in twice a quarter to see how they are meeting their goal.	Weekly ask students to plan and create goals for their reading. Encourage partner reading so that peers can hold them accountable to their reading. Try series books to develop stamina.	Inspire students to create a visual logo of where they think reading will take them. Divide the image into 50 parts. As they read books, they color in their logo. I do this for my house-saving fund . . . it works!

	Mild	Medium	Spicy
Whole Group Goal Setting	Post an in-class goal above the door such as "10,000 pages."	Maintain bookcase updates and include books that teachers are reading.	2013 is the year that my first year of students at KIPP Infinity will be going to college. In fifth grade, we made the goal that when the 85 kids read 2,013 books, we'd celebrate with 2013 Day. We made our goal, at around the end of the first semester, and celebrated with lots of whole school celebrations.
Make It Fun	Connect stamina to students' real lives. In what other ways do they build stamina? Encourage students to seek out those at-home stamina stories and bring them in to share.	Do an in-class read-a-thon. In lieu of a reading mini lesson, devote the entire class to reading straight through, with comfortable sitting, a variety of break books and snacks. The kids will think they are getting a break! Yes! Keep things active. According to John Medina, author of *Brain Rules*, being active increases brainpower 45%.[45] Halfway through the class, do jumping jacks. In the same way that you build reading stamina, build push-up power as a halftime brain boost.	Create a whole school read-a-thon. Invite teachers, parents, and school leaders to participate with coupons such as "Lunch with Ms. McCaffery," "Dance class with Mr. Vea," or "Arm Wrestling with Mr. Negron." Build fervor at least a month in advance for the big day.

	Mild	**Medium**	**Spicy**
Hold Students Account-able to Thinking	Set up i-Think journals in your classroom. Keep them organized so students are all on the same page each day. Keep them in the classroom so they don't get damaged. During independent practice, check in on student progress using i-Think journals. Let students personalize them!	Halfway through the reading period, encourage students to trade their i-Think journals and grade using criteria for the aim.	Use i-Think journals for classwork and homework. Once a week, during class assessments, collect i-Think journals and grade them. Mix it up by having students periodically use sticky notes or I Love Reading pages. Establish a class blog for homework a couple nights a week that represents their thinking. Or try a class Twitter page where students tweet their reading thinking.

FAQ

Q: How often should I check in about stamina?

A: At least several times a week, all year. Also, try to get kids in the habit of doing a stamina calendar each time they check out a new book.

Q: Should students always record the thinking in their heads? Doesn't that take away from their reading?

A: Make sure that you aren't making kids record their thinking daily in sentence form. That will take away from the love of reading. Mix it up. For instance, instead of asking them to use their i-Think journal, ask them to draw an eyeball on a sticky each time they visualize. You do need to hold them accountable, but accountability doesn't always mean writing out sentences.

KEEPIN' IT REAL

Here are some problems that we faced when building stamina. Address the pitfalls in advance and I hope they won't happen to you!

Book List

Students forget to update their personal book lists. Provide in-class time and reminders for kids to fill in the book list or the routine won't stay alive.

Series Books

In addition to boosting love of reading, series books are a great way to build stamina. Create a library checkout routine that is streamlined toward getting books, especially series books, back. It has certainly happened to all of us, but when a student can't find book three of your complete set, it stinks to tell them to move onto book four. Can you imagine reading *Chronicles of Narnia* out of order? What a drag.

Read-a-thons

Create a system for what students will do if they are tagged out of the read-a-thon. We create several rooms that different teachers run. The rooms aren't punishment, and usually incorporate literacy extensions such as reading games.

Magic Ratio

During independent practice, you will notice two types of students who, though they aren't the norm, need to be addressed. First, there is the Over Writer. These students usually have amazing handwriting and a ton of different pens. They love to write, and they write for most of your independent block about their thinking. Then there is the Over Reader. These students get caught up in their reading, and often with two minutes remaining they have nothing written down. Therefore, we taught our students the magic ratio, which we use in all reading and nonfiction classes. The magic ratio represents how much reading versus writing about your thinking you should be doing. It is 7:2. For every nine minutes, seven should be spent in deep reading and two should be spent writing down ideas. Why 7:2? Usually our reading time is between 25 and 30 minutes and students typically write down three ideas = nine minutes. One way to teach magic ratio is by ringing a bell after seven minutes then having the whole group write down their thinking for two minutes.

Blog

Do the blog at least once a week to keep the routine going. It can be hard figuring out who did their blog homework if they are creating user names like "CrazyD," so be specific about user names. You will notice that students also want to write ur posts in txt, and if that bothers u, let them know upfront.

FOR COACHES AND SCHOOL LEADERS

DEAR

Consider creating a schedule that allows for 30 minutes of DEAR (Drop Everything And Read) each day and criteria for what DEAR looks like. Ensure that this time is a sacred, pleasure reading time in addition to the time you already read during class.

I Love Reading Survey

With your reading department, create an I Love Reading survey and administer quarterly. Then, during a departmental meeting, together analyze trends. Using positive outliers, create an action plan to boost love of reading for the next quarter.

TO SUM UP

- Explicitly model what good and bad stamina look like. Break down exactly what you want to see your students doing. From there, give students strategies to build their stamina.
- Help your students make good book choices during choice reading.
- Build the state of flow in your classroom to boost rigor.
- Teach your students how to strategically read their choice books.
- Hold students accountable to their thinking.

Shared Reading to Teach, Reinforce, and Challenge
Why Reading Teachers Need to Be Like the Best Tennis Coaches

Adding shared reading to your literacy program will ensure that students have rigorous practice with difficult texts. In order to set it up, follow these steps:

- ❑ Create a schedule that allows for 30 minutes of shared reading four times a week.
- ❑ Choose the right text.
- ❑ Guide students through the text by doing close reading.
- ❑ Be strategic when assigning shared texts for independent reading.
- ❑ Scaffold shared reading for struggling readers.

Anyone familiar with sports knows the importance of coaches on the field. Players are given feedback to become the best they can be. A tennis player needs to master many different strokes. Each has their own characteristics. One must consider swing, body placement, grip, rotation, force, and where to hit the ball differently with each stroke. In order for tennis players to be effective, they need to master each stroke. A good coach teaches the stroke in isolation. For instance, she might show her player how to do a long stroke. A coach teaching her player how to get better at one type of stroke is like the teaching you do during choice reading. During a read-aloud/think-aloud, model one effective reading strategy that independent readers use. Teach that strategy in isolation.

But isolation isn't enough. Players need real-time feedback as they practice all the techniques because they can't only use a long serve while playing. That's what shared and guided readings do. In shared reading, you are a coach guiding

Figure 4.1 Set Up Lots of Time for Shared Reading in High School

your whole class through a text, like in a game of tennis, giving constant real-time feedback. You push your readers using lots of different strategies, not just one like in choice reading. Just like in sports, you need to learn skills not only in isolation. Shared reading is the opportunity to give constant feedback to your readers as they apply the skills you taught.

Shared reading is where you can push achievement and incorporate rigor by introducing difficult tasks to your students. As Lev Vygotsky, the famous educational theorist, argued, "The only good kind of instruction is that which marches ahead of development and leads it" (Vygotsky, p. 188).[47] One way to lead development is to guide students through difficult texts that span a variety of genres. In *With Rigor for All*, author Carol Jago cites a study by ACT that informed the standards. As Jago notes, "the students who were most likely to be successful in post-secondary education were those that could comprehend complex texts" (Jago, p. 66). Shared reading does just that.

Shared reading presents its own unique pitfalls. It's essential that you engage students in the text so that they can't wait to unpack it. I dis-

You maximize accountability with a shared text.

tinctly remember suffering through *The Scarlet Letter* in the 11th grade just as I'm sure you have had similar experiences. That doesn't mean that we should be switching out difficult texts with texts like *Gossip Girl*, a popular adolescent pick, or *Judy Moody*, a book you will often find in third graders' backpacks. One can easily teach symbolism using a nursery rhyme, and many teachers use simple texts to teach complex ideas. While I don't argue for banishing simple texts entirely, it's essential to also weave difficult texts into your teaching repertoire. It's for this reason that we are moving toward the Common Core Standards that highlight text complexity to ensure that students get exposure to difficult texts. Not all reading should be for plea-sure. As corroborated by the Common Core, we should pick books that are beyond our students' abilities (and outside their areas of interest) and build their capacity to not only understand the texts, but also to critically analyze and ultimately really enjoy the text. If that's what the best readers can do, then my kids should be able to do it too.

So this is why we incorporated shared reading in the *Reading Without Limits* program. This chapter offers specific strategies for how to make it a reality in your classroom.

SCHEDULING A SHARED READING BLOCK

In the Introduction, I shared the importance of including a block of time for shared reading in addition to choice reading. During shared reading, the teacher leads students through a text that everyone has in front of them. By rotating reading-aloud and questioning for meaning, the teacher pushes kids to work on a text that is difficult for them. In Vygotsky's zones of proximal development, there needs to be heavy guidance in the beginning before students become independent. The shared reading block, coupled with mini-lessons during choice reading, is that heavy guidance.

The shared reading block is a time where you slow down and spiral (or review) strategies previously taught in order to demonstrate that good readers use lots of strategies as they read in the same way that tennis players use many strokes. It's also a time to include those teachable moments that should not be included during a read-aloud/think-aloud. Guide students through a series of questions. Students demonstrate their thinking by going back and finding textual evidence. In the beginning of the year, there's less of a range of questions as students have learned fewer strategies up to this time. As the year progresses, so does their shared reading toolkit. Remember, you are building an arsenal for dependent readers.

The reason why shared reading is so important is that you maximize accountability with a shared text. While the i-Think journal and other checks for choice reading understanding are effective, you haven't read all of their books (unless you are a reading teacher machine, and then please disregard!). With shared reading you maximize accountability because you read the text beforehand, and therefore can direct students to find meaning using textual evidence. Shared reading allows the teacher to heavily guide students through a difficult text all the while pushing for meaning.

Choose the Right Text

The Common Core Standards pushes teachers to use texts that are just above students' ability level. The shared reading block is the perfect time to

Figure 4.2 Give Students the Text While You Teach a Shared Excerpt

do just that. The key is choosing the right text. There are a few things to consider when picking the best text for your kids.

Consider the Level

You are going to have a range of learners in your class. In fact, your learners might span at least six years in reading levels. Choose a text that is difficult for all of your students. We usually choose a text that is on the same grade level with potential for deep interpretation, so all readers including readers above grade level are pushed. If the text is on a student's frustration level, then we provide the text as a book on tape.

Consider Quality

If our kids want to read *Goosebumps* during choice reading, then let them. It won't go down in history as the finest literature, but it's pretty entertaining. Shared reading is an opportunity to choose texts that are written really well. We are so lucky because there are so many phenomenal young adult books out there! Following are some of my favorites. You can find references for these titles in Appendix A at the end of the book.

MID ELEMENTARY

Short Stories, Picture Books, Drama, or Poems

Revolting Rhymes

Dream: A Tale of Wonder, Wisdom and Wishes

Tar Beach

Nonfiction

Amelia to Zora: 26 Women Who Changed the World

Books by Seymour Simon

Novels

Sadako and the Thousand Paper Cranes

My Name Is Maria Isabel

Seedfolks

Fast Sam, Cool Clyde and Stuff

UPPER ELEMENTARY

Short Stories, Picture Books, Drama, or Poems

House on Mango Street
Thank You, Ma'am
Shortcut

Nonfiction

First Crossing: Stories About Teen Immigrants

Novels

Tiger Rising
Holes
Maniac Magee
Bud, Not Buddy

LOWER MIDDLE SCHOOL

Short Stories, Picture Books, Drama, or Poems

"All Summer in One Day"
Local news
"Priscilla and the Wimps"
Greek myths
"Raymond's Run"
"The Road Not Taken"
145th Street Stories

Nonfiction

My Life in Dog Years
Anne Frank: The Diary of a Young Girl
Narrative of the Life of Frederick Douglass: An American Slave

Rising Voices: Writings of Young Native Americans

Novels

Are You There God, It's Me Margaret
Dragon's Blood
Tangerine
The Giver
Roll of Thunder, Hear My Cry
The Outsiders
Chains

UPPER MIDDLE SCHOOL

Short Stories, Picture Books, Drama, or Poems

Maya Angelou's poems
Moonbeam Dawson and the Killer Bear
Laramie Project
Cool Salsa
From the Notebooks of Melanin Sun

Nonfiction

The Autobiography of Malcolm X

"Gettysburg Address"
Warriors Don't Cry: A Searing Memoir of the Battle to Integrate Little Rock's Central High

Novels

Of Mice and Men
The Chocolate War
Catcher in the Rye
The Devil's Arithmetic

LOWER HIGH SCHOOL

Short Stories, Picture Books, Drama, or Poems

Destination Unexpected
13: Thirteen Stories That Capture the Agony and Ecstasy of Being Thirteen
A Raisin in the Sun
"The Gift of the Magi"
Fahrenheit 451
"A Midsummer Night's Dream"
"A Brief Moment in the Life of Angus Bethune"

Nonfiction

"Letter from a Birmingham Jail"
Black Boy
"Hope, Despair and Memory"
"Common Sense"

Novels

To Kill a Mockingbird
Night
Things Fall Apart
The Joy Luck Club

UPPER HIGH SCHOOL

Short Stories, Picture Books, Drama, or Poems

"Because I Could Not Stop for Death"

"King Lear"

"Macbeth"

"Antigone"

Short stories by Jhumpa Lahiri

Nonfiction

Excerpts from *Collapse*

Walden

Books by Malcolm Gladwell

The Trial of Socrates

Novels

The Road

Their Eyes Were Watching God

The Great Gatsby

Jane Eyre

Mix Up the Genres

I love novels. I love them so much that I often choose them over other genres. Big mistake! Make sure that you are incorporating a variety of genres into your shared reading, with a particular emphasis on nonfiction, poetry, myths, drama, and folktales. We have an entire class devoted to nonfiction studies, but still incorporate nonfiction into our reading class. The Common Core Standards push that at least 50% of the texts that kids read are nonfiction. When choosing novels, avoid exclusively teaching realistic fiction. Incorporate science fiction, historical fiction, and fantasy. Mixing up text length also maximizes the breadth of material you can cover. Make sure to embed short nonfiction texts. The list above represents a good mix of genres.

GUIDE STUDENTS THROUGH CLOSE READING

Close reading, one of the foundations of shared reading, is where the teacher chooses excerpts from the text, and leads the class through questioning in order to analyze the text's meaning. It is extremely important in preparing our students for rigorous high school and college work.

Playing Soccer

MRS. WITTER: Do you think Holden has qualities that make him a good friend?

MONIKA: I don't think he would be a good friend because he judges people too much. At first I thought he was actually a nice person, but he lied a lot and I realized he was actually a phony person. He wouldn't be trustworthy which I think is an important character trait.

SIMON: I agree with Monika in that he's phony even though he claims he doesn't like phony people. Even though he's humorous, which is an important trait, at times he is very needy and depressing and on page 90 it says that he almost wished he was dead. I don't want that kind of negative energy.

LACY: Also, I think in addition to him having negative energy he's very judgmental. Like he was friends with the head master's daughter but noticed her big nose. He will bring you down even though he's not perfect.

MRS. WITTER: Can you show me where any of the qualities you've mentioned changed over the course of the book?

The point of close reading is not to pick the text apart piece by piece and to examine every word, but to find the important elements that contribute to meaning and help students find evidence for the interpretations they are forming. Determining what to zero in on and what to leave out is not always simple. That's why it is essential to carefully prepare and plan what you want to examine in the text or the analytical skills you want students to practice. The goal is to engage in a lively and stimulating back and forth with students.

When a team plays soccer no single player takes control of the ball. Instead, it is dribbled and then passed to different players who move it down the field with everyone participating in advancing to the goal. When you "kick out" the question to your students, ideally kids will be interacting with each other before they kick the ball back to you. After a student replies to a question, another student should build, revise, and critique their answer. There should be a back and forth between students before you are holding the ball again. Teach students to "talk into the silence." After asking a question, instead of replying to a student's answer right away, remain silent. This is a cue to the other students in the classroom that it's time for them to continue the thread of conversation as shown in Figure 4.3.

It is also important to allow students to do a really close inspection of the text, by pushing them to go back to the text. After asking questions, give students ample time to think about the questions. Avoid a back and forth with the kids, where you ask a question, a kid replies, you reply, a kid replies, et cetera. Instead, build in opportunities for students to build off of each other's answers.

The Elements of a Good Close Reading Session

Most close reading involves a process of moving from literal to implied meaning. First, students must figure out the text in order to paraphrase it. They might need to paraphrase to help figure out the text. Those two strategies are intertwined. After they are accurately able to paraphrase, then they can move onto inferential thinking (see Figure 4.4).

In the following short close reading example using *Tangerine* by Edward Bloor, the teacher starts by asking students to figure out what they are reading as they simultaneously paraphrase the

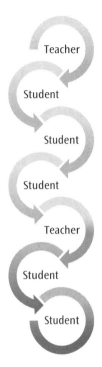

Figure 4.3 Playing Soccer to Increase Student Engagement

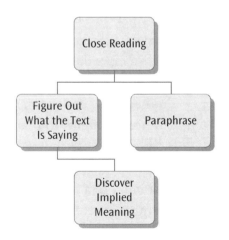

Figure 4.4 Criteria for Close Reading

text before moving onto the implied meaning strategy. The teacher does several things:

1. The purpose of all of the strategies is to figure out the meaning of the text.
2. As students attempt to figure out meaning, the teacher pushes them to paraphrase.
3. Once a concrete paraphrase has been established, then the teacher pushes for deeper implied meaning.
4. During each part of close reading (figuring out the text while paraphrasing and discovering implied meanings) the teacher anticipates pitfalls. He preplans questions that are directly related to those confusions.

Teacher: "*The house looked strange. It was completely empty now, and the door was flung wide open, like something wild had just escaped from it, like it was the empty two-story tomb of some runaway zombie.*"

- **Visualize to figure out meaning**: What images stood out?
- **Visualize to figure out meaning**: There's a key line that establishes what the house looks like. What is it?
- **Anticipate pitfall**: Some students might say, "The house looked strange." What does strange look like? Why would "It was completely empty now" create a more concrete picture for us to visualize? Some students might be tripped up by the word "zombie." Is this a book about zombies?
- **Connect to figure out meaning**: Why might the house be empty?
- **Connect to figure out meaning**: Students might say that the house is empty because the people are poor or have been robbed. Push the students to look at the word "completely empty" and have them rethink their interpretation.
- **Paraphrase/retell**: What's happening in the previous passage? How do you know?

- **Find a deeper meaning**: What mood is the author trying to establish? What clue words tell you that?
- **Anticipate pitfall**: Why is the mood not crazy or scary, even though the words "wild" and "zombie" are there? What word makes you think that?

Teacher: "'*Wait for me by the car, please. We can't have the new owners thinking we left a mess behind.' . . . We'd already packed up our sleeping bags, suitcases, and two folding chairs all neatly wedged into the back of Mom's Volvo wagon. Now only this ten-gallon, self-tying, lemon-scented garbage bag remained, and we planned to toss it into the Dumpster behind 7-Eleven.*"

- **Connect to figure out meaning**: What are the characters doing? What word or phrase can you connect to that helps you figure that out?
- **Paraphrase/retell**: What's happening? How can you tell? Use character names.
- **Find a deeper meaning**: Did anything surprise you in the above passage? Was anything described that people who are moving don't typically do or experience?
- **Anticipate pitfall**: Many students will be surprised that they are throwing a bag away. Push them to reread the line starting, "We'd already packed up our sleeping bags . . ." What is the author leaving out? How can you tell?
- **Find a deeper meaning**: What can you tell about the narrator's mom? What clue words make you think that?

Close reading guides students through their strategic thinking like a coach giving constant real-time feedback. It provides a different dimension of critical thinking for your kids. During close reading, you are a driving instructor guiding your students through stoplights, yield signs, and right-of-ways, so that when they eventually get on the freeway, they are independent drivers. You won't have readers "driving through stoplights" again if you include close reading in your instruction.

Take Your Close Reading Work to a Higher Level

I've just described an example of close reading. Here are suggestions that will improve the close reading you do with students.

"Change It" Questions

Take what students are now able to comprehend, and ask them to apply their knowledge by making an imaginary or hypothetical change to the text. For instance, let's use one of the Common Core Standards as an example: analyze how particular lines of dialogue or incidents in a story or drama propel the action. If you were teaching students this standard through close reading, after going through the steps outlined above, take it to an even higher level by asking students to imagine a change to the story.

"What do you think would have happened next if that particular line of dialogue was ____ (something different)?"
"How could the author have rewritten the line of dialogue to propel the action more?"

Students must be prepared to defend and revise their answers. Keep a mortarboard in your classroom. After asking one of these cognitively demanding questions, students vote on the most insightful response. The student who shared that response gets to wear the college cap!

Questioning Hierarchy

The following questioning strategy is excellent in that it slowly builds toward higher levels of cognitive demand while students still feel like they can do the task—both are necessary for engagement. George Hillocks developed a questioning hierarchy, which is a great way to check for understanding using a shared text. Similar to Bloom's Taxonomy, it is a series of question types that moves from literal to inferential.[48]

1. **Basic Stated**: Can students remember stated information?
2. **Key Details**: Can students recall an important plot point mentioned only once?

3. **Stated Relationships**: Can students synthesize two pieces of information?

4. **Simple Implied Relationships**: Can students make an inference that is not directly in the text?

5. **Complex Implied Relationships**: Can students identify important details and then make a conclusion?

6. **Author's Generalization**: Can students figure out how the text connects to real life or the world?

7. **Structural Generalization**: Can students determine how the structure creates meaning?

Ask a series of questions going through the above hierarchy after reading a small section of text in order to do a close reading. Here are some examples using an excerpt from Dr. Martin Luther King's "Letter from a Birmingham Jail." In the following questioning hierarchy sequence, the teacher wants students to see that the point of the paragraph is ultimately that Dr. King isn't happy because political leaders aren't supporting his nonviolent campaign in Birmingham, nor are they helping to find peace. The students read the following short excerpt from "Letter from a Birmingham Jail":

> In any nonviolent campaign there are four basic steps: collection of the facts to determine whether injustices are alive, negotiation, self-purification, and direct action. We have gone through all of these steps in Birmingham. There can be no gainsaying of the fact that racial injustice engulfs this community. Birmingham is probably the most thoroughly segregated city in the United States. Its ugly record of police brutality is known in every section of this country. Its unjust treatment of Negroes in the courts is a notorious reality. There have been more unsolved bombings of Negro homes and churches in Birmingham than in any other city in this nation. These are the hard, brutal, and unbelievable facts. On the basis of them, Negro leaders sought to negotiate with the city fathers. But the political leaders consistently refused to engage in good-faith negotiation.[49]

1. **Basic Stated**: Can students remember stated information? *Birmingham is suffering injustices. What are they?*

2. **Key Details**: Can students recall an important plot point mentioned only once? *What have African American leaders attempted to do?*

3. **Stated Relationships**: Can students synthesize two pieces of information? *What is the conflict between African American leaders and political leaders?*

4. **Simple Implied Relationships**: Can students make an inference that is not stated directly in the text? *How have the political leaders been neglectful according to King?*

5. **Complex Implied Relationships**: Can students identify important details and then make a conclusion? *In what ways is King unhappy? Rank them.*

6. **Author's Generalization**: Can students figure out how the text connects to real life or the world? *If King were trying to negotiate peace between warring countries, what would he push for? How do you know?*

7. **Structural Generalization**: Can students determine how the structure creates meaning? *How does the first sentence of the paragraph link to the concluding sentence?*

Questions higher on the hierarchy are very demanding. The teacher scaffolded the questions so that her students have a high degree of success. She started with easier questions, and worked toward more rigorous questions. Using this framework can really boost engagement as it allows for what Thomas Gunning, who researched ways to drive literacy achievement, recommends: a student success rate of 90 percent accuracy or higher.[50] Therefore, through scaffolding, students will feel like they can really accomplish the rigorous work, which encourages them to be engaged. When doing question hierarchy, try asking students to write their answers on whiteboards so you can check that everyone understands. It will also give you a baseline of what students can and can't do. Link it to a Jeopardy game with questions going up the dollar scale in order to make it kid-friendly.

Accountable Talk

Remember, people love videogames because they become co-producers of the videogame's outcome. It is important not to push your own interpretation of the text onto students. Instead, push for a high level of elaboration. Ideally, students should be arguing, defending, and modifying their ideas. The educational psychologist Lauren Resnick developed an approach to encourage students to engage in what she calls accountable talk, which involves giving students sentence starters that push them to build off of their classmates' ideas. Traditionally, teachers use accountable-talk sentence starters during class discussions or book club meetings. The key to accountable talk is that students are using what others say when they communicate to show that they are really listening to each other and that they also back up what they say with evidence. Students should use accountable-talk sentence starters as they agree to disagree.[51]

1. What I like/don't like about _____ is . . .
2. I'm not sure about/why . . .
3. If I were . . .
4. It makes me think . . .
5. I was surprised . . .
6. What don't you want me to do?
7. I'm curious about . . .
8. I don't understand . . .
9. I think . . .
10. It seems like . . .
11. I noticed . . .
12. It reminds me of . . .
13. Is it possible that . . . ?
14. That example is ___ than ___

Push for Textual Support

Donna Santman in *Shades of Meaning* (an incredible book for teachers looking to push for critical thinking in their classrooms) uses the term "justifiable interpretations" to show how important it is that students back up their critical thinking with textual proof. It contradicts the idea that the author intended one interpretation. According to Santman, "Learning how to interpret is about learning how to negotiate. It's about trying out a bunch of ideas and grappling over which seems most interesting and convincing. It's about cracking open the details of the text and using them to imagine new responses to the text and to your life. If you get into the habit of trying to see things in newer, fairer ways, then you will do so in a variety of contexts in your community—now and when you are adults" (Santman, p. 108).[52]

Encourage students to avoid one line of thinking while they read and instead work with a variety of ideas. Justifiable interpretations are imaginative. Push students to develop new possibilities about the text, the world, and their lives that are convincing. Teach students to persuade other students to believe their thinking by using *textual evidence.* Justifiable interpretations must be justifiable not because you are good at convincing people, but because you are good at finding textual support. Model how to avoid making overgeneralizations. If all students are reading the same text, they can build, argue, and defend their interpretations together. Ask,

"Where do you see that in the text? Which paragraph? Which sentence? Which word?"

Blog

Developing a class blog is a great way to keep the conversation going outside of class. After normalizing expectations, post debatable statements about the text for students to respond to. Then they can have a great argument to do as homework.

Road Map

As students back up their ideas using textual evidence and integrate others' ideas into their understanding of the text, they need to also be able to change their minds. Some adolescents want to stick to their original ideas even when further reading doesn't support those ideas. During close reading, many adolescents want to stick to their original interpretations as well. Praise new, different thinking over the course of the text. A few years ago my students made road maps as a metaphor representing how their ideas changed regarding the theme of the text. We did this because the students were becoming stubborn readers and sticking to their original interpretations. Their original theme could be represented by

Figure 4.5 Road Maps Push Kids to Come Up with Multiple Interpretations

a dead end, or it could develop into new streets. Themes that had a ton of textual evidence became arterials whereas less-supported themes turned into side streets. The end product was a visual depiction of how their thinking developed and changed over time. Notice how this fun, kid-friendly activity isn't just fluff like a book report: it is designed to push multiple interpretations.

Cognitive Empathy

Share your empathy regarding text difficulty before starting the text. As Carol Jago explains in *With Rigor for All*:

> No teacher with any sense would expect teenagers to love *Crime and Punishment* at first sight … For this reason, I always warn students that they are going to struggle a bit before they feel comfortable inside Dostoevsky's fictional world … If they want to know Raskolnikov, it is going to take effort … Instead of pretending that obstacles don't exist, I address the potential stumbling blocks directly. Forewarned is forearmed [Jago, p. 19].[53]

Four years ago, when teaching *Things Fall Apart*, I forewarned my students of an unfamiliar setting and culture, a complex vocabulary, and of unlikable characters. I even shared that the text was too hard for me in ninth grade, but I was confident that with their help, together we wouldn't just tackle this text, but would love it. Show cognitive empathy by sharing potential pitfalls that are going to make the shared text difficult. No one climbed Machu Picchu without knowing the challenges ahead.

ASSIGNED READING

Assigned reading is when you assign the shared text for independent reading. This independent reading should happen both in class and for homework. Since you want to avoid exclusively doing a close reading of the entire text and just do close reading of excerpts, there needs to be time built in for students to independently read the rest of the shared reading text. According to the new Common Core Standards, 30% of reading that students do should be difficult. Choice reading happens in students' comfort zones. Assigned reading of a shared text is beyond a student's comfort zone, and fulfills the standards' recommendation. Assigned reading is essential in getting kids ready for high school and college. However, there are many assigned reading pitfalls that occur that are avoidable. Giving kids specific strategies on how to manage assigned pages will make a huge difference. The following are guidelines for how to manage assigned reading.

Teach How to Manage Assigned Reading

Assigned reading prepares students for high school and college because it pushes students to meet deadlines. You must explicitly teach your students how to do this—especially if assigned reading is new or if there is prior experience of "fake reading." Show students how to create a calendar in order to meet assigned pages deadlines. Remember the goal-setting calendar students should make during choice reading? They should do the same thing for assigned reading. Teach students how to set their own *assigned reading stamina goals* by giving a week's worth of pages and asking them to plan out their progress individually. Each student's will be different! Consider requiring a set amount of pages weekly instead of nightly to allow for choice and flexibility. For instance, ensure that the total number of pages you assign for the week are reasonable: averaging no more than 30 pages per night. Your goal is for students to have a multi-night assignment. If you have built time in, students will have time to do some of their reading during class. Avoid frequently giving a certain amount of pages due in class, as each reader reads at their own pace. However, nightly assigned pages are a reality across high

Figure 4.6 Students Read Shared Texts Comfortably

schools and colleges so ensure that you teach students how to manage that type of homework as well. I recommend building in assigned reading once students have demonstrated consistent choice reading stamina for at least 30 minutes. Consider starting with short texts to build their assigned stamina.

The Loop

Give students ample time to begin independently reading the assigned text in class. This isn't just to be nice — it's an opportunity for you to assess their assigned independent reading habits. As students are reading, walk around the room and note the pages students are reading. By doing "the loop," you are assessing whether or not students did their at-home reading. Rarely will a student "fake read" when they get an entire 30 minutes to read in class — they will start where they left off. If they left off where they stopped reading *in class* the day before, then you know they didn't do their assigned

Figure 4.7 Check If Students Are Doing Assigned Reading by Doing the Loop

reading at home. When you find a student who is behind, call them over for a conference. Ask them what happened. Create a stamina calendar plan together. Avoid punishment because reading should never be punishment. If you avoid punishment, then students will more likely be honest as to why they didn't read the night before. Most often, students aren't doing assigned reading because they are leaving it for the last homework assignment of the day.

Annotations

Is it possible for students to purchase their own copy of the book? If so, ask students to annotate the text. Create a key for the different symbols they should use while annotating if you want students to use symbols. Figure 4.8 shows an example using "The Golden Bird," a Grimm's Fairy Tale.

Cold Calling

Cold calling is a questioning strategy where you call on kids without raised hands. This keeps kids on the edge of their seats. While it might at first seem the opposite of engaging, and a little scary, it actually motivates students to raise themselves to the cognitive demands necessary during beyond-comfort reading. Before starting close reading, cold call several questions. This is not an opportunity to check for low-level recall: "Caitlin, who escorted Ponyboy to the hospital?" Rather, continue to push higher order thinking questions: "Caitlin, what did Johnny's dying message to Ponyboy symbolize? What words make you think that?" If cold calling at the beginning of close

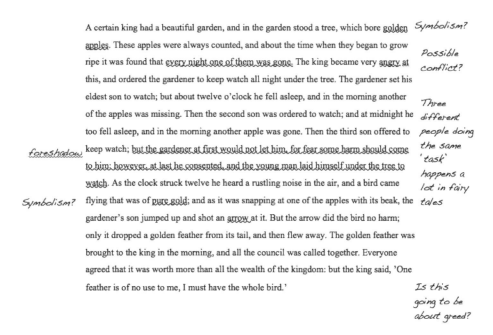

Figure 4.8 Sample Text Annotation

reading is a daily expectation, students will become highly accountable to the text.

SparkNotes

Let's keep it real. Kids might say they read the chapter when they didn't and instead read SparkNotes. It stinks, but it happens. There are ways you can prevent it and also catch it. For many teachers, SparkNotes are evil. Instead, embrace them. Teach students how to use SparkNotes: show them how to read a chapter summary if they found a chapter confusing, to determine other people's takes on thematic statements, and to get a description of the author's biography. SparkNotes are helpful. Be honest, have you ever taught a class text and checked out SparkNotes? In order to still keep kids accountable, avoid asking questions that can be directly answered by reading SparkNotes alone, and ensure that kids are able to directly reference the text when answering.

SCAFFOLDING SHARED READING FOR STRUGGLING READERS

The Common Core pushes that we use texts that are at or above grade level in order to increase rigor. As you read in Chapter 1, not all of our readers come into our classes on grade level. In fact, the average class has a span of six years of reading levels. Leveled reading needs to be a huge part of your reading program, so that readers are reading texts on their independent level during choice reading. However, the purpose of shared reading is to work with texts that are beyond students' comfort levels. As suggested, if the shared text is on a student's frustration level, we provide a book on tape. While most students have a listening level that's higher than a reading level, some do not — so make sure to assess your readers accordingly. See www.reading-without-limits.com for ways to manage books on tape. However, there are going to be kids in your class who will need you to scaffold the shared reading beyond books on tape and the questioning you do with the whole class. Below is a range of different ideas that work for fiction and nonfiction texts.

Gloss Notes

Copy a page from the text that you want students to read. In the margin, write assisted notes that include definitions for difficult vocabulary. Break down complicated concepts more concretely, and rewrite important sentences using simple syntax. Basically, you are making the text more readable in the margins!

Book Walks

One great strategy to increase readability is a book walk. Do a think-aloud, walking students through text features. Say, "I notice this subheading. I bet the chapter will be about ___." Or "Let's look at this picture. What do you think it tells us?"

Say Something

"Say something" stops a student as they are reading and gives them an opportunity to talk through their thinking. In partnerships, students read the text aloud and then pause to figure it out and paraphrase as they read. This strategy lends itself well to sentence starters.[54]

Steps to Say Something

1. With your partner, decide who will say something first.
2. Do one of the following when you say something in order to figure it out:
   a. Make a prediction
   b. Ask a question
   c. Clarify something you didn't understand
   d. Connect
   e. Paraphrase
3. If you can't do any of the strategies above, then reread.

Derived from Kylene Beers's *When Kids Can't Read.*

A complete reading program includes a synergy of choice and shared texts. Close reading allows for a high level of text accountability. You will develop students who prioritize figuring the text out and paraphrasing it as they read. In addition, students will develop group thinking, revision, and interpretation skills. Build close analysis of the text through questioning and going back to the text. Teach readiness strategies for high school and college to promote assigned reading stamina and remember to keep it kid-friendly.

ADDITIONAL RESOURCES

1. Transcripts of shared reading
2. Shared reading professional development
3. Video of teachers doing shared reading
4. Graphic organizers to support readers struggling to find meaning with shared text

MILD, MEDIUM, SPICY NEXT-STEP SUGGESTIONS

	Mild	Medium	Spicy
Find time for shared reading.	If you can't fit additional time in your schedule, do a read-aloud/ think-aloud every other day and shared reading the opposite days while still allowing time for independent reading on all days.	Lengthen your class so kids have enough time for choice and shared reading.	Put shared reading in the afternoon right before DEAR (Drop Everything And Read). This will mean in secondary school that multiple teachers will need to be trained on shared reading. Preplan questions for your team of literacy teachers and lead a series of professional developments. I have one on www.reading-without-limits.com you can use!
Choose the right text.	Make sure that you build prior knowledge about the text before jumping in. Go to www.reading-without-limits.com for an additional chapter devoted to building prior knowledge for readers.	Check out *The Book Whisperer* by Donalyn Miller. In it she has a long list of books that she recommends. *Shades of Meaning* by Donna Santman has a great collection of short stories recommended for teens.	Figure out your shared texts for the year and write a grant for them in advance so you have enough copies.

	Mild	Medium	Spicy
Figure out the meaning through whole-class questioning.	Read the book before you teach it!	Check out Doug Lemov's *Teach Like a Champion*. In it, he describes questioning techniques when students don't get an answer 100% right. It's very important during close reading to push for precision of response. This book is super helpful in developing your questioning skills.	In the margins of your text, preplan the questions you are going to ask. Incorporate questions that anticipate confusions like the example I gave in *Tangerine*. Don't spiral too many strategies in close reading session.
Build engagement for the shared text.	It's all about your language. Instead of "Take out your copies of *Holes*" in a boring teacher voice, try "We get more time with *Holes* today! I can't remember what happened yesterday. . . can someone remind me of the best part while we hand out the books?"	Create homework assignments with nonfiction excerpts that support the shared text. For instance, with *Holes* students read peach recipes, articles about Annie Oakley, and analyzed the desert biome.	In eighth grade, my English teacher Mrs. Toth had tea parties. She would bake yummy desserts and we would come in as characters from the book and have a party from the perspective of the characters we chose while the rest of the class watched. Make the food themed to the culture where the text takes place. Drink coconut water while reading *Lord of the Flies*, eat bagels to celebrate *A Tree Grows in Brooklyn*, and sip tea while reading a speech from Colonial times.

	Mild	**Medium**	**Spicy**
Assigned Reading Stamina	Give students reasonable deadlines of no more than 30 pages per night.	Teach students explicitly how to manage assigned reading while still enjoying pleasure reading by switching to break books, Manga, or a favorite series. Show them how to integrate assigned reading onto a goal calendar.	Read the book yourself and time how long it took you to read. Create a contest to see who can read the book at the same pace while still mastering questioning hierarchy.

KEEPIN' IT REAL

Here are some problems that we faced when introducing shared reading. Address the pitfalls in advance and I hope they won't happen to you!

Your Interpretation

Shared reading isn't a time to spoon-feed kids your interpretation of the text. They aren't going to become stronger readers if you do. Remember, this time for heavy guided practice is spent so kids ultimately can do the same work on their own.

Lost and Found

Bless them, but children lose things. Make sure to number books and identify which student received each book.

Read the Book Before Teaching It

While you aren't pushing your own interpretation of the book, do have a command of it before teaching it so that the book is aligned with your unit plan.

Vacation

Ensure that your units end before vacation. There's nothing like a two-week winter break to stop flow. Avoid assigning those last few chapters for spring break if you run out of time — trust me, I've learned this the hard way.

Avoid Pop Quizzes

I have never been a fan of low-level pop quiz questions at the beginning of class to check that students read and then punishing students who didn't read. As someone who consistently failed those quizzes in high school, I know what it feels like firsthand to be punished for not remembering things. It stinks. I was too focused on the bigger picture ideas and wasn't completely holding on to little details. Try establishing cold calling at the beginning of class that pushes for students to answer questions that involve justifiable interpretation.

Planning

It's really time consuming to preplan the best questions during close reading. You want to make sure that the questions really count. Preparing in order to anticipate pitfalls of understanding also takes time, but is really helpful when pushing thinking. Don't do it on the fly; your questions won't be as good.

FOR COACHES AND SCHOOL LEADERS

Extra Time

According to teachers I've spoken to, the biggest shared reading pitfall is finding enough time for shared reading (coupled with independent reading, vocabulary, mini-lessons, guided reading, etc.). From elementary through high school, that's the biggest complaint. That's on you! In order for your school to attain high achievement in reading, students need more time dedicated to reading.

Texts

Set aside money in your budget for students to have shared reading texts. If there isn't any room in your budget, start writing grants. Sample grants are available on www.reading-without-limits.com.

Book-of-the-Month

Try a book-of-the-month with your staff. Introduce a young adult book once a month. Incite discussion around the book during staff meetings. Promote dialogue and debate. Choose books that are aligned to character development that are also recommended shared reading texts. It's like an assigned text with your staff—and the cool thing is, they can bring the books to their classrooms to use for shared reading. This strategy works really well in high schools. All the texts I recommended in this chapter would be great.

TO SUM UP

- Incorporate at least 30 minutes a day into your schedule for shared reading (including close and assigned reading).
- Choose texts that are beyond your students' comfort zone and that span a variety of genres.
- Guide students through the text through close reading.
- Assigned texts promote college and career readiness. Teach students how to have great reading stamina with assigned texts.
- Make sure to scaffold shared reading for readers who need the scaffold.

Guided Reading to Move Students Along Their Continuum
Practice "Yet"

Guided reading will take your readers to their highest potential as readers. When implementing guided reading, include the following:

❑ Follow the same predictable structure of before-reading strategies, read-alouds, independent practice, and after-reading strategies.
❑ Group students homogenously and teach one grade level above their comfort level.
❑ Give kids tons of time to read aloud and at the same time have conferences to discuss grow goals.
❑ Be proactive to have successful guided-reading classroom management.
❑ Reassess every six to eight weeks.

Psychologist K. Anders Ericsson studied how those who are successful become successful. He looked at different types of ice skaters and discovered that aspiring Olympic ice skaters practice skills they have *yet* to master,

Guided reading is the opportunity to give your readers practice with texts that are a little bit difficult as you provide support so students can achieve what they weren't able to do independently before.

club skaters practice skills they have *already* mastered, and amateur skaters, like me, spend most of the time hanging out with friends and drinking hot chocolate. Even if these skaters spend the same amount of time on the ice, Olympic skaters achieve different results because they are practicing their "yet"—that which is just outside their ability. Ericsson studied fields such as music, firefighting, memory, and all sorts of different sports and the same held true for all: those who are successful practice a skill just outside their reach with guidance until they perfect the skill.[55] There are no short cuts in obtaining a new skill, as any mother who has seen her toddler repeatedly trying to stand can attest to. In order to develop lifelong readers, borrow upon what makes Olympic skaters great: practice "yet."

Guided reading is the final component of a well-rounded reading program. Guided reading is a set of training wheels for your readers. It's a toddler trying to stand. It's an ice skater working on her triple axel jump. It's the opportunity to give your readers practice with texts that are a little bit difficult as you provide support so students can achieve what they weren't able to independently do before. As students read on their comfort level in choice reading, guided reading gives them the opportunity to struggle with harder texts in small, differentiated groups. Shared reading accomplishes the same goal in a large class setting. However, during guided reading you work with small groups who have the same needs so you can offer more individualized support. Shared reading, while essential, is not differentiated in this way. In order to move students' zones of proximal development up, create a program keeping in mind what Vygotsky says: "What the child can do in cooperation today he can do alone tomorrow" (Vygotsky, p. 188).[56] Guided reading works with students on their instructional, or

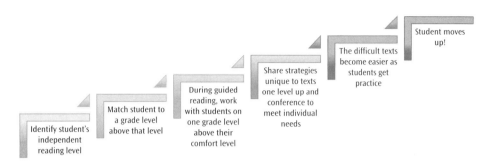

Figure 5.1 How Guided Reading Boosts Reading Achievement

"comfort-plus" level, so that it eventually becomes their independent level as shown in Figure 5.1. Unlike shared reading where all students are reading texts at the same difficulty level, guided reading groups students with texts that are a little bit too hard for them, so each group is reading on different levels. As a few weeks go by, these harder texts become less of a struggle, and voila! Your students' reading levels move up.

Now that I've described our thinking behind guided reading, the following chapter offers kid-friendly suggestions for making it a reality.

FOLLOW THE SAME PREDICTABLE STRUCTURE

Guided reading works with small groups of no more than eight students. Groups are divided homogeneously by their comfort-plus levels. I recommend that guided reading takes place at least twice a week. While it's possible for a teacher to meet with a guided reading group while the rest of her 25 students are doing independent work, it's much easier if guided reading occurs during a separate time in the schedule where all students attend guided reading. Additionally, I highly recommend that guided reading isn't the sole responsibility of the English or reading teacher. If multiple teachers pull guided reading groups during the guided reading block, it creates a more sustainable solution.

Guided reading is a 25 to 45 minute block divided up into four sections: before-reading, direct instruction, independent work, and after-reading. What I describe below is a predictable structure that occurs when a teacher meets with one guided reading group.

Before-Reading

(Two to Five Minutes) The goal is to build background knowledge about the text. Since the text is a little too hard, before-reading is like a booster seat for your kids to get them ready to read it on their own. It's important to connect to what kids know. All of the following strategies build on prior knowledge quickly, which is perfect for guided reading since time is valuable. Choose one from the list below, and feel free to mix it up! More before-reading strategies are available at www.reading-without-limits.com. You might have noticed that I didn't recommend any before-reading strategies during shared reading. That's because during shared reading, the purpose is to expose students to a text on its most "naked" level. Then, with the words alone, they need to unpack meaning. This is not the purpose of guided reading. The purpose of guided reading is to move kids up their developmental continuum, and doing before-reading strategies together will help them move on up.

Book Walk

For shorter texts with pictures, subheadings, or any other text features, slowly turn pages of the book from beginning to end, doing a think-aloud about what you notice. Make predictions about the book based on text features. For instance, "*I see a picture of a giraffe on this page. I wonder if this is a book about Africa? Let's keep looking. Here's a map of Tanzania. I know that's a country in Africa so I was right.*"

Tricky Vocabulary

For texts with high level, technical, or unfamiliar vocabulary, identify two to five words that you think will be tricky from the text, and teach them to the students by defining them in context. Encourage students to act out or draw the words.

Anticipation Vote

For texts with complicated themes, write out four to five controversial statements that align with a central theme, character choice, or event. Ask kids to vote on their positions about these statements and then discuss. For instance, "'Friends should never rat each other out.' Do you agree or disagree? Why? Today we will see that the characters must confront this theme."

Direct Instruction

During direct instruction, you will either be reviewing a previously taught strategy or introducing something new.

Quick Review

(Five Minutes) You are probably thinking, "Maddie, you've lost your mind! How am I going to teach kids how to be better readers in five minutes?" Guided reading is just one piece of the puzzle, and is one tool toward the bigger picture. Most of the time you will not be teaching a new strategy or skill during guided reading. The strategies that you teach during direct instruction will be review as you taught them during choice or shared reading already. I address when you will need to teach a new strategy to a group that they haven't learned in a later section. Guided reading, like shared reading, is an opportunity to review the strategies that turn dependent readers into independent readers. Those strategies can be found in Chapter 2. Just like choice reading, model the strategy with a read-aloud/think-aloud. Since your kids have seen that strategy before, you don't need to stop three times. Two is probably sufficient. You can also read aloud a shorter piece of text. Try not to go over five minutes because the work kids do independently will help them grow the most and you need to save time for independent work.

Choose a really short excerpt to work with. For instance,

- Sample text: *Frindle*
- Text grade level: Fourth grade (students in this guided reading group read on a third grade level comfortably, so this text is a little too hard for them)
- Strategy to model: analyze how characters remind us of people we know

Before-Reading
Introduce the vocabulary word "pestering."

Read-Aloud/Think-Aloud
There were only about 15 kids on the late bus because it was Friday afternoon. I sat near the back with Stephen, and he kept pestering me.

"Come on, Nora. I showed you my report card. I want to see if I beat you in math. Let me see what you got. Come on."

"No," I said. "No means no … But I have a choice about when I look at my grades, and right now I choose not to. So ask me on Monday."

Think-Aloud
"Nora reminds me of my friend Cady. She has great self-control. She can resist temptation in the same way that Nora is resisting opening her report card."

Think-Aloud
Stephen is my best friend, but I'm not sure he would have admitted it.

"I don't know anyone like Stephen so far. He doesn't want people to know that he is friends with Nora. I don't know anyone who has secret friends. Do you?"

Link to Independent Work
"Readers, today as you read out loud, I want you to identify different characters and consider how they do or don't remind you of people that you know. I will be checking in."

Teaching a New Strategy

If you are working with a group that is far below grade level, you might be introducing a strategy (like pausing at punctuation when you read aloud) that you didn't teach to the whole group during shared or choice reading because only a few students needed that strategy. In that case, and in the case of all guided reading instruction, stick to the tried and true read-aloud/think-aloud because it doesn't take a great deal of time. Stop a couple of times just as you would during a regular think-aloud; however, spend less time checking for understanding or questioning. Save that time for one-on-one work. A table below lists the strategies you should focus on based on students' comfort levels.

Independent Work

(15 plus minutes) During independent work, students read aloud quietly to themselves. While students read aloud, listen in and check for understanding.

Students Read Aloud

After direct instruction, immediately move to independent work. Here, students read the text aloud to themselves. Students do not read aloud to the group. Instead, each student reads aloud quietly to themselves and you work with them individually. Avoid whisper reading, as it does not help students as much in reaching optimal fluency. There should be a tonal melody in their voices. So, you will have six to eight students all reading aloud to themselves simultaneously. Push for all students to read aloud. This is important in

Figure 5.2 Encourage Students to Read Aloud During Guided Reading

order to build students' oral fluency. If students are spending time in reading class reading silently, guided reading is a time for something different. It is also the only way you will hear fluency issues or decoding miscues. A section later in this chapter describes the best questions to ask while students are reading aloud.

Part of the predictable structure is that students are reading aloud after you teach the mini-lesson. Some people believe that out-loud reading isn't developmentally appropriate for adolescents. I currently work with a population of incarcerated high-school-level kids and that's not the case. They are all older than 16, and love reading aloud. When I work with eighth graders, partner book units are a favorite. Maybe it's because kids like to hear themselves speak? Try mixing it up by having kids read in funny voices like monsters, mice, and cowboys in primary grades. Even give funny voices a try in high school. Trust me; a 16-year-old will giggle. But seriously, reading aloud for guided reading is essential so that you can listen to their fluency and decoding. Sometimes students will start reading aloud, and will switch to reading in their heads. In order to ensure that kids are reading the whole time, try to remind them or reinforce the strategy:

- I hear Ashley is still reading aloud.
- Who can remind me how our voices should sound for all of independent work?

Toobaloos

Some kids get distracted by other students reading aloud while they are reading aloud. Try toobaloos in lower grades, which are plastic fake phones that amplify whispered voices. Or spread kids throughout the room in upper grades so they can't hear each other. Ensure that each student starts reading aloud a few seconds apart so that they are not choral reading. Students are all reading at their own pace, and not at the same time so that you can listen in to the individual needs of each student.

Props

Annica likes to hand out props like sunglasses, a funny hat, or a Hawaiian lay, when it's time to start reading out loud. Delay each student's start by a few seconds so students don't choral read and are reading at their own pace.

Echo Reading

Instead of students reading on their own, partner students. First, a student reads a paragraph aloud. Then their partner rereads the paragraph to make it smoother. This strategy is great for high school students because adolescents love peer work.

What the Teacher Is Doing During Independent Work

As students read aloud, jump from kid to kid asking questions in order to ensure that they can do the strategy on their own. I offer a ton of different strategies for checking for understanding throughout the book. I spend a couple minutes with each kid and then loop around and meet with each student one more time. Is jumping around too exhausting? Get a chair on wheels or a mini golf chair so you can quickly pop from student to student.

You Be the Student

Here's a strategy you can use if a student is struggling more than others in the group. Start reading a book aloud to your student. Then model getting stuck. Have the student help you through a word or strategy. Switch, this time you put on the teacher hat and help your student through the word or strategy. Rotate a few times.

After Reading

(Three to five minutes) It's important to close your lesson with reflection. End your lesson by linking back to the purpose of the lesson. Here are some strategies you can use.

Figure 5.3 Jump from Student to Student to Give Feedback During Guided Reading

Summarizer

Ask students to summarize the purpose of today's guided reading lesson. Want to mix it up? Ask them to do it in a poem format. Or ask them to do it in three words or less.

Rank

Ask students to determine how well they understood the strategy that day by ranking their understanding from one to ten.

Transfer

Ask, "How does this strategy make us better readers? How could we use this strategy with our choice book tomorrow?"

Author's Chair

Ask students to show one time where they demonstrated the strategy that they practiced that day to the group.

Types of Text to Choose

For the mini-lesson text, I prefer any text as long as it takes under five minutes to do a read-aloud/think-aloud. It does not have to be the same text that students are reading during independent work. For the texts that students read, I prefer short texts. It can take a group of students much longer to read a novel or long text aloud. If I need to move kids around within groups flexibly, like after a few weeks, moving them into a novel group halfway through is confusing. The website www.readinga-z.com provides hundreds of short texts that are kid-friendly with an array of folktales and myths. With a low yearly subscription fee, it's worth the investment.

GROUP STUDENTS HOMOGENOUSLY AND
TEACH ONE GRADE LEVEL UP

Which strategies are best during guided reading? It depends on the student. If a student is reading on a third-grade level comfortably, then identify strategies that are helpful for fourth-grade texts. That's why guided reading is different from shared reading; each group is getting different strategies based on their needs. Below is a chart you can use that shows which strategies to teach. Teach to students' comfort-plus level: a level that is just beyond their reach. During choice reading, students read books that are comfortable. During guided reading, students read books that are a little bit too difficult for them. Table 5.1 is organized by student's comfort levels. If a student is reading comfortably on a second grade reading level, regardless of what grade they are on, guide them with a third-grade reading level text and its corresponding strategies.

CONFERENCE FOR GROW GOALS

While students read aloud, have a conference with each individually.

Conferencing

During guided reading, I pop from student to student usually spending about two minutes per kid. I listen in to help with decoding and I have comprehension questions ready to go. Sometimes students are so focused on reading aloud that they forget to read and think. Remember dependent readers? They don't think as they read, yet. Conferences help support the thinking behind the reading during guided reading.

Decoding
When I hear a student make a decoding error, or miscue a word, I prompt them in order to see if they can self-correct. Questions to Prompt Decoding in this section offers a list of great prompts derived from Fountas and

Table 5.1 Skills and Strategies to Teach to Different Developmental Groups During Guided Reading

Comfort Reading Level	Instructional "Comfort-Plus" Level	What to Teach
1st grade early texts	1.5–2nd grade level texts	**Paraphrase/Retell**: Beginning, middle, and end of whole text **Fluency**: Pause at punctuation **Decoding**: Look for sounds within words **Strategies**: Use pictures to get information **Common Core Examples**: Match pronouns to characters, figure out the setting
1st grade late texts	2nd grade texts	**Paraphrase/Retell**: Stop after a paragraph or page and describe who, what, and where **Fluency**: Pause at commas, periods, and paragraphs **Decoding**: Look for sounds within words to solve multisyllabic words **Strategies**: Make a character list, predict, visualize, and reread if you lose track **Common Core Examples**: Determine character traits, identify who is telling the story
2nd grade texts	3rd grade texts	**Paraphrase**: Paraphrase bigger portions of the text, such as two pages **Fluency**: Read lyrically, pause at punctuation, read dialogue in different voices **Decoding**: Look for sounds within words **Strategies**: Reread when you don't understand, keep track of characters with a list, visualize, and figure out what you already know, which helps you understand the text **Common Core Examples**: Analyze character change, determine impact of other characters on main character

Table 5.1 (*Continued*)

Comfort Reading Level	Instructional "Comfort-Plus" Level	What to Teach
3rd grade texts	4th grade texts	**Paraphrase**: Distinguish between fun and important facts **Retell**: Go back to the text explicitly, describe in depth a character, event, or setting **Decoding**: Use context to confirm or self-correct unknown words **Strategies**: Analyze how characters remind us of people we know, figure out unfamiliar settings, change mental visuals during time and place shifts **Common Core Examples**: Distinguish between resolved and solved conflicts, track plots of side characters
4th grade texts	5th grade texts	**Paraphrase**: Simultaneously figure it out and paraphrase the text in your own words **Retell**: Identify a theme in the text, distinguish between plots and subplots **Strategies**: Judge actions and decisions of characters, put yourself in characters' shoes, use nonfiction text features to find information **Common Core Examples**: Analyze mood or tone, determine how the setting impacts the story, analyze a setting's obstacles

(*Continued*)

Table 5.1 (*Continued*)

Comfort Reading Level	Instructional "Comfort-Plus" Level	What to Teach
5th grade texts	6th and 7th grade texts	**Paraphrase**: Paraphrase text in your own words **Retell**: Create an objective summary, determine what the author is trying to teach us **Strategy**: Distinguish your point of view or beliefs from those of characters and the author, (see all upper-elementary and middle-school strategies in Chapter 2 for a more comprehensive list) **Common Core Examples**: Analyze how complex characters advance a plot, analyze how the structure of a text (with parallel plots and flashbacks) creates suspense
6th and 7th grade texts	8th grade texts	**Paraphrase**: Include inferences within paraphrase **Retell**: Show how the structure of one chapter or excerpt fits into the text as a whole, determine a central idea and show how it develops **Strategies**: Develop theories about the writer's values and beliefs during different moments, discussing the fairness of different events **Common Core Examples**: Use text support to make inferences, analyze specific word choice and how it impacts mood or tone
8th grade texts	9th grade texts	**Paraphrase**: Paraphrase to determine the author's intention **Retell**: Determine how the structure of the book affects its meaning **Strategies**: Determine what the author left out, figure out how themes are expressed through different characters **Common Core Examples**: Analyze how an author's point is made clearer through particular words, lines, or excerpts of the text

Pinnell's *Word Matters*. The prompts give your students a strategy that they can use, like looking for a word they know inside of a larger word to figure this larger word out. The list below always helped me when I worked with students who needed decoding support.

Comprehension

You want to make sure that students really understand the text. Start by asking students to paraphrase what they just read. If they demonstrate confusion, choose a question listed below to help guide them through their confusion. Then ask questions that relate to the mini-lesson that you taught.

Fluency

Fluency refers to the melodic way a student reads aloud, including pausing at punctuation. It's a low-hanging fruit that students master pretty quickly, though they might fall out of habit and start reading in robot voices if you don't listen in. You can find fluency prompts as well in the next section.

The following is a handout that I *always* have on a clipboard while I am doing guided reading.

Questions to Prompt Decoding
- Do you see something that isn't quite right?
- Try saying the first sound.
- Look at the parts.
- Do you know a word that starts with those letters?
- Do you know a word that ends with those letters?
- What other word do you know like that?
- That sounds right and makes sense, but does that look right?
- It starts like that. Now check the last part.
- You almost got that. See if you can find what's wrong.

Questions to Prompt Comprehension
- Have you ever experienced something similar?
- What will happen next?
- What information do you remember?
- How will the character resolve this problem?
- How much time has passed? How does the author structure time?
- Reread that and see if it makes sense.
- What did you learn from the character's words on page___?
- What is the author saying about friends, family, love, conflict, et cetera?
- Retell the main events in your own words.
- How does the purpose of this chapter fit with the whole book?
- What literary elements did you find?
- How does the title relate to the story?

Questions to Prompt Fluency
- Listen to me read, and then reread what I read in the same way.
- Pause at commas and end-of-sentence punctuation.
- Can you read the sentence a little bit faster?
- How would the character say those words?

Derived from *Word Matters: Teaching Phonics and Spelling in the Reading/Writing Classroom* by Fountas and Pinnell (Source: Fountas and Pinnell, 1998, Figure 20–3).[57]

Planning Guided Reading

Table 5.2 shows how I plan out a guided reading group for seven weeks for students reading on a second grade level. That means I am going to show them strategies that would help them read on a third grade level. A list of which strategies to teach are found earlier in this chapter. I plan seven-week cycles in advance, since I usually assess every six to eight weeks.

For sample schedules for all of the different reading levels, go to www.reading-without-limits.com.

Table 5.2 Sample Seven-Week Guided Reading Plan for Students Comfortably Reading on a Second-Grade Level

Week	Tuesday	Thursday
1	When you miscue a word, find a word within the word to solve it (spiral later).	Pause at all punctuation when you read aloud.
2	Paraphrase two pages of the text at a time.	When paraphrasing bigger portions, make sure you aren't leaving out main details.
3	Keep track of characters with a list (spiral later).	Read dialogue with the mood that the character is demonstrating.
4	When you miscue a word, find a word with the word to solve it.	When you don't understand, go back to the start of the chapter and reread.
5	Figure out what you already know when figuring out a text.	Keep track of characters with a list.
6	Visualize to gain meaning.	Analyze how a character has changed.
7	Figure out how different characters are feeling and how those feelings change.	Do another running record to see if the students moved up in reading level.

BE PROACTIVE TO HAVE SUCCESSFUL GUIDED READING CLASSROOM MANAGEMENT

There are classroom management issues that are unique to guided reading that I suggest addressing in advance. They include:

- Students not reading aloud
- Students distracted by others reading aloud
- Where to sit during guided reading (if they are reading comfortably)
- What to do if a teacher is listening in
- What to do if you hear a student make a decoding error

Remind-and-Reinforce

To address the guided reading classroom management concerns from above, or any others that pop up, I recommend the remind-and-reinforce strategy.[58]

Remind: "Who can remind me of strategies we use so we aren't all reading the same words at the same time?"

Remind: "What level should I hear voices? Let's practice. Say the sentence (insert something silly)."

Remind: "When you are finished with the book early, what should you do?" (Go back and read it aloud again).

Reinforce: "Marcus, I noticed that you got out the whiteboard and started writing a word that you clunked. That's awesome!"

Beyond management, use the remind-and-reinforce strategy in order to repeat strategies that you want kids to do every time they read. For example,

"What's one thing you do before starting a book?"

"How can pictures help us get more information about what's happening on a page?"

"Who can remind me why the glossary is helpful?"

"What should you do if you lose track of what's happening in the book. Who can name three things?"

"Hakeem, I noticed that you are reading the captions aloud. Everyone should make sure to get all of the information on the page. You rock!"

Separate

Try separating students so they aren't sitting close to each other when reading aloud. That will also give you more room to conference with students.

RE-ASSESS STUDENTS EVERY SIX TO EIGHT WEEKS

This criterion is pretty self-explanatory. Allow kids a couple months to immerse themselves in a more difficult level, and after that time you will start hearing a lot less decoding errors and a higher command of the text. That means they are ready to move up levels during choice reading. Not all students in the group will move up. In my experience, about 80% will. Therefore, make sure someone (you or a literacy coach) is able to reshuffle and organize the groups every eight weeks. Each student will move at their own developmental pace. However, if it has been three to four months and you don't see progress, then immediately do a thorough investigation into their reading stamina and love of reading. Students who don't move up at the same rate are not reading at home 99% of the time.

In conclusion, a couple times a week, meet with a group of students to work with texts that are a little bit out of reach. Group students by their reading levels. By guiding them, you will get your students performing triple axel jumps in no time.

ADDITIONAL RESOURCES

1. Ready-to-print guided reading tracking sheets organized by reading level
2. How to help a student decode including videos
3. The complete set of prompts for teachers to use during reading
4. Ready-to-use guided reading lesson plans
5. Videos of teachers doing sample lessons
6. Professional development including a recorded PowerPoint and interactive notes
7. Ready to use grant template for guided reading resources
8. Sample seven-week scope for each text band

MILD, MEDIUM, SPICY NEXT-STEP SUGGESTIONS

	Mild	Medium	Spicy
Set-Up	Group students in homogenous groups according to their comfort levels. Print out materials from www.reading-without-limits.com. Create a schedule for when you will meet with each group, preferably at least 25 minutes twice a week. Prioritize meeting with students who are not yet at grade level.	In addition to www.readinga-z.com materials, print out rich nonfiction resources. For students at or above grade level, create larger groups of 16 or more students to do a text study. Choose books that are demanding yet highly interesting like *Of Mice and Men* or a nonfiction narrative.	Are you super organized and do you want to make schoolwide lasting change? Take on this very important project. Group all students, regardless if they are at or above reading level, in groups of 8 or less. Create a guided reading room that collects all texts by comfort level for your entire student body. Create a magazine bin for each reading level. When you come across an amazing short story, newspaper article, or short text, make a ton of copies and put it in the guided reading bin according to its level. Encourage teachers to put copies of a text they loved in your box so you can file it away in the guided reading bins later.

	Mild	Medium	Spicy
The Delivery	Low on time? Instead of targeted mini-lessons for each session, start each session with during reading. Use the time to conference. This will give kids even more out loud reading time.	Use the Guided Reading tracking sheet available on www.reading-without-limits.com to record miscues and misunderstandings. Make sure that these sheets are shared with the reading teacher so s/he can use it during O3s.	DonorsChoose is an online charity that connects donors to classrooms in need. You can submit a grant for anything that you think will benefit your students. Write a grant for toobaloos on DonorsChoose. Make guided reading kid-friendly by giving kids funny sunglasses, weird hats, or wigs to wear once it's their turn to start reading aloud so students don't all start at the same time.

SUGGESTED FURTHER READING FOR GUIDED READING

1. *Word Matters: Teaching Phonics and Spelling in the Reading/Writing Classroom* by Irene Fountas and Gay Su Pinnell
2. *When Kids Can't Read* by Kylene Beers
3. *Yellow Brick Roads* by Janet Allen
4. *I Read it, But I Don't Get It* by Cris Tovani
5. *Guiding Readers and Writers* by Irene Fountas and Gay Su Pinnell

FOR COACHES AND SCHOOL LEADERS

Schedule

Create a schedule that makes time specifically for guided reading. It will help all students whether they are struggling readers or students who are also taking Advanced Placement English. Put guided reading opposite an elective class so while half of the grade is going to gym class, for instance, the other half is doing guided reading. Set aside a closet or corner of a room for guided reading materials and keep it well stocked. As you find awesome short articles, make copies (laminated would be really cool) and add them to the guided reading bins.

Assess

Reassess your readers every six to eight weeks. Encourage guided reading teachers to do the assessing or allow the reading teacher to take a break from teaching classes for a couple days in order to get through the entire batch of students. Then reorganize guided reading groups. Some teachers like sticking with the same group of kids, some teachers like sticking with the same level. Do a temperature check to see what is the most sustainable for each teacher.

Readers Who Read on Grade Level

Some schools don't have the staff to put each student in a small guided reading group. Every school I've worked with has been there. For students reading on grade level, we didn't put them in guided reading groups when we didn't have enough staff to meet their needs in small groups. Their developmental needs were pushed during choice and shared reading.

Prioritize Guided Reading

I strongly believe that guided reading should either happen outside of the reading classroom, or that the reading teacher should get help from a supporting teacher. For teachers who are able to rock out guided reading groups during independent reading class, keep working it. However, I found myself a frenzied mess trying to organize guided reading on top of managing a classroom, checking for understanding, and the other one thousand requests that happen over the course of a class. School leaders should be intentional in how they schedule guided reading. It's too hard to expect reading teachers to hold guided reading groups for all of their students by themselves. Adding extra time for guided reading (in addition to extra independent reading blocks and shared reading) is an excellent way to increase student achievement quickly. If there are students in your school who are struggling readers, they need more time.

KEEPIN' IT REAL

Here are some problems that we faced when doing guided reading. Address the pitfalls in advance and I hope they won't happen to you!

Team and Family

Help! Reading teachers can't do this on their own. In our first few years at KIPP Infinity, we had all teachers, including content teachers, do guided reading in the fifth grade. Therefore groups were smaller and I really appreciated the help. I did professional development a few times a year to make sure that we were all on the same page and I helped by providing lesson plans and materials. We also hired part-time guided reading teachers to help out.

Collecting Resources

A wonderful website for guided reading groups with a low-cost yearly fee is www.readinga-z.com; however, putting together the guided reading books available there is time consuming. Find a time where you can get a lot of helpers and organize the guided reading texts for the entire year. Keeping your guided reading room organized is essential. When books aren't returned or if resources get mixed up, guided reading ends up falling apart.

Homework

Avoid using guided reading time as study hall for students to do homework and tutoring. Students should be using this time to read aloud. The amount of growth that will happen is insane. Coupled with stamina and love of reading, reading aloud should be a pillar in a reading program. Guided reading should also never be a homework assignment unless you plan on going home with your group.

TO SUM UP

- Follow the same predictable structure each time you do guided reading by activating prior knowledge, modeling a reading strategy in less than five minutes, giving kids tons of time to read aloud, and doing after-reading strategies.
- Group students one grade level higher than their comfort level.
- Conference while students read aloud using question prompts.
- Be proactive to have successful guided reading classroom management.
- Reassess every six to eight weeks and you will see your students move up!

PART 3

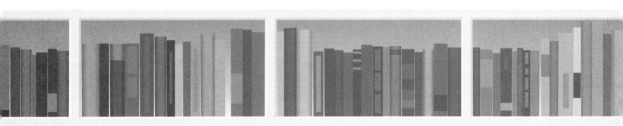

Putting the Power of Choice, Shared, and Guided Reading to Work in Your Classroom or School

6

Make It Visible
Borrow from Casino Developers and Interior Designers

This chapter shows specific guidelines for intentional classroom set-up, which include

❑ Comfortable reading spots
❑ Intentionality with what you put on your walls
❑ Mindful set-up of library and desks

Take a second and consider a time that you enjoyed a favorite reading moment. I find drawing helps me trigger memories, and I encourage you to grab a piece of paper so you can draw your favorite memory. See what I drew in Figure 6.1.

I drew my mom reading Dr. Seuss with me. My mom passed away 14 years ago, and I lovingly cling to memories of her. Snuggled up in her bed, she nightly read the same book until I recited the words with her. Another memory that vividly stands out was in college amidst stacks of reference materials under the glow of green glass shades. Figuring out how to tackle a

171

Figure 6.1 My Favorite Reading Memory

research paper gave me a great deal of pride. Both of these memories stand out as favorites.

Where were you? Were you reading with a family member as a young child curled up in an armchair? Were you hiding under your covers at night with a flashlight reading Judy Blume?

Wouldn't it be cool if you did this activity with your students in 20 years, and some of them drew your classroom? Continue your path toward creating *Reading Without Limits* readers with how you set up your physical space. In the beginning, in addition to determining reading levels, be very intentional with what you make visible in your classroom.

Dave Levin likens school and classroom design to Las Vegas. Casino developers are incredibly intentional at making things visible, and they want one thing: money. Every square inch of a casino is considered, from lighting to pumped oxygen to lack of clocks to placement of tables to free drinks. Their goal: make as much money off gamblers as possible. Although as educators our target is certainly different, there is much to learn from casino developers. What's my goal? As a teacher, I want an environment to encourage each of my students to be lifelong, confident readers.

I love teaching. I also love interior design. Though I never went to design school, I learned that one rule holds true for all designers (whether eclectic, modern, or traditional)—be intentional. Stacking mail by your door for a week is not intentional. Putting up a kitty poster that says "Hang Ten" in your classroom is not intentional. Leaving a roll of paper towels in the center of your dining room table is not intentional. A table runner lined with votive candles designed to provide warmth and color is. Learn from designers. Be intentional about everything that is visible.

In the beginning, you should assess your students' reading levels in order to figure out how to match them to texts comfortably. In addition, be mindful with sensible classroom set-up. Casino developers and interior designers show the importance of intentionality when setting up space. This chapter will show how to consider your classroom space just as a casino developer or interior designer does. Your goal is to create a learning environment that balances the intimacy students would get from reading a picture book with the academic rigor of a college library. I argue for a balance between an intimate and academic environment for two reasons: first, some of our kids prefer a cozier environment while some appreciate formal environments, and second, we want to promote a love of reading that celebrates hiding under the covers with a flashlight just as much as we want to promote strategically attacking a stack of books. If you make your classroom too intimate, it takes away the urgency of building stamina and strategic rigor. If you make your classroom too academic, it doesn't evoke the notion that love of learning can happen anywhere. Sensible set-up is equally important as finding students' reading levels in that the layout needs to strategically support boosting lifelong reading.

SET UP COMFORTABLE READING SPOTS

I've just described our thinking behind strategic set-up. Next I offer specific guidelines for making it a reality in your school.

Figure 6.2 You Can Work Rigorously and Comfortably
at the Same Time

If our goal is lifelong reading, our classrooms need to mimic what readers do in their real lives. When reading for leisure, as students do during choice reading, give them comfortable seating options.

Intentional Seating

When you read at home for fun, do you read at your desk? I sure don't. I read on the couch because it's more comfortable. Lift what you do from your life when designing your classroom. Create comfortable seating areas using beanbags, old armchairs, or sofas where students read during independent reading. Having beanbags for every student is probably not realistic: try this teacher strategy. Write each student name on a Popsicle stick. Then randomly draw sticks to see who gets beanbags. Or put up a schedule in your room designating kids' use of beanbags to certain days of the week. See the next chapter for how to set-up explicit routines so comfortable seating is easily managed. When students are being pushed rigorously during shared reading, intentionally match them to appropriate workspaces: desks. Arrange them in a U-shape to promote classroom discussion about the shared text.

I try to create little nooks with comfortable seating. For example, bean bag chairs and old armchairs. My favorite quote is "The library has become my candy store." Yesterday a student said to me, "The library really has become

my candy store!" I'm an avid reader, and I love to drink coffee in cafés while I read. The students can drink hot cocoa when they read as a reward.
—Theresa, 5th grade reading teacher

Set Up a Reading Café

The way I do library check-out on Mondays is I have my teacher timer set to three minutes. They get three minutes to find a book on their level. I call the first row and they know that when the timer goes off they have to have their book. Then the next row goes. That way I don't have more than seven kids in the library and I don't have to say anything. They just know when and how to go. I love it.

—Amber, 6th grade reading teacher

Many adult readers love working and reading in cafés. Whenever I try to get a table at my neighborhood bookstore, it is full of people flipping through magazines, working on their computers, or reading a favorite book. Theresa, former fifth grade reading teacher at KIPP Infinity, created a Cocoa Caliente café off to the side of her seating arrangement. Students get hot chocolate while they read their books at café tables. Kids earn café reading and love to sip-and-flip. The reading café is great for all independent reading, whether it's a book of choice or studious shared reading.

Vacation Reading

When introducing choice reading, I recommend trying to lift the qualities of what makes vacation reading great and transferring those qualities to your class. Instead of a reading café, put out some lawn chairs, beach umbrellas, and silly sunglasses.

Research Library

One of my favorite reading moments was studying under the green lamps at the NYU Bobst library. Some students will not want to read on beanbag chairs because it distracts them. Create a section that mimics a college library: find a long desk, put up dividers, and set up green lamps. Include reading supplies like sticky notes and different colored pens to promote rigorous learning. During independent reading, choice, or shared, allow students to choose if they want comfortable couches, café tables, or reading cubicles.

BE INTENTIONAL WITH WHAT YOU PUT ON THE WALLS

It might seem small, but what you put on your walls has lasting impact. Now that your seating is set up, design what will be up on the walls year-round. Next I offer specific suggestions of what you can put on your classroom walls that support big picture goals. Remember, all students have the right to an excellent education and you aim to build lifelong readers.

Make College Visible

KIPP's mission is for students to go to and through college. Consider painting your classroom in alma mater colors to give your room a collegiate feel. If you aren't able to paint, hang college banners throughout the room. Go all out and drench your entire classroom in a college theme. Name different sections of your library after real places in your own alma mater, such as your favorite café or the name of your library. You are sending the daily message that college is fun, rigorous, and attainable.

Inspirational Quotes

Paint love-of-reading quotations on the wall. A few of my favorites include the following:

Reading is to the mind what exercise is to the body. — *Joseph Addison*
When I got [my] library card, that was when my life began. — *Rita Mae Brown*

I used to walk to school with my nose buried in a book. — *Coolio*
The libraries have become my candy store. — *Juliana Kimball*

What quote did we post in the youth justice center?

He who opens a school door, closes a prison. — *Victor Hugo*

And don't forget to integrate those quotations into your instruction. Every day the principal of the justice center points out the quotation that hangs over the entrance to the students as they enter to remind students of its importance.

Bookcase Updates

Lifelong readers share books. Create a bulletin board that posts what each student is currently reading. I first got this idea from Ramp Up Literacy, an America's Choice program, and they call this bulletin board "Status of the Class." To play off Facebook, call it Bookcase Updates. Update what students are reading weekly, and display Bookcase Updates up front in your class. Ask teachers in your building to put their books up, too.

For Struggling Readers: Teach How to Self-Assess

Using Bookcase Updates, teach readers how to determine if they are meeting their total books-read goal. Allow time to evaluate progress by using an exemplary model that not only shows quantity, but variety.

Celebrate Student Growth

Celebrate student growth over achievement. In lieu of displaying student levels (How would Sofia feel if she saw she had a level lower than her peers?), track student growth with bar graphs. Post the graphs in the classroom so kids can see.

Figure 6.3 Make It Visible with Quotes

Figure 6.4 Bookcase Updates Are a Fun, Accountable Making-It-Visible Routine

INTENTIONALLY SET UP YOUR LIBRARY AND ROOM

Remember Vegas? Make your goal of lifelong reading visible. The library will become your students' "candy store" if you make it delicious.

Intentional Library Layout

Intentionally set up your library. Whether or not you level it, alphabetize it, or arrange it by genre, make it look beautiful. Spread the bookcases out so there isn't a traffic jam in one corner of your room.

Market Your Books

See how your neighborhood bookstore markets books. Which books catch your eye? Use the same marketing approach for your library. Bookstores incorporate flat tables with books that customers are more drawn to because they can see each book cover. I bet if you designed a similar table in your classroom, you would see more kids at that table, too. Consider intentionally grouping books by themes. Kids who are drawn to one type of book will see similar books and "buy" them. Have a new hot book that everyone wants to read? Put it on your bulletin board as you teach your lesson. It'll be gone in minutes.

Library Checkout

Students need to checkout their books when they go to the library. Avoid having just one library checkout station, as it leads to traffic jams. Instead, arrange several different stations by student's last name. Use a library checkout form like Table 6.1, arranged in several different stations by student's last name.

Intentional Classroom Layout

Be super intentional about how you lay out your classroom, as Figure 6.5 shows. Spread the choice library out. Put the bookcase update board front and center, along with a list of recommended books. Incorporate comfortable seating. Find desks that are movable so you can arrange in

Table 6.1 Book Checkout Form

Name	Book Title	Author	Genre	Day Checked Out	Day Returned

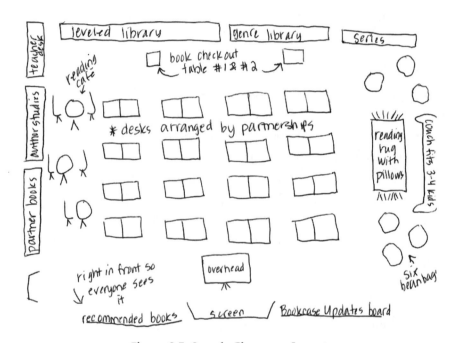

Figure 6.5 Sample Classroom Layout

partnerships or in a U-shape for shared reading. If you can, integrate café seating for older readers. Consider all pitfalls, such as congestion at the book checkout table.

Be intentional with how you set up your classroom, and design areas that evoke love of reading while maintaining an academic feel. What you make visible can have profound impact on the reading achievement in your classroom.

ADDITIONAL RESOURCES

1. A sample grant template you can use to get books in your classroom
2. A slideshow of reading classrooms
3. Suggested classroom seating layouts

MILD, MEDIUM, SPICY NEXT-STEP SUGGESTIONS

	Mild	**Medium**	**Spicy**
Comfortable Seating	Create an area for beanbag chairs or other comfortable seating options. Bring in stuffed animals for kids.	DonorsChoose lumbar pillows for kids to use at their desks during independent reading time.	Create a reading café in your classroom. Set up cubicles in the back that look like a college library.
Walls	Put up inspirational quotes using an overhead projector.	Find a favorite book cover and create a mural of it outside your classroom. Track how many books your students have read with a "goal thermometer."	Create a Bookcase Update bulletin board. Create a competition among teachers of number of books read and track the contest in your classroom. Track number of minutes you read each night on a line graph.

	Mild	**Medium**	**Spicy**
Library	Choose high interest books to display on your bookshelf.	Create a shelf where other teachers in your building recommend books to kids. Display adult books that you read last month.	Allow select kids to make their own recommendation shelf. Design regions for break books (comic books, magazines, manga) strategically throughout the room and cultivate a high-interest break book library through grants on DonorsChoose.
Miscellaneous	Play classical music while students read.	Create mood lighting with lamps.Take pictures of students reading comfortably in their homes, in parks, or on public transportation to show that reading comfortably happens everywhere.	Go to bookstores in your neighborhood and have them donate some standees (large cutouts advertising books that you will often see in bookstores). Paint your classroom in your alma mater's colors. Incorporate cocoa, juice, or water in your café.

KEEPIN' IT REAL

Here are some problems that we faced when making it visible. Address the pitfalls in advance and I hope they won't happen to you!

Bookcase Updates

When your students start building a love for reading, they will read many more books. Utilize a student helper so that Bookcase Updates can be updated weekly.

Classroom Library

Keep your classroom library neat and organized. Create a system of organization that both you and your students can maintain. Use color-coded stickers to sort books by their different sections. Build time within your class daily for leaving the space "cleaner than you found it."

Knick-Knacks

A cozy space does not equate to a cluttered space. Avoid overdecorating because it's too stimulating. While adolescent bedrooms are a source of comfort to many, that doesn't mean that a messy adolescent bedroom is our source of inspiration for classroom decorating. Instead of decorating with dozens of stuffed animals, choose a large one that a student can earn. Also, avoid too many posters, quotes, or wall colors to keep things simple.

Café

Do not start drinking hot cocoa on the first day of class; the purpose of making the café visible from day one is to provide a visual incentive for your kids. Your students will start drooling (maybe even literally) with anticipation when they see the Cocoa Caliente Café set up in the back of their class.

FOR COACHES AND SCHOOL LEADERS

Volunteers

Organize volunteer teams to come beautify your school. Using overhead projectors, the volunteers can trace inspirational quotes and book covers that later become murals.

Grants

Classroom libraries and bookshelves are very expensive. Utilize DonorsChoose, a grant service. Grants with smaller price tags are more likely to be funded; so if you need an entire library, split it up into multiple grants.

Staff Recommendations

Spend time each staff meeting as a venue to recommend books. It's a fun activity to start a meeting. If teachers are voracious readers, the enthusiasm will rub off on students.

TO SUM UP

- Design a room that invokes both love of reading and rigorous learning.
- Allow students to read comfortably during independent reading, mimicking how you read at home or on vacation.
- Inspire future mindedness and promote lifelong reading with intentional design such as designing a college-themed classroom and putting up love-of-reading murals and quotes.
- Be intentional with your classroom and library layout by considering how you organize your library, where comfortable seating best fits, what goes in the front of the room, and student traffic.

Muscle Memory Routines
Where Do You Put Your Keys?

Having tight routines ensures an optimal learning environment. This chapter shows how to teach reading routines to your students, and how to keep routines going for the entire school year. The following steps will keep your classroom running smoothly:

❏ Figure out all of the details of the routine before you teach it.
❏ Teach the routine using examples and non-examples.
❏ Incorporate something bizarre or creative so it sticks in students' memories.
❏ Use the remind and reinforce strategy as you keep the routine alive throughout the year.

Where are your keys right now? Are you sure? Do you put your keys in the same spot everyday, do they travel with you, or do you not know where your keys are? For those with a muscle memory routine, you know where they are. Muscle memory refers to procedural tasks done without conscious effort due to repeated exposure. For instance, riding a bicycle or typing. Putting my keys on a table when I came home was my muscle memory routine.

Four years ago was a different story. My husband and I recently moved. Instead of a desk beside our door, there was a mountain of boxes, along with a frenzied dachshund. We moved into our apartment, and the following day Mike left for the Utah class trip. Then I lost my keys. I was on the wrong side of my door and a screaming puppy at 11 P.M. Did I mention my phone was with Bubba, my dog? This was my first time locked out of an apartment. I didn't stick to my routine. My muscle memory was to use the table, and when my table was a mountain of boxes with a wiggly puppy, I messed up.

Muscle memory helps retain simple, everyday tasks through *repeated exposure*. Dave Levin likens it to getting clean. Let's go to your morning or evening shower for a second. Do you wash your face first or last? Last? Try mixing it up tomorrow and reverse the process. It's not going to be easy, because your routine has become ingrained in your muscle memory. Repetition got it there. Muscle memory is a positive, essential part of our memory. Without muscle memory, we wouldn't be able to do everyday tasks. As teachers, we want more tasks to become engrained in our students' muscle memories so that they become everyday tasks.

This chapter will show how to teach reading routines following the three criteria in Figure 7.1 in order for your class to run smoothly. One

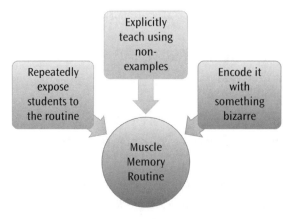

Figure 7.1 Criteria for Teaching a Classroom Routine

common mistake teachers make in establishing routines is succumbing to the temptation to tweak, adjust, and change. When establishing routines it is important to stick with them, so students can practice through repeated exposures and so no one, including you, "leaves the keys on the table" and gets "locked out." Also, when teaching the routine, you want to make it fun and bizarre so students remember. According to neuroscientist John Medina, author of *Brain Rules*, "Most of the events that predict whether something learned also will be remembered occur in the first few seconds of learning. The more elaborately we encode a memory during its initial moments, the stronger it will be" (Medina, p. 119).[59] If you elaborately encode the routine by teaching it in a bizarre way, students will be more likely to remember it. Finally, use *non-examples* when teaching your routine so that your students know what to do, and what not to do.

If routines become apart part of your students' muscle memory, you will not to have to call a locksmith, hope your landlord comes to help, or figure out a way to find your dog walker. And you won't have too many students with hands up asking questions, realize in January that half of your books are missing, or wonder why Shirley is out of her seat meandering through the library. In this chapter, first I share how to teach a routine through repeated exposure, elaborate encoding, and using non-examples. Then I provide routines that will help you manage choice, guided, and shared reading.

START BY FIGURING OUT ALL THE DETAILS OF THE ROUTINE

Step 1 in teaching a routine is figuring out all the details that will make the routine a success. Consider what you want to see kids doing when the routine is working, and what you don't want to see. It's best to preplan the little details.

Visualize the Routine

Before teaching a routine to your class, consider exactly what you want the students to do when they are doing the routine. Visualize the routine through from start to end before teaching it as you drive to work. Consider all that could go wrong when you are visualizing. It's essential to take the extra couple minutes to think through each of the details. Those two minutes will save you time in the long run. Lots of research has been done on the effects of mental imagery in sports. Olympic athletes who visualize their best training, corrections on feedback, and the actual event are outliers in their success.

For instance, on Monday you want to teach your students how to check out books from the library. Picture yourself teaching the routine by asking yourself the following questions:

❑   What do you want students to be able to do?
❑   Not do?
❑   What are details that would drive you nuts?
❑   What might confuse students?
❑   How should they do the routine tomorrow?
❑   Next Monday?

Examples and Non-Examples

After visualizing, break down what students should do into critical individual components. UCLA basketball coach John Wooden, at the first team meeting of the season, showed his players how to put their socks on. First, he rolled each sock over his toes, his foot, his ankle, then pulled it snug. He then went back to smooth it out, making sure there were no wrinkles. Wrinkles cause blisters, which aren't good for performance.[60] He broke down the details necessary for a routine's success in the same way that you need to break down reading routines. The hard part is striking the right balance. Wooden didn't spend too much time going over rules, rules, rules; otherwise, he would have droned like Charlie Brown's teacher. This chapter shows how you can make routines short and sweet and describes a management strategy that will keep them alive without your seeming like a teacher with too many rules.

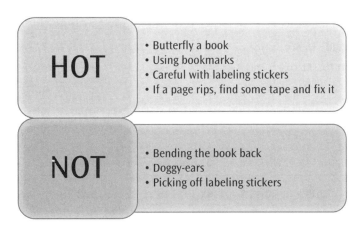

Figure 7.2 Examples and Non-Examples of Handling a Book

For instance, you want to teach the routine of how to handle a book. First visualize everything you want to happen and that could possibly go wrong. When you introduce the routine to your students, tell them what you do want to see (how to use bookmarks, find tape if a page rips) and what you don't want to see (dog-eared pages, bent spines, ripped pages, messed up labels) as shown in Figure 7.2. It's important that you also incorporate non-examples. Anytime you introduce a routine, show students what you

Figure 7.3 Routines Will Help Students Read for Longer

don't want to see as well. When introducing reading notebooks, we show one filled with graffiti, spilled pizza, and ripped pages. That's what we don't want to see. Then we show what we want to see. Incorporating non-examples is also one way to capture attention by showing something bizarre. Seeing a teacher's example tagged and covered in spaghetti sauce is definitely bizarre.

MAKE IT BIZARRE AND FUN

The more intense or vivid an experience, the more likely we are going to remember it. And we definitely want our kids remembering routines. Therefore, when teaching a routine, make it fun. Memory-training books, like Kenneth Higby's *Your Memory: How it Works and How to Improve It*, often recommend linking something bizarre to something you want to remember.[61]

Now that you've figured out all the details of the routine, you need to consider how to introduce it in a bizarre way to kids so it's encoded in their memories. For instance, one way to encode how to handle a book by making it fun and bizarre is by asking a student who takes really good care of his sneakers a couple days before class to bring them in. Before starting the lesson, jokingly treat him as if the shoes are museum quality. Show the sneakers off to the students. Ask why it's a good idea to take care of clothes. Then launch into the how-to-handle-books routine. Starting a lesson off by looking at sneakers is bizarre and helps engrain book handling into memory.

REMIND AND REINFORCE

When you teach the routine to your kids, you share all the details (what you want to see and what you don't want to see). You also teach it by including something bizarre to encode it in their memories. But that doesn't mean that everyone will remember the routine. We need repetition in order for something to be ingrained in our memory. First off, avoid changing the routine—that will confuse you and the kids. In order to keep the routine alive in students' memories, follow the Remind and Reinforce strategy introduced by Roxann Kriete. The remind and reinforce strategy is a management technique that helps put tasks into muscle memory.[62]

Remind

Before independent reading starts, ask students to remind you about a routine.

- "Who can remind me how we handle our books?"
- "What's one thing we shouldn't do when handling books?"

Reinforce

As independent reading starts, reinforce by saying,

- "Jonathan, I noticed that you butterflied your book. That's going to keep our books in good shape for a long time."
- "Eliza, you used your bookmark last night. Thank you for not doggy earring the pages."

Use the remind and reinforce strategy throughout the year.

READING WITHOUT LIMITS ROUTINES

I've just described our thinking behind planning and reinforcing a routine. Next is a list of routines that will help develop *Reading Without Limits* readers. First, read through the different routines. Determine which routines you want to make a part of your reading classroom. When considering the guiding questions, answer them for your own classroom style—there are no right or wrong answers. In the heading that includes suggested options for how the routines can work, circle the ones you like, cross out ones that don't work. Then modify to fit the needs of your students, your school, and your personal pet peeves. The following list shares routines necessary for choice, guided, and shared reading. Figuring out your routines on the front end will save a ton of time later on so you can develop *Reading Without Limits* readers.

CHOICE READING: BOOK CHECKOUT

Time Frame

First week of school

Questions to Consider

- How do you want your students to checkout books?
- Should they check out multiple books at a time in order to lessen library visits?
- Is your library layout spread out so there isn't overcrowding?
- How can you avoid a traffic jam?
- What are your behavioral expectations in the library?
- What should students avoid?

Options

- During designated times only, students put up a signal (like a hand gesture showing the letter L) to go to the library. Once the teacher nods, they go.
- To avoid overcrowding, students may go to the library if there are three or fewer students in the library.
- Students may not go to the library unless they have a book to return.
- Students go to a binder system, organized by last names (try having several binders to avoid long lines at the check-out) and write in the title of the book and any other information. There is one page per student.
- Students may use a whisper voice when checking books out.

Make It Bizarre

- Set excitement around the library unveiling by putting up caution tape or wrapping the library in wrapping paper that the students get to tear through.
- As an entire class, role-play Not Hot routines. For instance, have all 30 students go to the library to check out a book and then experience a traffic jam. Then, as a group, create the rule together for how many students can be in the library at once.

CHOICE READING: BOOK RETURN

Time Frame

First week of school

Questions to Consider

- What is the consequence if a book is lost or misplaced? How will you keep track of whether or not kids are returning a book each time they check out a new book?
- Should students demonstrate understanding of the books that they've read, either with an online quiz or a book summary sheet before returning the book?
- Should students put the books back where they found them or in a bin like at the public library?
- How can you use student librarians?
- What should students avoid?

Options

- In order to check out a book, students must show that they have their finished book to return. If they don't, they may either read a short story, picture book, newspaper article, or something assigned until they return the book.

- Each student gets four pieces of cardboard that are the size of a book writing their name on each. Every time they check out a book, they put the cardboard in the library as a spot holder. When they return the book, they take the cardboard back.[63]
- Students fill in a quick book coupon that can include a retell, five-star recommendation, or questions that they have about the book.
- Students return books to a book bin so books don't become disorganized. Librarians re-organize outside of class time.
- Students complete an online Accelerated Reader quiz.
- After returning a book, students get a sticker and fill in the sticker chart on their own.
- Before starting their new book, students fill out a stamina calendar.

Make It Bizarre

- Give students a stack of disorganized library checkout cards. Do a race to see who can organize and make them neat the fastest.

CHOICE, SHARED, AND GUIDED READING: KEEPING A CLEAN LIBRARY

Time Frame

First week of school

Questions to Consider

- What does a neat library look like to you?
- What are your cleanliness pet peeves?

Options

- Face books cover forward, if they are in baskets, and not upside down if they are lined up on a bookshelf.
- Return books to the right section of the library.

- Remove all sticky notes or any sheets of paper from the book before returning, unless you want students to keep a recommendation bookmark or warning signals in the book.
- Do not leave pencils, rolled up balls of paper, or any other material in the library.
- Avoid scribbling on or picking at book labels.

Make It Bizarre

- Trash one section of your library so that it is disgusting. Include lots of yucky things like half eaten pizza and even (gasp!) spilled soda. Make it appalling and act like everything is normal. Start off your routine by having students go to the library to check out books. Once a buzz has started, launch your clean library lesson.

CHOICE AND SHARED READING: READING BINDERS

Time Frame

First day of school

Questions to Consider

- Where will students store worksheets?
- Does the sequence of worksheets in your binder matter?
- How will you divide up the sections? Do-now? Classwork? Homework? Reading log?
- How often will you check the neatness of binders?
- May kids decorate their binders?
- What should students avoid?

Options

- Staple all sheets that students will be using for the day, from do-now through homework, so you only need to pass out papers once.

- Binder papers are numbered based on the class day. Students need to keep their binder sequentially organized.
- Twice a month, during reading assessments, ask the students to keep their binders out on their desk. Create a binder rubric and grade each binder using the rubric.
- Encourage students to decorate their binders invoking their love of reading.
- Encourage students to avoid making their binders yucky by picking at the plastic and stuffing papers in the pockets.

Make It Bizarre

- I tell the story of my binder when I was a kid (which was a gross mess) and how I constantly got in trouble for not being able to find anything. Try a "what not to do binder" that is so awful that when you pick it up, all of the papers fly out onto the students' desks.

CHOICE READING: ABANDONING BOOKS

Time Frame

One or two weeks after the library is opened

Questions to Consider

- Can students abandon books in your class?
- How will you keep track of abandoned books?
- At what point are students permitted to abandon books?

Options

- Students are allowed to abandon books following the 50-page rule. If they don't like the book after 50 pages, they can get a new book.
- Write "abandoned" on their checkout card and write what page they read to.

Make It Bizarre

- Break Up: Write a break-up letter, politely, with the book that you are no longer "seeing." Make sure to say why.

CHOICE, SHARED, AND GUIDED READING: COMFORTABLE SEATING

Time Frame

The second month of school

Questions to Consider

- At what point during class can students use comfortable seating?
- Do students earn comfortable seating? Is it a random selection? Is it on a rotational schedule?
- What should students avoid?

Options

- Sit comfortably, but if you look sleepy you may not be on a beanbag.
- Avoid plopping down heavily on beanbags to avoid spilling stuffing.
- Create a rotational schedule for who gets comfy seating.
- Write the name of students on Popsicle sticks and those students get to sit in comfy seating.
- Determine who demonstrated the best reading stamina from the day before and give those students a ticket for comfy seating.

Make It Bizarre

- Have students brainstorm fun places that they can read in your classroom. Some of my students like reading under desks.

CHOICE READING: BOOKCASE UPDATES

Time Frame

First week of school

Questions to Consider

* Is it sustainable for you to update every student's book each time they check out a book?
* How often do students need to "post" a Bookcase Update?

Options

* Reserve a place on your white board for Bookcase Update. White boards are great because you can easily erase and post new books. Stick index cards with the names of each student on the board.
* Submit an update in a basket when done with a book. The post can simply be the title, or it can include tons of other information.
* A site administrator helper writes in the new books weekly. When a student is done with a book, the site administrator sticks a sticker on their card.
* Once every couple of weeks, analyze how many stickers each student earned. Students should be getting a new sticker at least once a week.

Make It Bizarre

* Make your Bookcase Update board look like a Facebook page to mirror Facebook updates. Or instead of Bookcase Updates, you can have students do a "Twitter feed." Along with the title of their book, they need to write a quick description, and the total letter count cannot exceed 140 letters.
* Try making this bulletin board online.

CHOICE, SHARED, AND GUIDED READING:
TURN AND TALKS

Time Frame

Immediately

Questions to Consider

- Think/Pair/Share (what we call turn and talks) gives kids a chance to think and discuss with a partner before sharing with the whole group.[64]
- What volume is best for turn and talks?
- What do students look and sound like when turning and talking with a neighbor?
- Can students turn and talk as they wish or only when you ask them to?
- Can students turn and talk while on comfortable seating?
- If students can opt to turn and talk, what signal can they give to you so that you know they are doing the right thing?

Options

- Turn and talk volume should be at a "six inch" voice.[65]
- Face your neighbor.
- Students may not talk about off-task topics.
- When kids want to turn and talk during independent reading, they flip their reading coaster to green. Coasters are two-sided pieces of paper, often color-coded in green and red. Try laminating! For turn and talks, one side can mean silent reading and the other side can mean checking in with a partner.
- Students may use sentence starters when turning and talking.
- Teach students to raise their hand to give a gesture, such as pointing to their partner, which indicates they want a quick check-in.

- Students may talk on comfortable seating as long as they are using coasters.
- Students during independent reading may opt to turn and talk two times, but no more; otherwise, they are taking from their independent reading time.
- Avoid talking that disrupts others.

Make It Bizarre

- Create want ads for partnerships. In the want ad, students list qualities that they have as a reader. They also list qualities that they are seeking. These qualities should be traits that they don't yet have as a reader. Then cut slips on the bottom where students can rip off. Students may pick five different "slips" from partners, and you decide from their top five who will be their partner.
- Teach a song for turn and talks set to Katy Perry's "California Girls":

I know a place, a place where everybody reads now

And in this place the kids can read and can talk now

You can travel the world but nothing comes close to us

When we're ready to sha-re this is how we go (oh o oh o oh)

Turn and talk, it's hot, but it's not loud at all

Six inch voice, polite and on task

When you speak, I track, I keep my head up

(oh o oh o oh)

Turn and talk, it's hot, because we read so much

Sentence starters kick things off right

KIPPsters love to read, and love to turn and talk (oh o oh o oh)

CHOICE, SHARED, AND GUIDED READING:
HOW TO HANDLE A BOOK

Time Frame

Before students checkout books

Questions to Consider

- Should students always use bookmarks?
- How should students carry books as they go home?
- What should students avoid?

Options

- Avoid doggy-earring pages. Use a bookmark or write down where you stopped in a book log.
- Butterfly a book (hold it open rather than bending it back) to keep it in good shape.
- Feel free to read wherever you are the most comfortable.
- Try to turn pages carefully so that they don't get ripped. If the page does get ripped, it's OK. Get some tape so another reader can read it, too.
- While traveling keep books in one gallon zip lock bags so that they don't become damaged or get wet if it rains.

Make It Bizarre

- Use your life questions. Some students take very good care of their clothing, especially sneakers. Share how and why they take good care of them and then link that to book care.

- Here's a song on how to handle a book set to Adelle's "Rolling in the Deep":

There's a fire, burning in my heart, my book's been treated bad and it's tearing me all apart

It's been doggy eared and now it is all bent, there is no hope for it, I'll have to replace it

The scars from the book thugs, they leave me breathless. I can't help thinking my book has had enough.

The scars from the book thugs, they are so careless, I can't help thinking

You could have saved your book, if you had butterflied instead, you ought to keep it in a zip, zip lock bag after reading

You could have saved your book, a bookmark is the way to go, it's got doggy ears, and now, it's too late, it's been cheated.

So be nice to what you're readin'.

CHOICE, SHARED, AND GUIDED READING: STUDENTS LISTENING TO A READ-ALOUD

Time Frame

Before the first read-aloud

Questions to Consider

- What do the kids look like when you are reading aloud to them?
- What should they avoid?

Options

- Students should be tracking the book or the speaker (if it's a picture book). Tracking means looking at the speaker.

- Avoid fiddling with shoes, paper, pens, hair, et cetera.
- At KIPP schools, we teach the acronym SLANT. SLANT stands for

  S: Sit up/Stand up straight

  L: Listen

  A: Ask and answer questions

  N: Nod

  T: Track the speaker

KIPPsters are asked to SLANT during each of their classes during direct instruction. Some KIPP schools add an extra S at the beginning to make it SSLANT. Can you guess what the S stands for? Smile ☺.

Make It Bizarre

KIPP Infinity taught SSLANT to the whole school, all at once, during morning announcements. Teachers create poster boards standing for each letter of SSLANT like cheerleaders at a football game. As one teacher holds up the letter, other teachers model the right and not right thing to do. The not right thing often gets a few giggles. Here are some ways to model the "not right way" to make it kid-friendly:

- S: Model a big, goofy fake grin.
- S: Hang over the desk, completely sprawled out.
- L: Whisper to a neighbor or dreamily looks out the window.
- A: When the class is asked a question, just sit there. Another teacher, the eager beaver, wiggles fingers and jumps out of their seat saying "Ooh! Ooh!"
- N: Nod like a head banger.
- T: Whip your head around whenever someone is talking, making a spectacle out of the neck movement.

SHARED READING: ASSIGNED BOOKS

Time Frame

The first time you introduce a shared text

Questions to Consider

- Are you providing whole class shared texts or do students buy them?
- Are students allowed to write in the text to record their thinking?
- What happens if they lose the text?

Options

(If students buy the text)

- All students need to purchase the same edition, so everyone is on the same page.
- Students are allowed to write in the text to record their thinking, but they must keep it neat.
- Students must write their names on the inside cover in case theirs gets jumbled with someone else's.

  (If you provide the text)

- Assign a number to each book. Write down which student received each book in case a book goes missing.
- Students don't write in the book.
- Students are required to replace the book if damaged or lost. You have extra ones on hand, and tell students in the beginning of class how much it will cost.

Make It Bizarre

Play the following game. Give every student a piece of identical wrapped candy. Before they eat the candy, tell them that you are going to take the candies back, put them in a bag, and jumble them up. The only way they can get the candy is if they find the exact candy they started with. So students start noticing all the details that make their candies different and write them on a scrap piece of paper. Take the candies and jumble them up. Then ask kids to find their candies.

The point is that they won't be able to find the candies. That's why they have to be sure when using shared texts to write their names in or always notice the number. Then let them eat the candies!

Remember the story with the keys? Building muscle routines and keeping them consistent will be as powerful as any home routine such as where you put your keys.

MILD, MEDIUM, SPICY NEXT-STEP SUGGESTIONS

	Mild	Medium	Spicy
Break It Down	Create posters in your room that list routine expectations.	Before school, visualize students going through the routine from start to finish in real time. What does that look like? Visualize all of the details. Then, break it down to your kids that day.	Create a routine 'zine that kids keep in their binders. In the 'zine include pictures modeling what to do and not to do. Take pictures of what not to do, like the library with pizza in it, and blow them up as visuals.
Remind and Reinforce	Before you spiral a routine taught from earlier in the week, ask, "Who can remind me how we do this routine? What should we be careful not to do?"	Incorporate routine-based questions in your do-nows during the first month of school. Include non-examples that students analyze.	Create homework questions that spiral routines connecting to different modalities, like creating a comic book, movie script, or advertisement for the routine.

	Mild	**Medium**	**Spicy**
Miscellaneous— Student Organization	Staple all daily work together. When you collect the homework the following day, collect the whole packet to keep students' binders neat and empty.	Create a rubric for a binder check that includes neatness and completed work. During testing periods, look through students' binders to give them a quick grade.	Number each handout daily starting with #1. Teach students to organize their work sequentially. Direct to a place in the room where you keep all old handouts to make up what's missing.

KEEPIN' IT REAL

There are times well-planned routines don't work as planned. Here are some problems that do come up; now they won't happen to you!

Coming Soon

The following is a list of routines that are detailed in other chapters.

Library

Since our students are reading so many books, it can be difficult to make sure that books aren't getting lost or buried in lockers. The easiest solution is to require students to present their finished book in order to check out a new book. Make sure your library routine is airtight; otherwise, as I've found in my own class, it can turn into the mall with lots of off-task chitchat. The following are additional pitfalls that occur in the library that need to be addressed as non-examples:

- ❏ Lost books
- ❏ Books returned inappropriately
- ❏ Too many kids in the library
- ❏ Talking in the library
- ❏ Taking too long checking out a book

Visit www.reading-without-limits.com for additional ways to solidify your library routine.

Student Organization

Unless I check binders regularly, some of them turn into a garbage dump. I totally get it, as I lived with a garbage dump in my backpack all throughout school. Why? No one checked my binder. The best times to check binders are during do-nows or assessments, as it won't take away from instructional time. At the end of each term, consider a throw away system in which the whole class cleans out their binders.

ADDITIONAL RESOURCES

1. An entire chapter dedicated to the first week
2. A binder quiz rubric

3. A ton more routines are available
4. Interviews with teachers about their routines

FOR COACHES AND SCHOOL LEADERS

Ready to Use Webinar

Go to www.reading-without-limits.com where you can find professional development resources on Muscle Memory Routines that you can use with your staff. Included with these resources is a ready-made professional development on the first week of reading classes and a narrated webinar.

The Essential 55

One resource that I really love is *The Essential 55*. In Ron Clark's book, he lists routines, which are not reading specific. What makes them so awesome is that he teaches each routine with a vivid hook. Sometimes it can be hard to come up with a creative hook for each routine, and so I highly recommend sharing this book with your teachers.[66]

TO SUM UP

- Before teaching the routine, figure out all the details.
- When teaching the routine, break down all the details, including non-examples.
- When teaching routines, hook your students with something fun in order to help retention.
- Stick to your routine so that your students can get repeated exposure to keep it in muscle memory. Remind and reinforce throughout the year.

8

What to Do When Choice, Shared, or Guided Reading Isn't Working

Why *Can't, Low*, and *Doesn't Care* Are Ugly Words

This chapter will show you how to find a solution to common pitfalls that do come up during choice, shared, and guided reading. When your class isn't going as planned

❑ Use growth mindset when thinking about students.
❑ Use whole class and one-on-one management tricks.
❑ Tweak your teaching to address common pitfalls.

Brandon McCarthy is a major league pitcher who was almost pushed out of the league in 2010. In 2012 he is considered one of baseball's best pitchers. Why? He looked at what wasn't working, and he fixed it. In the minors, McCarthy had success on the mound and focused on striking players out. But, when he was transferred to the major leagues, he went downhill, losing game after game. He was benched, traded, suffered from injuries, and became famous for giving up homeruns and walks. He continued trying to strike players out, yet it wasn't working. Inspired by sabermetrics, now made famous by the book and movie *Moneyball*, McCarthy studied excellent pitching and noticed a trend among pitchers who win games: they all don't necessarily strike players out; they get players to hit ground balls that can be easily fielded for outs. One of the most successful pitches, known as the two-seamer, grounds balls out. With tweaks and attention to detail, McCarthy changed his pitch from one that tried to strike players out to the two-seamer that gets players to make ground outs. What happened? He became one of the best pitchers in 2012.[67]

McCarthy didn't resign himself to losing games. Instead, he analyzed ways he could increase performance and made the change. The McCarthy story reminds me of what I love so much about teaching. No matter what, there's always hope. It also reminds me of my greatest pet peeve—when schools lose faith in their students. I currently consult with a youth detention center for boys. Many students have a vocabulary that could make a grandmother squirm in her seat. They use some ugly words. But these words don't bother me. What bothers me are words that teachers use sometimes. These words include: can't, low, and doesn't care. When we say that a student can't read, we are perpetuating a fixed mindset. We are losing faith in our students. We are resigning ourselves to the fact that that student won't move up his developmental continuum. All too often I see schools abandoning choice, guided, or shared reading. I hear, "They can't read independently together." "They don't care about reading aloud to themselves during guided reading." "They are too low to read *Catcher in the Rye*." Unlike McCarthy, these schools *hang up their cleats*.

This chapter shows what to do when elements of choice, guided, and shared reading aren't working in your classroom or school. Strategies will be targeted so you can change your pitch. One of KIPP's mottos is, "If there is a problem, we look for a solution. We will either find a way, or make one."

CHANGE YOUR THINKING TO GROWTH MINDSET

Sometimes our students aren't going to meet our expectations during choice, shared, and guided reading . . . yet. In fact, I'm 100% confident that your class will have some students who aren't there, not yet anyway. But, 100% of your students will get there with your help. First, we must continue thinking hopefully about their progress by trusting growth mindset popularized by Carol Dweck.

(**Ugly Word**: Can't) Instead of: Seb can't read.
> *Think: Right now Seb can identify many common sight words, and tomorrow I want him to try getting information from pictures on the page.*

(**Ugly Word**: Low) Instead of: Sarah's reading level is low.
> *Think: Right now Sarah is on an L reading level. In the next few weeks she will be on level M with my help and her hard work.*

(**Ugly Word**: Doesn't Care) Instead of: Kris doesn't care about reading class.
> *Think: Kris is sitting in class with her head down. I wonder if something happened at home? I will give her some space and speak with her one on one shortly to see if she's OK, then make a goal for her tomorrow to have her head up.*

Do you notice the difference? The italicized examples all demonstrate growth mindset. Start with "just the facts" and suspend judgment. Assume the best, and then brainstorm short next steps. With just a couple tweaks in the language, thinking about a student's behavior is immediately switched to a "yet" mentality. If anything isn't working in your classroom, that's the first step in facilitating a change: think "yet."

CONSIDER WHOLE-CLASS AND INDIVIDUAL MANAGEMENT STRATEGIES TO ADDRESS COMMON PITFALLS

Many schools abandon choice, guided, or shared reading because the students aren't doing them perfectly. It's frustrating when this happens, because students are human beings and aren't going to do things perfectly all the time. And, that's OK. It's our job to identify when things aren't going well and make an action plan to address it. Remember, they will get there even if they aren't there, yet. You can fix common pitfalls by either addressing them to the whole class or by chatting with individual students. Following is a list of common strategies you can use to help fix common pitfalls in your choice, guided, or independent reading programs that work regardless of the drawback. Within each category, I offer one solution-based example.

I reteach reading stamina by modeling my love for reading. I talk to the kids about how I "get lost" in my book and how amazing that feels. I do this especially if I perceive their stamina to be off track. They quickly latch onto that idea. After independent and DEAR time reading are over, I say "welcome back" to support the idea that they have "been lost" in their books.

—Annica, 5th grade special education teacher

Remind and Reinforce Routine Expectations

- Who can remind me what we do when we are done with a book?
- I noticed that Monika brought her shared reading book to class today.

Remind and Reinforce Individually

- Jacinta, for tomorrow, can you remind me what you should bring to class?

Explicitly Model What You Do Want to See and What You Don't Want to See

During guided reading, students aren't reading out loud. Bring in another teacher to help you out. Model starting to read aloud together at the same pace, then drifting off to read in your head. Share with students that you don't want to see them doing that. Then, together, model reading at the same time word for word. Share with students that you don't want to see them doing that, either. Then model what you do want to see: each reading aloud at his or her own pace. Remember John Wooden? He explicitly taught his players how to put on socks because he knew that doing it well would increase performance. Don't worry about being pedantic when sharing, reinforcing, or reteaching your expectations.

Hook Them into the Lesson by Making It Bizarre

During shared reading, some students are not reading assigned pages. Get students really excited about a movie that you want to show. For a few days share how it was your favorite movie and you can't wait for them to see it. Then at the start of class, only show a few minutes halfway through the movie. Ask, "Didn't you just love the movie?" Then explain that when you don't do the assigned reading, it's just like starting a movie halfway through. You don't know what's going on. Say that it's going to be your priority to focus on strategies so 100% of the class is meeting their assigned pages goals.

Positive Reinforcement

Make a phone call home when a student who was struggling to meet your expectations shows growth. Share specifically the behavior that he is now demonstrating, not the negative behavior. "Jordan is now able to read without looking up for five minutes. I'm pleased with his progress, and next week I want him to do it for seven minutes."

Negotiation

Instead of punishing students when they don't meet their goals, negotiate by giving them a strategy that helps fix it. "Miranda, I noticed that you aren't reading at home. Would it be OK if we met for 15 minutes today during lunch so you could have some quiet time to read?" Or, "Harry, I noticed that you aren't using your i-Think journal. Would it be OK if you did one entry today, and an I Love Reading Page instead of three entries? Is that a fair compromise?"

Figure 8.1 Give Students Many Opportunities to Read Aloud

ADDRESS PITFALL TRENDS

There are going to be times when choice, guided, or shared reading doesn't go as planned. That's why we included Keepin' It Real at the end of each chapter. Common pitfalls occur because we are asking our kids to do something extremely rigorous and pushing them to their highest limits. When kids are demonstrating trends that don't meet your expectations, don't give up. Instead, use it as an opportunity to teach. When McCarthy was benched, traded, and suffering from injuries, he didn't give up. He let sabermetrics teach him. We are the teachers who will get our kids back on a winning streak. It takes time, patience, and some creativity.

Here are some common pitfalls that occur during choice, guided, and shared reading and strategies that you can use to address and ultimately change those pitfalls. But change might not happen overnight. Don't abandon hope!

Books not Brought to Class
- ❑ Remind and reinforce with the whole class.
- ❑ Call home the night before as a reminder.
- ❑ Set up a buddy system so their peer calls to remind.
- ❑ Utilize positive reinforcement when they bring the book to class.

Choice Books Frequently Abandoned

❏ Negotiate: Would it be OK for the next book that you read at least 30 pages before you decide to give it up?

❏ Narrow choice: I want you to read one of these three books. Which one do you think you can read from beginning to end?

❏ Mix up the genres: Try a manga or nonfiction book.

❏ Try books on tape or www.audibles.com with an MP3 player.

❏ Ask students to read the book aloud to themselves using a Toobaloo.

❏ Set up a reading partnership so the students are reading the same book as their peer. They set up their reading goals together.

Not Interested in the Plot During Choice, Shared, or Guided Reading

❏ Demonstrate cognitive empathy by sharing how difficult the book was for you at first.

❏ Incorporate I Love Reading pages once a week.

❏ Do read-aloud/think-aloud lessons on whether or not the book is meeting your expectations.

❏ Do read-aloud/think-aloud lessons on strategies to get "into a book" during the beginning chapters.

❏ Give students the strategies to fix misunderstanding so they can paraphrase.

❏ Try action strategies. Action strategies are a means to get students interacting with a book through drama. Check out www.reading-without-limits.com for a list of action strategies.

Unfocused Stamina

❏ Make sure that the book they are reading is matched to their reading level.

❏ Try books on tapes or www.audibles.com and MP3s.

❏ Make a stamina calendar with the student.

❏ Check in on their home reading patterns. Would it be better to do homework reading at school if they get distracted at home?

❑ Set up a partner book with the student.

❑ Negotiate: "Would it be OK if you read for seven minutes today, and for the rest of independent reading looked at this magazine?" (Then increase stamina goal over time.)

❑ Make a positive phone call home when students meet a stamina goal (not a whole-class stamina goal, but their personal stamina goal).

❑ Try putting a piece of Velcro under their desk. They can rub the Velcro if they get distracted.

Distracted During Read-Aloud

❑ Give students a copy of the text.

❑ Actively engage the students during the read-aloud by dip sticking.

❑ Actively engage the students during the read-aloud by cold calling.

❑ When doing a think-aloud, keep students engaged by having them annotate your thinking on their copy of the text.

❑ Do the read-aloud in an animated voice.

❑ Avoid reading aloud for more than five minutes.

❑ Move around the room and employ proximity as you read aloud.

❑ Make sure students are turning the pages when appropriate. Say, "I noticed that Roland flipped at the right time."

❑ Instead of using texts daily, try incorporating famous paintings. Show a famous painting to your class. Do a think-aloud (about a painting). Many of the strategies that good readers use can be applied to paintings: questioning, determining theme, identifying story elements, and inferring. Just make sure whenever you use a painting that you go back to details in the painting in the same way that students should use textual references. Interested? Check out www.reading-without-limits.com for a lesson that uses a painting instead of text.

Refuse to Write Their Thinking Down

❑ Negotiate: Would it be OK if you did one i-Think notation today? Avoid giving students a quota of journal entries, as good readers don't authentically "think" six times a page.

❑ Instead of writing out their thinking, they can draw their thinking.

❑ Instead of writing out their thinking, they can talk through their thinking. Ask them to put their fist in the air when they are ready to demonstrate the strategy and you will chat with them.

❑ Give more opportunities for students to turn and talk during reading.

❑ Share a checklist of strategies students can use. Ask them to self-assess. They put a check mark next to strategies they aren't doing yet. Then they focus on that strategy for the next couple of days.

Rush Through Reading

❑ Share with the whole class that you value thorough understanding over number of books read.

❑ Avoid praising students who race toward reading a million words or 50 books. Instead, praise students who demonstrate great paraphrasing.

❑ Give students individual tasks that they do at the end of each chapter. For instance, they can fill in a paraphrasing graphic organizer or rank their favorite events that occurred in the chapter.

Once They Meet Their Goal They Say "I'm Done" and Don't Want to Continue Reading

❑ If some students' goal is to read seven minutes, while the rest of the class is reading 25, avoid letting them "sit there" when they are done. Instead give them a checklist that provides a list of ways they can "assign themselves." Make sure that everything on the "assign yourself" list involves rigor and strategic thinking. I provided a checklist on www.reading-without-limits.com.

❑ When students have completed their goal, they can apply strategies to a break book.

❑ Students can do more "reading is thinking" tasks, such as an I Love Reading page or a blog entry.

❑ Call home to praise your students when they independently assign themselves without reminders.

Avoid giving up a routine if it isn't working. Instead, reteach. If kids aren't using their i-Think journals properly, reteach the routine. If Malik isn't caught up with his stamina and is distracting other students, create an individualized grow plan. If your class gets distracted after a couple minutes of reading, then push for them to read three minutes tomorrow. And four minutes the next day. It's better to do three perfect push-ups than 30 sloppy ones. If students aren't engaged with your shared reading text, throw in more engagement strategies. But don't give up on choice, guided, and shared reading. Remember the research: by incorporating these three elements into your day, students will make remarkable achievement. Why? Because reading is cognitively demanding and really rigorous. By not giving up on choice, shared, and guided reading you will also meet the greatest goal of all: building lifelong learners and readers.

In 2002, Teach for America taught me to do whatever it takes for my students. But doing whatever it takes doesn't mean breaking my back or staying up all night lesson planning. Doing whatever it takes means analyzing what's working and what's not working yet, and making a plan for the future. Analyze pitfall trends, and address those trends by reteaching, reminding, reinforcing in and sprinkling in other strategies mentioned in this chapter. Will you see a change on Monday? Yes. Will the pitfall be "fixed" on Monday? Probably not. To keep choice, shared, and guided reading thriving in your classroom and school, you must continually address common pitfalls in the same way that Brandon McCarthy is still analyzing his game.

MILD, MEDIUM, SPICY NEXT-STEP SUGGESTIONS

	Mild	**Medium**	**Spicy**
Growth Mindset	If a student is resistant or refusing to do work, assume the best. Give them a little space and then ask, "Is everything OK?" "What can I do to help?"	Put up catch phrases in the back of your classroom that you can see to remind you to demonstrate a growth mindset with your students. For instance: Celebrate growth Focus on grow goals Yet	Start a staff "curse" jar in your teacher's lounge. Any time someone accidentally says an ugly word like *can't, low,* or *doesn't care* (I catch myself saying them from time to time), drop a quarter in the jar. Use the money for a charity of your students' choice.
Use Management Strategies	Try to use a remind and reinforce one-liner daily in class.	If you see a trend that you aren't happy with, pause your "curriculum" and teach a lesson focused on the routine that you do want to see. Model by explicitly showing what you do want to see versus what you don't want to see. It's not about "getting through the lessons." Remember, you are trying to build lifelong readers, and pausing your content-related work to focus on a routine will make huge payoffs in the long run.	Commit to one positive phone call a day to families.

	Mild	Medium	Spicy
Tweak Teaching to Address Pitfalls	Pause your "curriculum" to address common pitfalls. Reteach a stamina lesson. Reinforce a routine. Do engagement strategies to hook students in the shared reading book. But don't give up!	Allow students to choose whether or not they want to do an i-Think journal or another way to show strategic thinking. Create a poster in your classroom that shares the options.	Create a "What to Do If You Are Finished" center in your classroom. Fill it with strategy-appropriate graphic organizers. Go to www.reading-without-limits.com for reproducibles that you can include.

KEEPIN' IT REAL

This chapter was all about keepin' it real. Everything discussed in this chapter has happened to teachers at the KIPP schools I've worked with, teachers who work in schools across the country devoted to building lifelong readers, and the high school students in the juvenile justice center. What's important to note is that each of the pitfalls is fixable. Don't hang up your cleats!

ADDITIONAL RESOURCES

1. Sample calling home scripts you can use when making positive phone calls
2. Videos of teachers reflecting on routines that have worked and haven't worked
3. A self-reflection checklist that you can use to evaluate how often you are using different strategies that fix potential pitfalls

FOR COACHES AND SCHOOL LEADERS

Ready to Use Webinar

Go to www.reading-without-limits.com where you can find professional development resources on common pitfalls and ways to address them.

One-on-Ones

Meet with each of your staff members one-on-one or twice a month. On the agenda, ask them to do a case analysis of a student who is demonstrating a pitfall. Together create an action plan, and then follow up during the next one-on-one. For example, a teacher comes to you with the following scenario:

> Jose continually comes to class saying he read, but I have reason to believe that he didn't. He has abandoned a book several times this month, and in class frequently gets distracted to the point where he is distracting others. When he self-assesses on his stamina progress, Jose gives himself high marks.

First, notice how the above scenario is "just the facts." When meeting with a teacher, try to keep it as objective as possible. The first step is asking the teacher what he has tried. He says,

> I tried standing near Jose while he's reading, which helps, but when I move away he gets distracted. I met with Jose last week and told him that he can't abandon the next book, so he's still reading the same book he read last week. I can't stand next to Jose the entire period, because there are other needs in the class.

The next step is to assume the best about Jose. Remember, it's not that Jose "doesn't care" about reading. Are the books on his reading level? How much stamina can he muster on his own? Brainstorm a list of immediate next steps, and try a few with Jose next week. The following strategies would work with a reader like Jose:

❑ Using a book on tape or audibles on MP3s
❑ Setting a mini-goal with Jose that's two minutes past what his current stamina is
❑ Starting a series
❑ Utilizing partner books
❑ Reassessing to determine his reading level (the books might be too difficult)
❑ Giving him time to read by himself in school
❑ Showing him how to self-assess, and how you prioritize humility over top marks

Just as reading conferences give us *aha* moments, so do looking at common pitfalls with students. Try looking at one student each time you meet with a teacher, and remember to follow up.

TO SUM UP

- Use growth mindset when thinking about students, and avoid ugly words like "can't," "low," and "doesn't care."
- Try management strategies like reminding, reinforcing, positive praise, negotiation, explicitly modeling, and making it bizarre so students remember the routine. Address pitfalls with the whole class and with individuals.
- Avoid giving up on choice, guided, or shared reading if you are experiencing negative trends. Instead, make an action plan. Be prepared to modify the action plan if it isn't working. Continue to reteach your expectations all year.

PART 4

Steps to Enhance Lifelong Readers

The following chapters show ways to enhance the skills of your lifelong readers. Through small tweaks to an already thriving guided, shared, and choice reading time, your readers will be on their way to and through college and careers of their choice.

9

Reading Conferences,
Our *Aha* Moments

Reading conferences allow you to address individual needs. Conferences can occur during choice, shared, and guided reading. Do the following in order to keep conferences streamlined:

- ☐ Start with halftime and racetrack conferences.
- ☐ Create a grow goal for each student for O3s (one-on-one individual conferences).
- ☐ Take notes to track student growth.
- ☐ Hold students accountable to their goals.

Legend has it that Archimedes, a Greek mathematician and physicist, was enjoying an unhurried soak in his bathtub. During his bath, the force on his feet became less. Suddenly he jumped up, scurried out his front door, and in his birthday suit ran through the streets screaming, "Eureka, I got it!" As he frightened his neighbors, Archimedes gleefully celebrated his *aha* moment: how to calculate density and volume, leading to . . .

$$d = \frac{m}{v}$$

225

Fast-forward 2,000 years, and another scientist has an *aha* moment, though his came differently. Whereas Archimedes was in deep contemplation, Nobel Prize winner Dr. Edmond Fischer experienced a serendipitous *aha*. Fischer is my great-uncle and recounted this story to me about 15 years ago. Fischer was working on an experiment that he was cultivating in Petri dishes around his lab. Distracted by something driving his insatiable curiosity, he forgot about the dishes and accidentally left them overnight. The next morning, while collecting the dishes, something caught his eye and immediately he got out his microscope. It turned out that the cells had a fun slumber party, which led to his *aha* moment: the discovery of reversible protein phosphorylation. Archimedes' eureka occurred in contemplation. Fischer's arose from serendipity.

John Kounios, professor of psychology at Drexel University in Philadelphia, describes an *aha* moment in a 2010 *Wall Street Journal* article as "any sudden comprehension that allows you to see something in a different light. It could be a solution to a problem; it could be getting a joke; or suddenly recognizing a face. It could be realizing a friend of yours is not really a friend." As teachers, although we may not be discovering scientific breakthroughs, our *aha* moments are equally profound. As Fischer recounted in describing his process, "one knows where one takes off, but one never knows where one ends up." Unlike Archimedes or other scientists who wait decades for their *aha* moments, as teachers we get ours all the time, but in order to do so we must follow Fischer's advice: see where you end up.[68]

Mike, an eighth grade English teacher and recipient of a national teaching award, recounted the story of one of one of his favorite *aha* moments to me.

> In the midst of a lesson on character analysis, I approached Jerome during independent reading. I asked him about the character in his book. Jerome was using reasonable adjectives to describe the character. But when I pressed him further, he wasn't able to articulate his reasoning about the character with evidence. So I asked him to retell what he had

just read. And he couldn't. Jerome wasn't able to recall what he read. So, we reviewed recall strategies. From there, Jerome initiated the next few conferences, eager to share what he read. My *aha* moment was realizing that Jerome needed to return to a previously taught strategy. His goal was personal, achievable, and highly motivating. His goal gave him the power to understand his book.

Teachers need *aha* moments. They offer the data that drive our teaching forward. This chapter shows that student errors are goldmines. As Mike recounted, he discovered that comprehension had completely bro-

Students are on their own developmental continuum, and conferences allow you to lead them through their continuum.

ken down. Without that conference, Mike had no idea that Jerome didn't understand what he was reading. In this chapter, I describe how to launch reading conferences in your classroom, conferences that will lead to many *aha* moments. I describe three types of conferences, which range from whole-class to individual conferences. Conferences can happen during choice, shared, or guided reading; they can mean anything from chatting with a student during independent work on the fly to a scheduled conference. Therefore, this chapter is right for you regardless of your classroom structure.

As I described in Chapter 4, during close reading, you are like a coach giving constant real-time feedback on your players' performances. But each of your players has his or her own unique needs. Feedback for Venus Williams might not be the same feedback that Roger Federer needs. Once you experience the "*aha*" that helps you see how to lift your player's performance, conferences allow you to individualize your real-time feedback. Students are on their own developmental continuum, and conferences allow you to lead them through their continuum. It's like a toddler trying to stand. Any parent knows that learning to walk doesn't happen at a set stage. Once you've determined: "*Aha!* My baby is learning how to stand," you may coach them through walking by getting them a push toy. This chapter shows you how to determine the individual needs of each of your students (*aha!*), and then how to individually coach them through their needs.

First off, we have to bury the following putdowns about conferences: *I'm not doing enough. I haven't met with her in too long. My notes are totally disorganized.* There is no fixed definition of a reading conference. I've gone ages, too, without doing conferences. It's OK. There are no recommendations for how long each conference should take or for how many you should do in a period. Do I have my preferences? Of course. However, I know that my preferences are peculiar to my classroom, my management, and the constraints of the 60-minute class period. There are so many different ways to do conferences with your students, and these simple ways to check for understanding are key to our *aha* moments. Reading conferences enhance your reading program to help your readers become lifelong readers. Take the advice of my uncle and what worked for Archimedes and Mike . . . "one knows where one takes off, but one never knows where one ends up."

START WITH HALFTIME AND RACETRACK CONFERENCES

There are two different types of conferences I recommend as a starting point: halftime and racetrack. These conferences are the easiest to manage, require the least number of notes, and do not need to be planned in advance. They can be done during shared, guided, or choice reading daily or as often as you wish.

Halftime

The purpose of halftime conferences is to look for trends to address to the entire class. During independent practice, while students are independently reading or applying a strategy that you taught, walk around and write down positive qualities and areas that need improvement that you notice from your class as a whole. You are looking for trends that many or most of the students demonstrate. Then describe the trends to the whole group halfway through the class period. Avoid interrupting students while collecting data; look over their shoulders. Give students a target to work on for the last half of the period.

Example One

In a fifth grade class, after introducing how to ask questions, I noticed

- Students were stopping to ask questions
- Students were writing questions only when they started reading, and once they got in the flow, they stopped writing questions

After making the rounds for half of independent time, I read aloud the conference notes to the kids.

I said, "*I love how many questions you are asking, particularly about what your characters are doing! I am looking to see that you spread your questions out more for the rest of independent reading. Avoid clumping your questions on one page.*"

I praised and then gave one piece of specific feedback that benefitted all students. If students are already spreading their questions out, they will continue that good habit. Trends can vary from class to class, which I always found interesting!

Example Two

During a high school shared reading block in a youth detention center, I noticed that students were rapidly reading the assigned pages, but they were not carefully reading.

- Students are meeting their stamina goals
- Students are reading too quickly, and therefore not leaving with a deep level of understanding

I said, "*I love how committed you guys are to your stamina goals. You are definitely going to be able to read tonight's assigned pages. One thing I noticed is that many of you are reading too quickly. For the next half of class, I want to see you guys slowing down, spending more time on each page. Let's see if you notice a difference in how much you can remember and how much you enjoy the experience when you take a bit more time."*

Pacing

Halftime conferences take two minutes when you address the whole class.

When to Do Halftime

To celebrate success and clarify one thing that could be improved.

Notes

Notes are *simple* for halftime conferences. Jot down positives and areas of improvement that you notice on a piece of scrap paper. Then from your list decide which to share.

Halftime conferences work in any class, from math to dance class!

Racetrack

The purpose of racetrack conferences is to check in individually with as many students as possible during independent work to see if they understood the lessons. Racetrack conferences are speedy. The check-ins are exclusively about the daily lesson's aim. (In Figure 9.1, notice how Amber crouches down to eye level when doing racetrack conferences.) In the racetrack conference, move around the room in a loop aiming to check in with as many kids as you can by the end of the period, much like a car in a race. Focus racetrack conferences on

Figure 9.1 Racetrack Conferences Give You Real-Time Data

the day's aim. Determine whether or not each student mastered the aim using their i-Think notes (sticky notes, double-entry journal, or whatever tool you are using) as a way to assess. With each student, ask one of the following questions:

- Which is your best i-Think note (or sticky note, etcetera)? Why? Which is your weakest? Why?
- What's confusing about today's lesson?
- Can you tell me about a time today when you used the strategy? Can you tell me about a time today where you didn't use the strategy?

Praise, and then if the student is partially right, redirect the student to what you taught during the lesson.

For example, I say, *"Tim, I noticed that you are asking questions as you read. That's such a good reading habit! One thing I brought up during the lesson is to question the main character. Right now I notice that you haven't done that yet. In the next 10 minutes I want you to ask a question about the character and what she's doing. Can you think of anything right now?"*

If students are rocking out their i-Think notes and have fulfilled everything you taught, say, "Rank your i-Think notes in order of effectiveness and when I come back, be prepared to say why."

With racetracks, you can fix misunderstandings on the spot. It's another way for you to see if students are using the strategy or not. It will also offer *aha* moments. If you didn't look

For Struggling Readers: Provide Frequent, Specific Feedback.

Halftime and racetrack conferences provide feedback in real time. Avoid generic feedback like "good job." Ensure that it's specific by leveraging one strength ("I noticed you did X criteria") and pushing one area to improve ("For the next 15 minutes work on Y criteria").

at Tim's notes during independent time, you wouldn't know that he wasn't doing exactly what you taught.

One pitfall of racetrack conferences is when other students have their hands raised. You have less time to meet with each student because you want to address the raised hands. To anticipate this pitfall, before independent work starts, address any questions that relate to the task at hand. Then tell your students that you are doing racetrack conferences that day. Ask them if it's OK if you don't answer raised hands that period so you can get through as many questions as possible.

Pacing
About two minutes per kid.

	ask questions	clarifying questions
Deion	✓	✓
Shakira	✓	○
Alondra	○	✓
Kimberly	✓	✓
Samuel	✓	○

Figure 9.2 Racetrack Conference Checklist

When to Do Racetrack
When class is using i-Think notes, sticky notes, double entry notes, or worksheets.

Notes
Try using an Excel spreadsheet or graph paper. Check students who mastered the objective, and make a mark for students who didn't, as shown in Figure 9.2.

CREATE A GROW GOAL FOR EACH STUDENT

O3s (O3 refers to one-on-one) are individual conferences. Remember Mike's *aha* moment with Jerome? They were doing an O3. O3s involve the most teacher prep on your part. They are preplanned. To do them well I suggest the following:

- Identify a grow goal for each student
- Stick with goal until the student masters it

- Give specific next steps
- Take notes
- Hold student accountable to the goal

The following sections describe how to do each of these steps.

Establish Grow Goals

Grow goals are based on stamina, love of reading, reading strategy, and state standard needs. Determine an individualized grow goal based on data you collect during halftime, racetrack conferences, and other assessments. But where do you start? Which goals should you prioritize? What if students have many needs? Table 9.1 is a chart that I use to help in my O3s that shows what I prioritize. The second column describes common errors that students may demonstrate.

These grow goals are the most common ones I see with all the kids. You may have students who don't struggle with any of the areas mentioned.

Once students have shown that they are doing well with stamina, engagement, and paraphrasing, go to your weekly assessment data. Identify a skill in which they didn't yet master and reteach that skill. Have them apply the skill to their current book as

Figure 9.3 Strategically Station Yourself at the Front of the Classroom When Doing O3s

their grow goal. But prioritize stamina, engagement, and paraphrasing first.

Table 9.1 Suggested Grow Goals in Order of Priority

What to Prioritize	Common Errors	Questions to Ask	Quick Suggestions
Stamina	Student slowly reads books	When did you check out your book? What's slowing you down?	Create a quick goal calendar for your book so you are done with it by ____. Consider after school activities when making the calendar.
	Student is distracted during independent reading	What's distracting you? How long do you think you can read without looking up? How many pages do you think you can read in that time?	Give the student a timer and set it to the time they identified. After the timer goes off, allow one minute to look around the room, stretch, or tap fingers on Velcro under the desk.
	Student struggles with magic ratio and either reads too much and writes too little or vice versa	Why do you (write more than read/read more than write)?	For students who overwrite or underwrite, put three sticky notes on their desk and say they can only use those three sticky notes to demonstrate their thinking. As you go around the room, touch their shoulder three different times to signal that it's time for them to write an i-Think note.
	Student struggles with at-home reading	What's slowing you down at home? When do you have more time to read? In what space are you most able to focus? How can you make up the pages?	Create a stamina calendar. If students have a home environment that's not conducive to reading, set up a time at school when they can get reading done. Consider giving students a book on tape to take home.

Engagement	Student is not choosing just-right books	What books do you not like to read? Why? Choose one topic of interest.	Give the student a small basket and help create a playlist about that topic. Suggest movies to put in the basket, and if you can, order one from Netflix. Create a reading calendar.
	Student abandons too many books	Rank the last few books that you've read. What makes you abandon a book?	Give the student a book on tape cassette, or have the student read with a partner out loud. Present a task that takes an entire book, such as tracking a character's emotions over time and comparing those emotions to something that the student knows well (a movie, television show, or own life). Choose books that you always reject and focus on them for the month. Choose books recommended by peers.
Paraphrasing (for more strategies, go to Chapter 2)	Student reads through confusions rather than fixing it	Ask clarifying questions: Who is talking? How is time moving in this story? How do you keep track of multiple plots?	Each time you are confused, write down a question. Track dialogue by writing the name of the character who is speaking on a sticky note if it doesn't say "said ___,"

(continued)

Table 9.1 (*continued*)

What to Prioritize	Common Errors	Questions to Ask	Quick Suggestions
			Draw your own Delorian time machine and identify the time and place you are traveling each time there is a shift. Get color-coded Post-it flags to track multiple plots.
	Student struggles with paraphrasing	Can you tell me about what you read last night? What just happened? What's the 30-second gist? Recall earlier chapters from the book.	Choose one paraphrase strategy: 1. Remember to use character names. 2. Always start from the beginning. 3. Go back, skim, and flip as you retell. 4. Use the back of the book to help determine the big idea or theme. 5. Describe who, what, and where. 6. Write the gist on a sticky note at the end of each chapter in order to show that you can remember the book from beginning to end.
	Student doesn't connect to what he or she knows	What do you know about this topic? What's confusing?	Create a playlist around that topic so you can become an expert in this topic. Print out a couple nonfiction articles for your student to read.

STICK TO ONE GROW GOAL UNTIL MASTERED

Choose a grow goal for your student using Table 9.1 as a guide. Then ask your student to come over to the conference station. Go through the following steps as shown in Figure 9.4:

- Quick check-in and leverage one of the student's strengths, focusing on small wins
- Refer to the student's last goal
- Ask the student to share how he or she has been working on that skill
- Reteach the goal if necessary and offer one way to work on the goal
- Have the student try what you taught before returning to his or her seat
- Hold the student accountable

Next I describe each of these steps in detail.

Leverage Strengths

It's essential that you leverage the positive when starting a conference. By leveraging strengths, it makes overcoming a goal seem less challenging. If a student is working on stamina say, "I noticed that you didn't look up for ten minutes yesterday. Your stamina for the first ten minutes was focused. Today I want you to push that focus to fifteen minutes by reading a break book for the last five minutes."

Small Wins

Break up the goal into mini, bite-sized chunks so that kids can have "small wins." According to psychologist Karl Weick, author of "Small Wins:

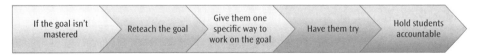

Figure 9.4 What to Do If the Student Didn't Master the Goal

237

Redefining the Scale of Social Problems," focusing on small wins has many benefits, one of which is reducing the importance of any single goal and so reducing the fear of failure. It also "reduces demands ('that's all that needs to be done'), and raises perceived skill levels ('I can do at least that')."[69] Instead of making the goal to have excellent stamina, teach the small win goal to grab a magazine when longer texts become distracting.

Reteach the Skill If Necessary

After praising, go back to check for understanding, and reteach the goal if necessary.

Check In

"How's your day going? Tell me about what you are reading."

Check for Understanding

"Last time we met your goal was to stop when you didn't understand and ask a question to clarify meaning. How's that going?"

(After student shares) "Let's go back to chapter ___. What happened in this chapter? What was confusing? What did you do to fix it? Please share with me the questions you asked."

Giving students sentence starters is a great way to reteach, and scaffold, a previous goal.

Reteach

If the student demonstrates that they didn't ask questions: "I noticed that you aren't yet going back to ask questions each time you are confused. Here are four stickies with questions where I already filled in sentence starters. When you read a chapter, I want you to ask a question about a character, the setting, a problem, and dialogue. After asking these questions, you will be able to paraphrase better. Use these sentence starters."

1. Why did the character ___?
2. Where is the story taking place?

3. What's going to happen with the problem about ___?

4. Why did the character say ___? What does it mean?

Try the Skill Together

"What was something that confused you in the last chapter? Let's go back and find a part to reread. Using the sticky notes, what's a question that you have?"

Hold Student Accountable

"I'm going to check in with you in a couple days, and I want to see how the next couple chapters go in your book. I will look to see that you use these sticky notes, and we'll look at the questions you ask in your i-Think journal together."

What to Do If the Student Masters the Grow Goal

In the above example, I showed what to do if a student hasn't yet mastered their goal when you conference with them. But what if the student did? Follow these next steps, as shown in Figure 9.5.

Praise

"Work it! You are asking questions each time you get confused, which is what great readers do. I do it each time I get confused, too. Keep doing it because it will make reading a ton more fun."

New Goal

"Now I want you to try something new. I want you to consider the 30-second gist of your book each time you finish a chapter." Show the student how to summarize in 30 seconds. Notice how I chose another paraphrasing skill.

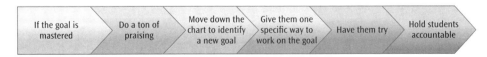

Figure 9.5 What to Do If the Student Did Master the Goal

Accountable

"Over the next couple days, work on the 30-second gist at the end of each chapter. Write it in your i-Think journal. Let's check in next time we meet."

Give Specific Next Steps

First, a quick activity. Get out a watch or another timing device. In the space below, answer the question. Then write down how long it took you to answer the question. The goal is to do it fast!

Make a List of Five Silly Things

1.
2.
3.
4.
5.

Total Time: _____

Did the silly things pop up immediately in your head? Did you figure some out at first and struggle getting the last ideas down? Do the same activity one more time.

Make a List of Five Silly Things Clowns Do

1.
2.
3.
4.
5.

Total Time: _____

Most likely you were able to generate the second list faster. The reason is that the prompt asked you for something more specific. While there are more silly things in the world, narrowing the list down to Five Silly Things Clowns Do gives our brains an entry point and therefore higher performance according to the Heath brothers in *Made to Stick*, a book that researches the criteria that helps ideas become memorable.[70]

Therefore, when giving students a task for their goal, make sure that it's as specific as possible. Instead of saying, *"For the next two weeks I want you to work on your stamina."* Instead say, *"Create a goal calendar where you are done with your book on Thursday. Read five pages on the night you have baseball and thirty pages the following night when you have more time."*

TAKE NOTES

During O3s, I tend to take less copious notes. I write down the date I met with the student, the goal, and what I asked him or her to do. I do this in shorthand. The reason I take fewer notes is because the more notes I take, the fewer kids I can reach in that period.

There are many ways to organize your notes. Here are the easiest:

Flip Cards

Thirty cards can be kept in one folder. Stack cards then tape the bottoms so they can flip down. This system is easy to move around if you teach in multiple classrooms.

Include the date, the student's grow goal, and check off the grow goal once it has been met, as shown in Figure 9.6. It might take the student a couple conferences before they meet the goal.

Excel

Another way to take notes is using an Excel spreadsheet, as shown in Table 9.2. The shaded boxes mean the student got a new goal. Notice how Beatrice gets more attention than Ahmed. That's because she is struggling with stamina. Students don't get an equal number of O3s.

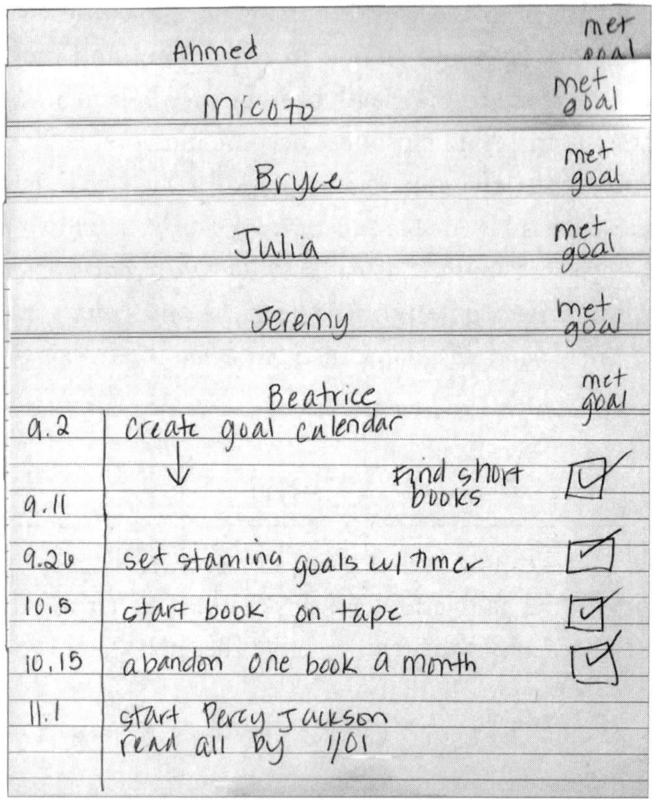

Figure 9.6 O3 Conference Flip Cards

Pacing

Keep O3 conferences fast; try to do a few a period. I like to limit them between five and ten minutes. If I'm also trying to do a racetrack conference, I may do only one. You don't have to do them daily. Do what works within your schedule. You can do them during choice, shared, or guided reading. Remember, Vygotsky said that the best teaching is teaching that leads development. If you conference, you are pushing students to even higher level of rigor by pushing grow goals. The stamina, engagement, and paraphrasing conferences usually take under five minutes. The skill O3s, where I need to reteach a skill that wasn't mastered, take a little longer.

Table 9.2 Sample Excel Notes for Conferences

	Ahmed	**Beatrice**
Sept	(9.9) Asking questions	(9.2) Create goal calendar
	(9.23) Asking questions gave sentence starters	(9.11) Find books that aren't too long and put on goal calendar
Oct	(10.4) Track dialogue	(9.26) Set stamina goals in class using timer
	(10.18) Identify each time shift	(10.5) Start book on tape—STAMINA MUCH BETTER!!
Nov	(11.11) Identify each time shift—look for past tense verbs	(11.1) Start series books—Percy Jackson. Read all in two months

When to Do O3s

Do O3s once your independent reading time is sustained so you don't have to manage stamina. Conferences can happen during choice, independent reading, and the assigned reading part of shared reading.

HOLD STUDENTS ACCOUNTABLE TO THEIR GOALS

Because students have at least five classes a day, a home life, a social life, lots of different books that they want to read, and so on, they have a lot on their mind. Therefore, make sure that they remember their grow goals. Otherwise, you won't see progress as quickly as you might want.

Make Sure Students Remember Their Grow Goals

Encourage students to keep their own conference notes in the back of their i-Think journals.

- Give them a new grow goal bookmark that states their goal and specific next steps every time they get a new goal.

- Before you launch independent reading, ask students to turn and talk and tell their partners about their grow goals. Repeat, remind, and reinforce and they will remember.

For Struggling Readers: Create Tasks That Are Challenging, But Doable

When giving students goals, ensure that the tasks are at their "yet" level— the level a little bit outside of their reach. Aim for a student to be able to master the goal in a couple of weeks.

In conclusion, by mixing halftime, racetrack, and O3 conferences, you are giving frequent, immediate, and nonjudgmental feedback that will push individual students to meet their grow goals. You can integrate all three types of conferences in every grade level. They also work if your school mandates a reading curriculum because it's a teacher tool that works regardless of the curriculum you are using. Mix up all three during choice, guided, and shared reading. Do the conferences while students are independently working and you will discover a multitude of *aha* moments. What works for Venus might not work for Federer. What works for Sofia might not work for Alex. Conferences will enhance choice, guided, and shared reading because you can work with students on their individual needs that they demonstrate during choice, guided, and shared reading.

ADDITIONAL RESOURCES

Check out www.reading-without-limits.com for these conference-related materials! There you will find

1. Paraphrase graphic organizers
2. More ways to organize your conference notes
3. Conference strategies for students who need help with decoding and fluency

MILD, MEDIUM, SPICY NEXT-STEP SUGGESTIONS

	Mild	Medium	Spicy
Halftime and Racetrack	If students don't yet have sustained stamina, stick to halftime and racetrack conferences. During halftime ask, "What's one thing we did well as a group with our stamina? What's one thing we can work on for the next 15 minutes?" Chart student responses.	If you don't get to all students during a racetrack conference, then do an exit slip as the final check for understanding in class. Then check the exit slips for kids you weren't able to get to during racetrack.	Encourage a student helper to lead the halftime conferences in your class. Give them the notes you have, and ask her to facilitate the class's conversation.
O3 Conferences	Avoid scheduling conferences at your desk because it can take away from intimacy. To make it more personal, create a comfortable seating area where you and the kids can crouch down on beanbags. Want to make it really kid-friendly? Set up two laptops on either side of the room and Skype the conferences.	Post a schedule for the next two weeks that lists reading "dates." To make your conferences more collegiate, call them "office hours." Teach students a lesson on how conferences will work. Show them what you will do and what they need to do. Spend a class period going through mock conferences.	In the back of i-Think journals, create a section where students take their own conference notes. In that section include the date, their goal, next steps, and a self-assessment as to where they think they are toward meeting the goal. Before launching independent practice daily, instruct students to look at their conference goal.

KEEPIN' IT REAL

There are times when conferences don't work. Here are some problems that happened to us; now they won't happen to you!

Racetrack

Check mastery of the objective for all students throughout the lesson. If you can't get to all students, no problem. Analyze the exit slips of the students you didn't get to. If you incorporate exit slips the days that you do racetrack conferences, you won't feel frenzied trying to get to every student because you can look at half of the class during racetrack and the other half's exit slips.

O3s

The biggest pitfall that I see is a teacher starting O3s too early in the year, getting frustrated managing a class and a conference simultaneously, and then abandoning conferences. Take it slow . . . even if you start in the second term; wait until the time is right. Get the classroom routines up, ensure the room is managed, and build sustained stamina first.

Accountability

Like many things, if we don't remember to hold students accountable, students might not follow through with their goal. It's completely natural to forget. To ensure that kids aren't forgetting their goals, and that you don't have to do the same conference over and over, build in a routine. Consider giving students a bookmark where they write their grow goal, and then ask them to self-evaluate their progress each day after independent reading.

FOR COACHES AND SCHOOL LEADERS

Co-Analyze Data

Every couple of months during a time where you can sit down with individual teachers, together analyze O3 conference notes. Look for trends. Is there any way that students can be grouped together? After grouping students together by need, consider covering another teacher's classes for the day. Then while you are covering, she can pull those groups and do longer conferences with the groups.

TO SUM UP

- Start with halftime conferences. Use in-the-moment data to push your kids' learning for the second half of class.
- Racetrack conferences are a great way to spot check accuracy.
- One-on-one conferences should be personalized to the individual needs of your student. Create a grow goal for each student and use O3s to help students meet their grow goals.
- Keep O3 conferences short, give specific feedback, and hold students accountable to that feedback. Don't forget to praise!
- Take notes to track student growth.

Teaching Vocabulary
Become a Word Whisperer Without Being "On" All Day

It can be hard juggling everything we do as teachers. Often, finding a way to incorporate vocabulary can be daunting. This chapter shows how to integrate vocabulary into the *Reading Without Limits* program.

❑ Devote lots of time to independent reading to boost vocabulary.
❑ Speak using high-level vocabulary.
❑ Choose the right words to teach.
❑ Explicitly teach new words, and create an organized review and application schedule that extends to homework.
❑ Assess weekly.

Yesterday evening I watched a segment on the local news about a baby whisperer, a woman who teaches positive routine management to parents who want to change a behavior of their child. The mother of a toddler was frustrated because her daughter threw fits whenever it was time to get dressed or brush her hair. Sound familiar? Mom was at her wit's end, so she called the baby whisperer. The baby whisperer unleashed a parenting technique that you typically see in parenting (and teaching! books). She explicitly taught the baby girl by combing her doll's hair, then with firm, positive directives did the same thing with the girl, who a few minutes later had lovely flowing locks. Sound familiar? It's just like a read-aloud/think-aloud!

Unlike teaching reading strategies, where the list is finite (as shown in Chapter 2), there are infinite vocabulary words to teach. The sense of urgency to teach as many words as possible might be that much higher for teachers of students from low-income households. Betty Hart and Todd Risley spent two and a half years comparing language acquisition between professional, working class, and welfare families. By the age of three, students from the families on welfare heard on average about 30 million fewer words than their more affluent counterparts, often known as the 30-million-word gap. Per hour, students in low-income households hear 616 words compared to 2,000 or more in middle class or higher households. These figures instantly start me panicking, and I try to calculate how to teach 30 million words to kids without exploding. Does that mean we need to teach our students 30 million words?[71]

It's just like my fear of parenting. As an expectant mother, sometimes I start to panic and think that in order to be an excellent parent, you need to *constantly* be doing amazing parenting techniques like the one the baby whisperer did above, otherwise your daughter will start to have a fit. It's almost like I need to teach my daughter 30 million different things. Do parents need to be *on* every minute? Obviously, that's ridiculous. What I forget is that while those parenting techniques are super crucial in raising a happy, healthy child, the other 90% of your time isn't straight-on teaching while you are parenting, it's spending positive time with your child that doesn't involve thinking through each step. For instance, taking your daughter for a walk in her stroller is fun, and you can do it on autopilot without explicit behavior modeling.

Don't panic. We can learn from the metaphor of parenting. Not all parenting involves explicit instruction. Teaching vocabulary is similar to effective toddler rearing. It's necessary to do explicit teaching, as the baby whisperer's suggestions. There are so many reasons that teaching explicit vocabulary is essential; in the same way that modeling how to brush hair for a toddler is essential. But at the same time a great deal of word acquisition will happen implicitly. The same thing that holds true for good parenting holds true for good vocabulary instruction. This chapter shows that much like parenting, kids will learn about 90% of their words incidentally, so you can directly teach 10% of their words. In the same way that you can be a baby whisperer before brushing a toddler's hair, but then go to the park and have fun, you can be a word whisperer without explicitly instructing vocabulary all day. It just takes 10 minutes of intentional vocabulary planning daily, and your kids will become word wizards in no time.

If you have an existing vocabulary program that works, this chapter still works for you. Simply integrate some of the suggested mild next steps. If you have an existing mandated program that isn't working for you, this chapter will show ways to supplement it through homework in order to lift students' mastery of words. No program at all? Then read on! All strategies in this chapter are recommended for elementary through high school.

DEVOTE LOTS OF TIME TO READING TO BOOST VOCABULARY

If students are reading a lot, they are encountering many new words by reading or being read to. In fact, researchers have found that the best predictor of a kid's vocabulary size is based on the amount of time they spend reading. Therefore, if you have established choice, guided, and shared reading, your students are encountering heaps of new vocabulary. At KIPP Infinity, we interviewed high and low student outliers on a national vocabulary assessment, and we came to the same conclusion: those who read the most had the strongest vocabulary. What does that mean for us? If your kids are reading a lot, they are acquiring vocabulary through *incidental learning*. That is a relief. Devoting all of that precious time to independent reading in my class made lasting payoffs across many learning targets, including vocabulary. While it can be useful to engage in explicit vocabulary instruction I still feel it is something you can *add to* your schedule, not something that should eat into any choice, guided, or shared reading time. That means that you don't need to spend a lot of time explicitly teaching vocabulary. In fact, research backs this up because more vocabulary instruction doesn't equate to more words learned. While different researchers give different numbers, in general, we shouldn't teach more than eight to ten vocabulary words per week or students won't retain them. If you are already doing the math in your head, that means that no more than 400 words can be taught a year. That's not enough, right? Especially given the 30-million-word gap. Here's the cool thing. Kids learn on average 2,000 to 3,500 distinct words yearly. So how are they learning the words if we can only teach 400 a year? *Through independent reading*. I was always terrified that I wasn't teaching enough vocabulary, even though I knew that I couldn't simply pile on more words. If you continue to devote extended time to independent reading, during choice, shared, and guided reading, students will be incidentally learning vocabulary at a rapid rate. In fact, most of the words students learn will be learned incidentally, so keep on reading! If most of your class time is devoted to building lifelong readers, your students will build a robust vocabulary. Phew. Doesn't that take the pressure off?[72]

In conclusion, one of the best ways for students to learn new vocabulary words is by independently reading. With your choice, guided, and shared reading programs in place, students will be learning vocabulary incidentally. Logistically, if you have independent reading blocked out during the school day, students will incidentally be learning a bunch of new words.

SPEAK USING HIGH-LEVEL VOCABULARY

In addition to independent reading, another way students learn vocabulary incidentally is based on the amount of high-level vocabulary you use while you talk.[73] Don't talk like a college professor. It's imperative that when you use high-level vocabulary, you use the words strategically.

Instead of: Jian, please close the door.

Say: Jian, you left the door ajar. Can you please close it?

Instead of: Maria, I noticed you read so many pages today.

Say: Maria, I noticed you read so many pages today. I can see your fervor for your book. Why?

Try it yourself!

Instead of: Ahmed, please catch up. You're slowing down the line in the back.

Try: Ahmed, _____.

By embedding the meaning of the word through context, students are able to incidentally infer the word's meaning. If you want to bring it up a notch, repeatedly use the same high-level words in your language for a couple weeks like *ajar* and *fervor*. Be strategic when choosing words, and try to incorporate big words when going over routines or other nonacademic activities. You can use this strategy during any content class at any grade level, and since it doesn't take up a bunch of classroom time, you can weave it in seamlessly during the day.

CHOOSE THE RIGHT WORDS TO TEACH

Less is more with vocabulary so students can retain the words. In this section I offer specific guidelines for how to choose which words to explicitly teach, since you only get a few. If you don't have a vocabulary program, the following section is just right for you. If you have an already existing program, use the suggestions in order to evaluate what your program is and isn't offering.

In my classroom, I usually taught five words a week. Most vocabulary programs teach *too many words* per week even though research contradicts that approach. Slow it down and you will have a higher rate of mastery. What's hard is deciding which five words to teach. You want your approach to be strategic and not willy-nilly. Often, if schools don't have set mandated lists, teachers choose words from their shared reading books. That's a good place to start, but don't stop there. There are four different categories of words to consider when choosing words. I recommend ensuring that you cover all four categories. If you are teaching 200 to 400 words a year, shoot for a minimum of 50 words within each of the following categories.

Academic

One group of words to consider is academic vocabulary. Academic vocabulary includes words like *symbolism*, *stamina*, and *caption*. Academic vocabulary includes words that show up in your lesson's objective and are particular to the content you teach. In *Building Background Knowledge for Academic Achievement*,[74] Marzano and Pickering share that compared with students who have no vocabulary instruction, students with direct academic vocabulary instruction perform 33% higher on standardized tests (83% compared to 50%).

Tier Two from Shared Reading

When choosing words, consider frequency and usefulness. In *Bringing Words to Life*, a fantastic book on vocabulary, the authors categorize words into three tiers[75] (not to be confused with the four categories I recommend teaching):

Tier One
These are words that most students are likely to know like *brother, dog*, and *lamp*.

Tier Two
Kids are less apt to know these words, but the words are likely to appear in a variety of texts and the oral language of mature readers and speakers. Words include *pillar, simplify*, and *hazardous*.

Tier Three

These words are considered rare because they don't appear in texts often and they might be specific to particular content. For instance, *pallet, inoculate,* and *timorous* are tier three words. Avoid exclusively teaching tier three words.

Choose tier two words from your shared text. That doesn't mean you shouldn't teach tier three words, but teach many more tier two words. Students are more likely to see tier two words during independent reading and use them eventually in their everyday language. With only a maximum of 10 words a week, don't choose too many tier two words from the shared text because you also want to save room for the types of words mentioned next.

Morpheme Families

Morphemes are word parts that make up a word. They include root words, prefixes, and suffixes. More than 60% of English words have easily identifiable morphological structure. There are many prefixes and suffices in the English language, and that can become overwhelming. My seventh grade science teacher taught us several a day for the entire year and I think my brain melted from boredom. And guess what? I remember very few. Fortunately, nine prefixes account for 75% of words with prefixes.[76] Thank goodness! I recommend spending less time focusing on suffixes because some suffixes are obvious (-s), (-less), while others can be confusing like (-ious).[77]

Want to "kill two birds with one stone"? Choose tier two or academic words that fall within one of the most common prefixes. Group words in morpheme families, by studying words with the same prefix. Focus on the most common prefixes instead of trying to teach all morpheme families.

Most Common Prefixes

1. Un- (not)
2. Re- (again)
3. In-, Im-, Il-, Ir- (not)

4. Dis-

5. En-, em-

6. Non-

7. In-, im- (in)

8. Over-

9. Mis-

Character Traits

Character trait words such as *ambitious, carefree*, and *flexible* are great because they apply to literature and our real lives. Many are also tier two words. And based on my own informal noticing, which cannot be backed up with any research—so take it or leave it—character trait tier two words are all over standardized tests. I think trait words are powerful vocabulary words that help students deconstruct literature. There is a list of our favorite words ready to print on www.reading-without-limits.com put together by the deans of students at KIPP AMP, Autumn and Liz. They even vertically aligned the words by grade level. Thanks Autumn and Liz!

If your school has mandated vocabulary lists, see which categories the lists cover and which categories are missing in order to improve the lists.

Now that you know which types of words to choose, how do you manage to squeeze four categories of vocabulary into your instruction? I suggest the following:

Planning a Four-Week Word Cycle

Choose a few academic vocabulary words that relate to the content you teach: 5–10 tier two words that are in one morpheme family, 5–10 tier two vocabulary words from your shared text, 5–10 character traits that are relevant to your shared text.

❑ *Week 1:* one academic vocabulary word, four words from shared text or character traits
❑ *Week 2:* one academic vocabulary word, four words from shared text or character traits

❑ *Week 3:* morpheme study-group, five words with the same common prefix

❑ *Week 4:* one academic vocabulary word, four words from shared text or character traits

Keep following a similar schedule and you will have a good balance of all four categories by the end of the year without overwhelming or confusing kids. You are becoming a stress-free word whisperer.

EXPLICITLY TEACH NEW WORDS ON MONDAY

Now that you know which types of words to prioritize, the following section shows how to explicitly teach new words to students that follows a day-by-day routine, including recommended guidelines for how to schedule word instruction. I know how hard it is to fit vocabulary into an already full schedule. The following is a recommended routine that shares how to keep vocabulary to 10 minutes or less a day.

Schedule Vocabulary into Your Class Period

As mentioned, aim to teach between five and ten new words a week. I prefer to teach five a week, as I find that doing more can result in speeding through words rather than mastering words. Those words can include tier two words, a prefix study, character traits, or academic vocabulary. In general, it's best to reserve 10 minutes a day for word study. Unless you make it a hard routine in your classroom, you might find that you run out of time if vocabulary happens at the end of class. Therefore, you might want to start class with vocabulary. In order to hold myself accountable to a vocabulary routine, I posted a weekly schedule on the board that we followed to the tee. Without a schedule, I found myself running out of time. Students knew what we'd do every day for word study and appreciated the consistency. Notice in Table 10.1 how I did a different activity both in and out of class daily. The following sections describe each of the activities.

Table 10.1 Weekly Vocabulary Schedule

	Monday	**Tuesday**	**Wednesday**	**Thursday**	**Friday**
In class	Explicitly teach five new words	Chant and charades	Synonym Slide	Buddy Check	Assessment
Homework	Example/ Non Example	Create Illustrations	Generating Examples	Sentence Stems	Context Clues for next week's vocabulary

How to Explicitly Teach New Words

Inspired by the work of Dr. Robert Marzano, author of several vocabulary instruction books, I adapted how to explicitly teach new words to fit in busy teacher schedules.

Introduce in Context

First, introduce the word in a sentence that implies meaning through context and storytelling. *"You guys have been working really hard. You read at least 60 minutes everyday. When you are confronted with a difficult task, you do whatever it takes to work hard in order to accomplish it. When you are in class you are on task the entire time. You are diligent students."*

Elicit Meaning

Then ask kids to turn and talk to determine the meaning of diligent. During whole class Q&A, ask kids to define the meaning of the word. If their response isn't precisely accurate, go back to the story you told to highlight clues in order to push for 100% accuracy. Heavily guide this stage, and ensure students are accurately determining the correct meaning. If they aren't, correct. If this process takes your students too long, then move onto the next step.

Provide Kid-Friendly Definition

After giving students time to wrestle with the meaning, provide a kid-friendly definition with an additional example. For instance, "*Diligent means hard-working. My brother is diligent because he stays at work late to finish working for his clients.*"

Echo and Respond and Show

Then set up the chant. The chant can be sing-songy or monotone. The chant includes four parts: echoing the word, spelling the word, defining the word, and doing a charade of the word. Either provide the quick charade gesture to the class, or ask students to come up with a good example. The entire class should do the same charade gesture together. Bold is what the teacher says, italics is what the students say. When teaching the word, keep the word and definition on the board. "**Diligent**. *Diligent*. **Spell it**. *D-I-L-I-G-E-N-T*. **What does it mean?** *Hard-working*. **Show me**. (Students mime deep reading.)

Repeat the same process for the new words you are introducing that week. Vocabulary instruction on Mondays usually takes the most time.

REVIEW TUESDAY THROUGH THURSDAY

Chant and Charades on Tuesday

On Monday, you introduced the new vocabulary and students started the chant. This time, you want to do the chant without having the word or its definition on the board. Go through the chant multiple times. Each time you do a round, erase a couple letters or parts of the definition. After three or four rounds, students can say the chant from memory. Then tack on another word. Go through the same process until you've done all of the week's vocabulary words, including spiraled words, or words that you already taught. This activity builds rote memory of the words.

Diligent				
Lazy	Careful	Hard-Working	Painstaking	Industrious

Figure 10.1 Synonym Slides to Boost Application During Vocabulary

Synonym Slide on Wednesday

Sarah, a fifth grade teacher at KIPP Academy, introduced me to synonym slide eight years ago. You can find an example in Figure 10.1. It's a great way to build shades of meaning of the word as well as thesaurus skills. In order to teach synonym slide, first model how to use a thesaurus. That means students must be able to alphabetize, skim and flip quickly, and distinguish between synonyms and antonyms of the word. In synonym slide, students write down five synonyms of the vocabulary word on a horizontal scale as shown in Figure 10.1. In the middle is the kid-friendly definition you provided to the class. The word on the far left is a non-example of the word. The word to the far right is an extreme example of the word. Students color code it from blue meaning Icy Cold (far left) to red meaning Hot Synonym (far right). Students are encouraged to include words only that they've seen before. They may not know the complete definition of the synonyms, which is OK. However, they may not write words that they've never seen before.

Buddy Check on Thursday

On Thursday, students set up a study guide. They fold a piece of paper in half. On the left-hand side is the word. On the right-hand side is the kid-friendly definition and example. First, their buddy quizzes them. If a student gets a word wrong, the buddy puts a check by that word and returns to it in the next round of quizzing. Incorporate words from previous weeks to make it more challenging. If you want to organize all words in one spiral notebook, that will help spiral old words. Students can use the study as their own study tool at home. All they have to do is fold the piece of paper over so it only shows the word and covers up the definition.

Therefore, in class students this week have reviewed the words through rote memorization, higher-level thinking, and a study tool. But that's not enough. That's why we include word study for homework.

INCORPORATE APPLICATION IN CLASS OR IN HOMEWORK

If you suffer from time crunches like I do, it's essential to include vocabulary work for homework. Avoid cloze activities, where you give sentences and ask students to fill in the blanks with vocabulary words. Instead, push for higher-level thinking that pushes students to develop word mastery. If you follow the schedule discussed previously, the synonym slide was the only day of the schedule that included higher-level thinking. Each of the activities discussed in this section, derived from *Bringing Words to Life* by Isabel Beck and others and *Building Background Knowledge for Academic Vocabulary* by Dr. Robert Marzano and Debra Pickering, take about ten minutes. If you can fit these activities into class, that's awesome. But don't sacrifice guided, shared, or choice reading to do so. If you can't, they work really well for homework. However, it's super important that the following day you check for student understanding of the homework questions to ensure that students are on the right track. I include five homework assignments, as well as questions to ask the following day, next. For more, check out both resources.[78]

Example/Non-Example

Beck and others share Example/Non-example. First, provide several examples and non-examples of a vocabulary word. Ask students to identify which are the non-examples. Don't make the non-examples obviously wrong. Try to make them address common confusions regarding the word. For instance,

- Muhad is diligent because he likes to paint.
- Jericho was diligent when he signed up for after-school tutoring each day next week.

- Aronys diligently prepared a four-course dinner for his mom on Mother's Day.
- Mary Ellen diligently visited the museum.

Questions to Ask in Class

1. Why is Jericho diligent?
2. What word better describes Muhad? Why can't we be sure he's diligent?
3. If you do what you are supposed to do, are you diligent?
4. Why are Jericho and Aronys more diligent than Mary Ellen and Muhad in those circumstances?
5. Can you be diligent some of the time?

Illustrations

Ask kids to draw a picture of the word.[79] Tell students that the picture must be detailed enough that a stranger could infer the meaning of the word by looking at the picture. I push kids to include diagrams, captions, or any other text features that they think will help capture the meaning of the word. Figure 10.2 shows how a teacher can use her own illustrations to reinforce definitions.

Figure 10.2 Using Illustrations for Vocabulary

Questions to Ask in Class

1. Based on the picture, is the word a noun, adjective, or verb? How do you know? How does the picture show this?
2. How does the example you drew show the meaning of the word?

Generating Examples

This activity also comes from *Bringing Words to Life*. It's a great pen and paper homework assignment. Each of the following examples are variations on the same activity where students generate examples of the vocabulary word.

- What might a diligent student do when applying to college?
- What would a parent say to a diligent child who is becoming stressed out?
- How might a football player show he is diligent?

Questions to Ask in Class

1. How does your example show the meaning of diligence?
2. What other details could you add to your example to show diligence?
3. Turn it into a non-example. For instance, "How might a football player show he isn't diligent?"

Sentence Stems

We all know how important it is to encourage kids to use the words in their writing and oral language. Otherwise, why are we teaching the words? Do you ever have your kids write sentences with the words, and end up with something like, "*My mom is diligent.*" Sorry, but that isn't going to cut it. Instead, give them a sentence starter.

- Kate's mom is diligent because

  _____.

Questions to Ask in Class

1. How does your example show the meaning of diligence?
2. What other details could you add to your example to show diligence?

3. Turn it into a non-example. For instance, "What could Kate's mom do that isn't diligent?"

Context Clues

Remember the stories you tell when you introduce words on Monday? Give those stories as Friday's homework, and ask students to try to determine the meaning of the words in context. Monday, retell the stories. It's a great way to give your class a head start.

ASSESS ON FRIDAY

Add a short vocabulary assessment to your weekly assessment, as described in Chapter 13. Integrating weekly assessments will keep your data up-to-date, and allow for a steady flow of feedback to your students. There are a few criteria to consider when putting together a vocabulary assessment.

Start with Recall

Initially, include a section that asks students to match words with definitions. Try to scaffold it by doing the following:

Directions: Match each of the words with their definitions

Diligent	Column
Arid	Hard-working
Pillar	Very dry

Application

All of the homework activities just listed are great assessment questions. Ask students to do a couple different application questions for each vocabulary word. Make sure you have more application questions than recall questions.

Make It Kid-Friendly

Vocabulary tests can definitely raise the pressure in the room. Keep the assessment kid-friendly by intentionally crafting fun questions. For instance,

- Who is the least diligent movie character you have seen? Be prepared to support your answer with at least three details that show your understanding of the word.
- Your plane crashed in an arid land. Describe your immediate inner thoughts that show your understanding of the word.
- What are three creative ways you could use a pillar? Explain how with pictures.

Choice

Matt, a high school teacher who works with incarcerated youth, loves giving students choice on assessment. It helps ease the pressure. Instead of asking kids to answer all questions on the assessment, ask them to answer five to ten. Or give students three options that all demonstrate the same skill. For example, students can draw a picture with captions of a word, do an example/non-example question, or generate their own example, but not all three.

Spiral

Don't drop old words like hot cakes! Keep them in the rotation. I like a nice 50/50 split. Assess all new words, and throw in equal parts old words. Incorporate words that your class struggled with in the past. If you put them on a test, don't blindside your kids. Include them also in your homework rotation over the course of the week or you won't see a word mastery improvement.

This chapter showed that independent reading is going to dramatically help close the word gap for your students. You still need to explicitly teach words, but less is more. Follow a daily in-class and homework routine on a weekly schedule and your students will become word masters in no time. The best part is that it's also going to be sustainable for you.

ADDITIONAL RESOURCES

1. A list of character trait vocabulary words that are vertically aligned by grade level

MILD, MEDIUM, SPICY NEXT-STEP SUGGESTIONS

	Mild	**Medium**	**Spicy**
Incidental Learning	Ensure that your kids are reading at least 20 minutes everyday.	Use tier two words when students are packing up, such as, "Lee, I notice how industrious you are being."	Build guided and shared reading in your school. That way, students are reading texts that are a little bit out of their reach and getting great vocabulary exposure.
Choosing Words	Choose words from your shared reading book that meet the tier two requirements.	Do academic vocabulary instruction using your aim. For instance, To analyze (_____) character strengths by investigating text details such as how characters overcome obstacles.	Follow the schedule that I provided that mixes tier two, academic, character trait, and morpheme studies.

	Mild	Medium	Spicy
Teach New Words	When students are trying to come up with the meaning of the word, don't allow for partially correct answers. Push for 100%. Instead of just giving students the definition right away, make them go back to the story that you wrote so that they can analyze the context clues. Check out *Teach Like a Champion* by Doug Lemov for great ways to push for 100%.	Put up a word wall in your classroom with words you taught. Each time students find one of the words in their book, encourage them to write it down on a sentence strip and put it under the word on the wall.	Build in a routine where students create word cards for each word that you teach. The word *diligent* would make two cards: diligent and works hard. Then, once students start compiling cards, they can use them for games like Go Fish and Memory.
Application and Review	The best time saver is doing some vocabulary work as homework. Ensure that you are pushing high-level application questions for homework. Also, question students' understanding the following class period.	Add application and review questions to your do-now.	Do the vocabulary chant everyday as a transition. Ask a student to lead the chant. Give students a packet of 10 words that you want to spiral from previous weeks, and make sure kids are being zesty! And make the gestures fun so kids can wiggle around a little in your class.

FOR COACHES AND SCHOOL LEADERS

Technology

There are kid-friendly computer programs that boost vocabulary. Use them as an after-school activity.

Cognates

If you have a large population of ELL students who are native Spanish speakers, then push your teachers to instruct using cognates. There are between 10,000 and 15,000 Spanish/English cognates.[80] Table 10.2 shows how cognates can build tier two vocabulary.

Early Childhood Education

Much research has been done on the importance of early childhood education. If you have early childhood in your school, then you have the opportunity to make a significant difference by becoming a word whisperer early. Ensure teachers have lots of independent reading in their classrooms, incorporate high-level vocabulary words in their oral language, and push kids to talk as much as possible. Rich oral language and reading environments promote vocabulary development and will help close the 30-million word gap.

Table 10.2 Using Cognates

English Common Word	Examples of Tier Two Words in English	Latin Root	Spanish Common Word
Brave	Valiant, valorous, valor	Valere (to be strong)	Valiente

Derived from *A Focus on Vocabulary* by Fran Lehr, Jean Osborne, and Dr. Elfrieda H. Hiebert.[81]

KEEPIN' IT REAL

Here are some problems that we faced when teaching vocabulary. Address the pitfalls in advance and I hope they won't happen to you!

Dictionaries

Just like thesauri, dictionary skills need to be explicitly taught. Do not ask students to look up dictionary definitions as their definition in their notes because when teachers ask students to look up words and write definitions there's little word knowledge gained.[82] Effective dictionary instruction takes a lot of time and must be explicitly taught. Teachers model how to look up an unknown word and then think-aloud how to select the best definition for the appropriate context. Teachers must also model what to do if the definition itself has unknown words.

Context Clues

A lot of state tests ask students to use context to determine the meaning of an unknown word. I hate these questions, because often the context is elusive and the multiple-choice answers also include unknown words. Also, context clues don't always work for independent reading; they work if you have partial understanding of the word, but less so if you have no understanding of the word. It's an important skill, but by no means the most important word work skill.

Vocabulary Teachable Moments

As mentioned, try not to stop too many times during shared reading or a think-aloud to address a teachable moment. But there are going to be times when you find a great tier two word that you aren't planning on teaching explicitly. If you want to teach that word right away, try *Text Talk*, developed by Beck and McKeown.[83] In their example, a teacher comes across the word *absurd* while reading aloud a story. He does quick teaching and checking for understanding. Here's what the teacher said after he read the word in the shared text.

Teacher:

Hey guys, I really want to share with you that word we just read: absurd. If I told you that pigs could fly, that would be absurd. If I told you the school will travel to Mars today, that would be absurd. I'm going to tell you a few things. Raise your hand if you think they are absurd:

- *My dog Bubba speaks Chinese. (Absurd)*
- *The trees in my backyard are made of spaghetti. (Absurd)*
- *I saw a great program on television last night.*

Then, the teacher resumed reading aloud.

Morphemes

You don't need to go crazy on morphemes. Stick to the morphemes shared in this chapter instead of making kids memorize hundreds of word parts like my science teacher did.

TO SUM UP

- Students learn vocabulary incidentally by reading a lot.
- Speak using high-level vocabulary words especially during nonacademic times.
- Be thoughtful and organized when choosing which five words you teach each week.
- Explicitly teach new words and create an organized review and application vocabulary schedule that extends to homework.
- Assess weekly.

Class Discussion
Interview Skills Go Beyond
Trying to Get a Job

Classroom discussions will give your students the opportunity to demonstrate their strategic thinking in a different application. In order to set up smooth discussions,

❏ Before the discussion, create great discussion questions.
❏ Before the discussion, give students time to prepare their thinking in advance.
❏ During the discussion, hold kids accountable with formative assessments, summative assessments, and self-assessments.
❏ Explicitly teach excellent communication skills.
❏ After the discussion, summarize and reflect.

Colleges and organizations frequently offer workshops for how to master an interview. Interviews are divided into three categories: before, during, and after the interview.

Before the interview, you need to do a lot of preparation. First, research the organization so you come prepared with knowledge. You also want to review your resume so you can discuss further details if necessary. Then practice interviewing with a friend. It's recommended to go through the most common interview questions and get feedback from your friend so you can do even better on the big day.

During the interview, the key is excellent pragmatics, or being able to communicate effectively. Speak with professional courtesy. Get your main points

Figure 11.1 Be Strategic with Classroom Discussion Seating

across while speaking succinctly. Don't just answer questions; come prepared with your own questions. Avoid rambling or appearing overly flustered. Pragmatics isn't just about back-and-forth communication. It also involves proper body language. Make eye contact, avoid fidgeting, and keep your arms uncrossed. And, my favorite, don't forget to smile!

After the interview, send a thank-you card or e-mail summarizing your main points again, and thank everyone who was part of your interview one last time.

For potential hires I've interviewed, those who follow these tips stand out. But interview skills go beyond trying to get a job. The above skills are just practical real-life tips. Shouldn't we always try not to ramble? Common courtesy should be a norm in life, and the best conversations are not one-sided.

The best interviewees have confidence, poise, and willingness to ask questions, which scores them jobs. I bet these interviewees did a great job during class discussions throughout school, because those are the exact traits you need to have for a successful conversation. In this chapter, I show that to build the best classroom discussions about texts, you need to follow the same advice as you would to land a job. To be successful during a classroom discussion, follow before, during, and after criteria in order to demonstrate a high level of communication proficiency. If we build high levels of pragmatics, our students can steal those same techniques for life. In addition, if we incorporate classroom discussion, students' reading skills are going to benefit. If reading is part of an accountable, monitored discussion, students will have a deeper more thorough understanding of their shared text.

As mentioned in the Introduction, classroom discussion works best during the shared reading block. This is true because everyone has read the same text, so the discussion can revolve around shared knowledge.

Next I offer specific guidelines for successful classroom discussion in your class. These guidelines work for any grade level, as classroom discussions are differentiated by the complexity of the text discussed.

BEFORE THE DISCUSSION

Just like in a job interview, better discussions involve preparation on your part and your students' part. For teachers, I recommend creating questions that guide the discussion in advance. This doesn't mean that students can't bring their own questions to the discussions. However, preplan a couple questions that you want students to unpack using their shared text.

Creating the Best Questions

Before launching a class discussion, preplan two to three debatable questions that can be justified using textual evidence.

Question Criteria

- Debatable — you don't want 30 kids agreeing and saying iterations of the same thing. Trust me, I've been there . . . boring!
- Justifiable through evidence

- Invites inference or interpretation
- Specific—overly generic questions produce overly generic answers
- Avoid recall or comprehension questions because once a student has answered the question, the discussion stops

Table 11.1 shows some classroom discussion questions that worked really well, and some that didn't.

Notice the differences between the following two questions:

"*Is ___ a good friend, leader, father, etcetera?*" versus "*What inferences could you make about the main character?*"

While both invite interpretation and can be supported by using textual evidence, the latter question is too vague. It also doesn't feel debatable.

Give Questions in Advance

In order for students to be prepared, they need the questions in advance. Unless you have a photographic memory, it isn't easy to find text evidence right on the spot. During shared reading, as either a homework assignment or independent work, give students the questions a couple days in advance

Table 11.1 The Difference Between Great and Not Great Discussion Questions

Great Questions	Not So Great Questions
Do you agree with the author's ending message?	What did you think of the ending?
Is ____ a good friend, leader, father, etcetera?	What inferences could you make about the main character?
Do you agree with the author's views on ____?	What do you think of the theme of the story?
Did ____ change for the better or worse? Did ____ change enough?	How did ____ change over the course of the story?

so they have time to prepare for the discussion. That way, students can track their thinking, change their minds, and find lots of textual evidence.

Use Think, Pair, Shares, and Partner Checklists

Partner Checklist

✓ My partner came prepared for seminar
✓ My partner was courteous to other students
✓ My partner paused and thought before speaking
✓ My partner listened well to others
✓ My partner kept an open mind
✓ My partner acted as a positive role model for other students
✓ My partner built on what was said before giving an opinion
✓ My partner used examples from the text to back up his or her statements
✓ My partner spoke clearly and stayed on topic
✓ My partner interrupted others (−1)
✓ My partner did not make eye contact with the speaker (−1)
✓ My partner talked off topic (−1)
✓ My partner talked too much (−1)

After giving the questions well in advance, and before launching a class discussion, give time for your students to practice a mini discussion with their partners. Allow them to bounce ideas off of one another. Together they can rank their best arguments. Using the partner checklist, together they can identify what criteria they are prepared for and where they need support. This gives them time for a quick feedback session right before the real deal in the same way a great interviewer practices and gets feedback before the big day. Allow five to ten minutes before a discussion for think, pair, share, and peer feedback.

Self-Reflection Checklist

I . . .

✓ tracked both questions by annotating my ideas in the book
✓ have multiple ideas to share that are justifiable
✓ am prepared to move the conversation forward with questions
✓ have several pieces of text evidence to support my interpretations
✓ am open to others' ideas
✓ will track the speakers at all times
✓ am prepared to participate at least twice
✓ will be succinct as I'm speaking
✓ will speak up and enunciate at all times
✓ will be respectful when others are sharing

Incorporate Self-Reflection

Before, during, or after a discussion ask students to self-reflect. It's a reminder of how they will be assessed when they participate.

HOLD STUDENTS ACCOUNTABLE WITH DIFFERENT ASSESSMENTS

All too often I held class discussions and didn't track the skills of each student. Therefore, I wasn't able to give individual feedback. Guess what happened? They didn't grow quickly. I needed to come up with a system that allowed me to give students feedback. But that's not easy when 30 kids are participating simultaneously. The following strategies not only give individual feedback (which you can use in a grade book if you choose), but they are also manageable with a large class. The strategies are also kid-friendly!

Fishbowl

Assign half of your students (A) to a partner (B). All As go into the center of the classroom. Then they have a class discussion answering the first question. While they have a class discussion, their partner evaluates their performance using a rubric or checklist. Then partners switch. Bs go into a circle and have a class discussion about the second question while their partners evaluate. With our class sizes getting larger and larger, I liked to do this model because it made it easier for all kids to speak.

Whisper in the Ear

While the first discussion is happening, pause it halfway through. Allow partners to come in and whisper in their partner's ear for 30 seconds, providing some coaching feedback based on how they are doing so far. Then, the discussion continues. Repeat this process for the second class discussion. Kids like the halftime pep talk in the same way athletes regroup halfway through a game.

Rubric

The following chart shows a rubric that you can use to assess students during a discussion. Teach students how to evaluate by using the rubric so during a fishbowl, partners are filling in the rubric. I do not recommend that you use the rubric during a discussion. You will be flipping through 30 sheets of paper and it's too hard to manage. However, I explain "Seating Chart," which shows a manageable way you can evaluate students yourself using the rubric.

Seating Chart

It can be difficult to grade 30 students in real-time while they are having a class discussion. Teaching students to evaluate each other is really helpful. But you don't want to exclusively depend on peer evaluations in case they aren't accurate. Here's an idea from the Brooklyn Latin High School and

Table 11.2 Classroom Discussion Rubric

	4	3	2	1
Speaking	Speaks clearly Speaks loudly Speaks in complete sentences Uses appropriate tone Makes eye contact and tracks the speaker	Speaks clearly Speaks loudly Makes eye contact and tracks	Some comments unclear (might be rambling) Volume is too low Words mumbled Language is too colloquial Doesn't track	Comment is unclear so it is not understood
Using the Text	Every comment is grounded in the text Makes direct references to specific parts of text, including page number Paraphrases before going deeper Closely reads the text to make inferential comments Shares confusions about the text so class can help figure out confusions	Every comment is based in the text	Comments are sometimes about the text Comments are based on their own experiences	No comments are based on the text
Listening	Moves conversation forward by summarizing student ideas, linking student ideas, questioning ideas or clarifying ideas Listens closely Brings out missed ideas Brings up relevant idea that changes conversation Uses accountable talk lingo	Moves conversation forward Doesn't dominate conversation Uses accountable talk lingo	Doesn't move conversation forward Comments do not connect to ideas previously discussed	Takes no responsibility Shows lack of interest or disrespect Body language shows lack of interest Doesn't speak

Figure 11.2 Classroom Discussion Seating Chart

the Great Books Foundation.[84] Create a seating chart for the discussion like the one shown in Figure 11.2. It can be the same chart that you always use, or if students are meeting in the center of the room, assign them seats in a circle. As recommended in Making It Visible, I love U-shaped or circle configurations for classroom discussions during shared reading.

Each time a student talks put a check mark. Create other symbols for insightful comments (*), textual evidence (T), succinct responses (S), etc. as shown in Figure 11.2. Therefore, instead of writing out comments, you are only writing symbols, which is manageable. When you are done grading the discussion, it will look akin to the chart in Figure 11.2. Then, using the symbols, you can go back and fill in individual rubrics.

Literary Essay

If you teach writing as well as reading, align your discussion question to the literary essay prompts that you assign. Students will feel a lot more engaged, and will feverishly write down their teammates' responses so they can "steal" their ideas for their essays. Also, students will be more prepared for their essays once they start writing. When students are watching a fishbowl, require them to take notes so that they can use other kids' interpretations in an essay. Grounding the discussion in an essay will make the discussion more relevant and the essays of higher quality. Teaching students to lift each other's ideas is particularly important in high school, as this is a necessary strategy for college seminars.

EXPLICITLY TEACH CLASSROOM DISCUSSION SKILLS

Review Goals

Right before starting a discussion, ask students what they did well as a group during the last discussion. Then ask students if there was something that they need to work on as a group. Use the partner checklist or the rubric for ideas. A primary teacher could say, "*Last time we did a great job waiting our turns. We didn't interrupt each other. One thing we want to work on is ensuring that we make eye contact. I will be looking for that today.*" A high school teacher could say, "*Last time we did a great job going back to the text as we discussed. This time, before we make inferences, I want to hear you guys paraphrase what's happening in the text.*" I like to have charts up that list the most important criteria for discussions.

Classroom Discussion Criteria for Primary Students

1. Speak so everyone can hear you
2. Make eye contact
3. Try not to fidget
4. Ask and answer questions
5. Use language like, "I agree with _____ because . . ." or "I disagree with _____ because . . ."
6. Share new ideas and avoid repeating what someone already said

---

7. Go back to the book by using a page number
8. If some students haven't spoken, ask them if they'd like to chime in
9. Flush out an idea before asking a new question

Classroom Discussion Criteria for Secondary Students

1. Enunciate as you speak
2. Avoid repeating your point many times—speak succinctly
3. Offer new ideas, not stale ideas
4. Reference the text, but not awkwardly
5. If some students haven't spoken, ask them if they'd like to chime in
6. Flush out an idea before asking a new question
7. Agree to disagree
8. Use your schema to make insightful inferences

Explicitly Teach Strategies

Explicitly teach strategies that make classroom discussions excellent. Start with low-hanging fruit like accountable talk sentence starters (as described in Chapter 4), and not interrupting and ensuring that students are tracking the speaker at all times. As the year progresses, teach new lessons that will make your classroom discussions even better. Each of the criteria could be a lesson in itself. I like to teach classroom discussion strategies by modeling what to do, and what not to do. Try acting them out! Or create scripts. Write a classroom discussion script that excellently highlights the strategy you are trying to teach. Write another that is a non-example. Ask students to discover the differences. Remember John Wooden? He showed his players how to put on socks before a big game. Think like him. You are modeling exactly what you do want to see, and don't want to see, so kids will emulate what you want to see.

Videotape

One of the best ways to improve the quality of class discussion is by watching a videotape of a previous discussion for several minutes with your class. Using the rubric, ask students to evaluate the class's performance, then goal set from there.

Assign Roles

Here's a kid-friendly idea: assign roles that will boost the class discussion. You can choose to assign the roles to a few students or assign the same role to multiple students so that all students have a role. This role is something they do *in addition* to what is normally expected during a class discussion. Here are roles I gave my fifth graders, and they work for all grade levels. I was inspired by the work of Harvey Daniels's *Literature Circles: Voice and Choice in the Student-Centered Classroom*, and lifted the idea of student roles and adapted it for whole class discussion.[85]

The Summarizer

The job of the summarizer is to summarize multiple student comments that address one idea. For instance, *"So far we are saying that Bud acts brave on the outside when in reality he's probably really scared."* This role is important so kids can see how their comments synthesize. Have a student who really likes a challenge? This is the role for them.

The Paraphraser

The job of the paraphraser is to make sure that students paraphrase the text before making connections or inferences. Paraphrasers can either remind students to paraphrase or paraphrase themselves.

The Questioner

The role of the questioner is to find the best time to ask a new, but related question. Questioners need to wait when the original question has been flushed out, but not to the point when the class is getting bored because ideas are being repeated. This role is important because it keeps the discussion moving.

Big Ideas

This is one of my favorite roles. This student is expected to think outside the box, offer something that hasn't been discussed and make really creative (though substantiated) inferences. If you have kids that you want to challenge, the big idea is a great role to assign.

The Connector

The purpose of the connector is to connect ideas to previous read texts. It's important that the connector makes text-to-text connections with texts that everyone in the class has read before. This is a great role to introduce midway through the year.

The Clarifier

When students say something confusing, which they will, the role of the clarifier is to ask them to clarify or when possible, to clarify for them.

KEEP IT KID CENTERED

Classroom discussions are a time for kids to work together. Play soccer, not catch.

Intentionally Interrupt

You need to determine how much you want to play catch (teacher to student participation) versus playing soccer (teacher to student to student to student participation). I have no recommended ratio, but try to be silent as much as possible. This is a time for students to develop their language skills—and the more you talk, the less likely every child will be able to participate. However, you need to guide your students so that they become even more masterful at discussion, so you can lead their development.

Therefore, determine *in advance* how often you will interrupt. I try to use the remind and reinforcement strategies while the discussion is happening, and I also use the halftime strategy when the discussion is at its halfway point. Try hiding in the back or outside of the circle so students stop looking at you when they speak and start looking at each other.

- *(Halftime)* I love how much you guys are participating! For the second half of the discussion, I'm looking for you to go back to the text.
- *(Reinforce)* I noticed how Marilyn didn't awkwardly quote the text. She summarized it for us, and still included the page number.
- *(Remind)* Who can remind me what we should do if someone hasn't participated yet?

In general, try not to interrupt too much. Unlike close reading, you aren't heavily guiding. Classroom discussion picks up the quality that I argue for during choice reading: extended stamina. We need our kids to practice communicating clearly and effectively for long periods of time, and that's only going to happen if we give them those opportunities for extended practice. If you notice negative trends during classroom discussion, those become your *aha* moments. Use those aha moments as teachable opportunities the next time you do a classroom discussion.

Talk into the Silence and Pass the Mic

Another way to make the discussion as kid centered as possible is to consider how to call on each student. In Talk into the Silence, students literally talk into the silence as if they were a large group of executives holding an important meeting. They don't raise their hands! At first it will be awkward, because multiple students will want to share simultaneously. Teach students to forgo their turn if someone talked into the silence at the same time. Pass the Mic[86] is another kid-friendly strategy. After a student shares, students who want to share raise their hands and the student who shared last calls on the next student. This will keep your teacher talk time down even more and keeps the discussion kid-friendly.

Snowball to Avalanche

Have a really debatable question? Start the discussion. When a student answers, they become a "snowflake." As students agree with the original student, they move their bodies closer to that student to "build on that snowflake," making a snowball. If you choose a great question, there should be several snowballs throughout the room that eventually, if one side is more convincing, turn into an avalanche. Kids will love showing allegiance to their classmates' ideas. And they can definitely change their minds. Snowball to Avalanche requires some management. If doing Snowball to Avalanche, try no chairs. That way, kids don't have to move their chairs while they discuss. It's for this reason that many teachers choose to do classroom discussions on a rug. If no chairs for an entire discussion sounds daunting, do Snowball to Avalanche for only a few minutes. Getting kids out of their seats and moving is a great way to keep things fresh.[87]

AFTER THE DISCUSSION SUMMARIZE AND REFLECT

One thing that many potential job hires forget to do is follow up with a thank you e-mail summarizing their takeaways. In a classroom, one thing many teachers forget to do is close the discussion with after-discussion strategies. The closing only needs to take a couple minutes. Avoid ending your discussion as the bell sounds. Instead, try one of these after-discussion strategies.

Summarize

Use the last five minutes of the discussion to summarize your students' learning akin to Jerry Springer's "final thoughts." Discussion isn't a free-for-all, and there are going to be textual takeaways that you want your kids to remember. Encourage note-taking during the summary. I recommend that this summary is teacher-centered, but do not use this time to lecture on your interpretations of the book. Summarize your students' interpretations.

Reflect

Since the class made whole-group and individual goals, ensure that you save time for self-assessment. If you have time, show a clip of the discussion immediately afterward so the group can get immediate, actionable feedback. Cameras on jump drives are a great tool. Or hand out the rubric or self-assessment and ask kids to evaluate themselves.

If you find classroom discussions aren't working in your classroom, don't "hang up your cleats." Instead, do what pitcher Brendon McCarthy did. Analyze your game. Look for positive and delta trends. Remind and reinforce. Explicitly model. Analyze videos, establish roles, redirect when necessary. But don't give up on it.

In the same way that the best job interviewers prepare before, during, and after an interview, the best discussions are also prepared. I like to do a class discussion twice a month during the shared reading block. Remember, in advance of a discussion, hand out the questions. Give students ample time to prepare for the discussion in partnerships. Explicitly teach students excellent oral communication skills. Hold students accountable to those skills during the discussion, and don't forget to wrap up!

ADDITIONAL RESOURCES

1. Videos of classroom discussions
2. Lessons that launch classroom discussion at primary and secondary levels
3. Student self- and peer assessments for class discussion

MILD, MEDIUM, SPICY NEXT-STEP SUGGESTIONS

	Mild	Medium	Spicy
Before Discussion	Share discussion questions in advance. Push for high level, debatable questions.	Assign roles to students who don't normally participate voluntarily. Share the roles the night before.	Do a mini-discussion fishbowl with five willing students and then ask the whole class for feedback.
During Discussion	Try discussions with all genres, including paintings.	Halfway through the discussion, allow partners to whisper into their partner's ear some feedback.	Students vote on the discussion leader, the student who demonstrated the most insight, clarity, and textual evidence.
After Discussion	Encourage students to do a self-assessment.	After handing back your evaluation, create one bite-sized goal that you want each student to work on, using the rubric.	Using a video camera, watch a couple minute clip of the discussion with the class and generate goals together.

FOR COACHES AND SCHOOL LEADERS

Across Disciplines

Classroom discussion lends itself across disciplines and is especially fun in science and social studies classes.

Video

Video cameras are invaluable tools for class discussion and easy to use. If you buy a few for your school, teachers can sign them out and share clips with their kids.

KEEPIN' IT REAL

There are times when classroom discussion didn't work for us. Here are some problems that have happened to us; now they won't happen to you!

Um, Like

Teach teenagers? Like, I do, like, too. And they have social tics. The top two in my classroom are *um* and *like*. Talk about a brevity killer. A few years ago we did a little experiment. Each time a student said *um* or *like* the entire class had to stand up. There was a lot of standing at first. A lot. But I really wanted to nip it in the bud. Once, Barbie, an awesome kid in her junior year in high school, couldn't stop the tic, and we continued sitting and standing for five minutes. But this little consequence worked and put smiles on our faces.

Text Based

Interpretations must be justified with text proof. But sometimes students reference awkwardly by either not citing the best proof or directly quoting the text when a summary sounds better. Model and reteach how to find and cite the best proof during discussion. Often, paraphrasing textual evidence comes across less awkwardly.

Off Track

When you create debatable discussion questions, you still have an end point in mind. For instance, the question "Is *Of Mice and Men* sexist?" is intended for students to analyze character roles, the author's choice not to give Curly's wife a name, and other textual references. It's not a complete free-for-all. Sometimes kids can take the discussion off its track and it's your job to make sure they stick to the original point.

100%

I taught Reggie for four years, and he's also one of the hardest working kids I know kids — an amazing trumpet player who in 2013 will be graduating high school. But Reggie wouldn't speak during class discussion. Once you've identified which kids are less apt to jump in, try this strategy: while they are practicing the discussion in their partnerships, listen in. Then tell them that you really liked a specific point and ask them to share it during the discussion. Tell them you will call on them so they don't have to worry about it. Or ask them if it's OK if they start the next discussion.

TO SUM UP

- Choose debatable, high-level questions for discussion and allow time for students to prep and practice before the discussion.
- Hold students accountable using rubrics, self-assessments, and partner assessments.
- Explicitly teach excellent discussion and speaking skills.
- End the discussion with a summary and reflection.

12

Standardized Tests
You Don't Need to OD
on Test Prep

Here are guidelines you can use to craft a successful standardized reading test preparation unit that works for any grade level.

- ❑ Teach standardized tests just like you teach reading strategies.
- ❑ Build test-taking stamina.
- ❑ Recognize leveled reading.
- ❑ Design intervention groups.
- ❑ Include standardized tests weekly and spiral in daily do-nows.

Before I get into how to prepare students for standardized tests, I need to share why. Some folks believe that if you are authentically teaching your students how to become phenomenal, independent, confident readers, there is no need to teach any test preparation. On the other extreme are folks who think that since many of our schools are measured by our students' performance on standardized tests, we need to prioritize preparing our kids for the test above other instruction. As in life, extremes are usually not the way to go. In addition to integrating do-nows and homework throughout the entire year, what I found effective is shortly before the test, design a unit that prepares students for the state test.

One of the best ways to increase your student's likelihood of doing well on a standardized test is by doing lots of reading.

Being able to do well on a standardized test is a life skill, and the skills created through frequent independent reading can translate to success on standardized tests. Standardized tests are used for school entrance exams, drivers licenses, technical certifications, and graduate schools. One of the best ways to increase your student's likelihood of doing well on a standardized test is by doing lots of reading. Students who read more do better on standardized tests.[88] Students who read independently in schools and who stick with independent reading at home do even better.[89]

However, standardized tests are unlike the other genres in your classroom. Sitting in a silent, high-stress room for 45 minutes while you have to answer 35 questions based on 10 passages is not akin to reading *The Hunger Games* on a beanbag. Nor is it akin to a lively discussion about *Tom Sawyer* or the Gettysburg Address. It's its own beast. However, by using the same teaching strategies that you use during choice, guided, and shared reading, your kids will tame the beast and increase their test scores.

TEACH STANDARDIZED TESTS LIKE YOU TEACH STRATEGIC READING

Great test prep teaching is also great teaching. Not a lot should change when you are preparing your students for a standardized test. I recommend teaching a unit that runs two to four weeks on how to beat the test. Here are strategies that you can lift from your choice, shared, and guided reading blocks.

Make Goals Visible

First, design a goal for your kids and post it. Below are a few you can choose from:

- To be strategic readers as we move up __ % on the standardized test (growth based).
- To be strategic readers as we score a __ % or higher on the standardized test (achievement based).
- Attack the test by finding proof for each question (strategy based).

Make Goals Kid-Friendly

Then, *sell* the goal with even more visuals. Create a visual anchor and a slogan. At KIPP Infinity, one year we told the kids that if they achieved a certain percentage increase in their growth the teachers would all dye their hair blue. Eeek! The slogan was "Think Blue." We took a picture of teachers with a blue wig on their head and put the pictures up around the school. Another year we told the kids that if they made a certain percentage growth, kids could throw a cream pie at a teacher of their choice. The slogan was "Got Pie?" The visual was a pie. *Attack the test by finding proof for each question* was the test prep unit's goal that I used for 10 years. The slogan was "Attack!" and the visual was an axe. Another year, an incentive we made as a school was that teachers would shave their heads if students did really well. 100% of our sixth graders passed the test so Mike, their sixth grade reading teacher, and the math teacher got on stage in front of the entire school and kids shaved the teachers' heads. They had a ton of bald spots, but it was worth it for the glee of 350 screaming adolescents. While you certainly don't have to go to that kind of extreme, it's something that our kids will remember for a long time.

Strategically Read a Standardized Test

After you determine how you are going to make your goal visible, scope out the strategies you need to teach. First start with the big picture. In the case of standardized reading, there are two big picture strategies that students must master:

1. **To confidently comprehend the passage by using fix-it strategies and paraphrasing as you read**: Sound familiar? This was the big goal for choice, shared, and guided reading as well. Since you're spending so much time teaching this strategy to students as they read a variety of different genres during the year, it will translate to the standardized passages.

2. **To attack the test by finding proof for each question**: In this strategy, you want students to go back and underline and label all proof for each question that they answer. Students must underline the exact proof in the passage that got them to their answer. When students label, they write the question and answer next to the proof (for instance '2b'). You've spent all year ensuring during choice, guided, and shared reading that their thinking is textually relevant. They demonstrate that they can do this during class discussions, close reading, using i-Think journals, and annotating shared texts. Now it will translate to standardized reading tests.

In the same way that we are teaching our kids to use reading strategies for their choice, guided, and shared books, we want them to be strategic readers as they test. The following are strategies that good test takers use. Devote an entire lesson to these strategies, or reinforce the strategy during halftime. How do you teach the strategy? Model with a read-aloud/think-aloud, using a standardized test passage.

Test-Taking Strategies

1. Know the structure of the reading assessment, the number of passages, number of questions, and that passages get progressively harder.
2. Build stamina for the length of the test.

3. Read the directions before reading the passages and answering the questions.

4. Go back and underline the parts of the passage that answer the questions.

5. Flip back and forth from the passage to the questions when underlining important information.

6. Identify how many questions you can hold on to as you read.

7. Hold the test book open so you can see the passages and questions simultaneously.

8. If the text is really difficult, chunk the passage into parts—especially in informational texts without subheadings.

9. Read all text features.

10. Read all the words on the page—including pictures, captions, charts, etc.

11. Eliminate answer choices that absolutely cannot be the correct answer.

12. Know how the test writers write the answers: the ridiculous answer, the teaser, the most right answer, and the kind of right answer.

13. You often have to think hard between two possible answers—reread relevant parts of the text and select the better answer choice.

14. Jot some sort of symbol, like a star, next to questions that are a bit difficult, do not waste time on these questions, go back to these questions when you are otherwise done.

15. Mark the passage during important parts so you can go back and find them later.[90]

16. Fill in the answers in the test booklet first before filling in the scantron.[91]

Depending on the length of your standardized test, especially if you have unlimited time, encourage your students to use their the following strategies as well. They can write in the margins of the test, or if rules allow, on sticky notes. The following reading strategies are ones that particularly resonate with test passages:

1. Stop, reread, or read on when you are confused.

2. Paraphrase as you read.

3. Determine the overarching theme.
4. Question in order to clarify meaning.
5. Track time and place shifts.
6. Determine the author's most important message and what details support that message.

In New York State, the test is timed and our readers don't have time to jot notes in the margin. In fact, finishing in time after the thoughtful reading we've done all year is a big challenge, so we have to practice not only stamina but also speed. If your students have been doing these strategies all year, then make sure they transfer the same strategies using test passages whether or not they show evidence of their thinking.

BUILD TEST-TAKING STAMINA

In 2010, New York State changed the state test. It got longer with more passages. We gave our students a diagnostic in the middle of the year. Would you believe that for the first 25 minutes of the test (the first few passages) the kids were scoring almost perfect accuracy? For the next 25 minutes of the test, their accuracy plummeted to 50%. Why? The kids lost their stamina. Their stamina was built to 30 minutes, but not for longer. That's because they get to read for 30 minutes daily.

First things first, you need to find time for your kids to build reading stamina that goes beyond 30 minutes. Whether that's read-a-thons, DEAR time, or a day where kids read for your entire class without any lesson plan, make sure you are building that extended stamina.

You also need to build students' test-taking stamina. Start by giving them 30 minutes of independent practice daily where they apply testing strategies to test passages. Just as marathon runners practice short runs and build to longer runs up to the race, you need to do the same thing during your testing year. But the analogy for marathon runners holds true for building stamina in our test takers as well. Find a couple times in your schedule where you simulate extended test taking that mirror the length of the real test—but you don't need to do it a lot. If you do test simulations frequently, your students will burn out.

Building stamina for test taking is so important; in fact, in my experience, a student's ability to focus and apply test-taking strategies from beginning to end of a test makes them an outlier in test performance. Use the same strategies for building stamina during independent reading that are listed in Chapter 3 for building stamina during test preparation.

Standardized Stamina Strategies

Standardized tests are pretty much one of the least kid-friendly things out there. So we need to bring out all the bells and whistles to keep kids engaged. Here are even more, standardized test specific, stamina-building strategies developed by the reading teachers at KIPP Infinity: Joiselle, Amber, Sayuri, Mike, Annica, Ekene, Lynn, and Sheena. Thanks guys!

Musical Chairs
Play music for 10 minutes (or the length of time students should take reading and answering questions for one passage). When 10 minutes have elapsed, stop the music and students switch chairs. The purpose is for students to feel how long 10 minutes should be so their pacing becomes better. Some students rush or take too long on each passage.

Challenge
See who can get a higher score on the second half of the test versus the first half.

Test-a-Thon
The last student testing with great focus (with 80% or higher accuracy) gets an amazing prize.

Relay Race

Assign partners for a full-length test. The first partner starts while the second partner independently reads. The first partner hands over the baton (or the test) when they feel their stamina starts to wane and the second partner finishes it. Their goal is to get the highest combined score.

Push-Ups

Start each lesson with push-ups so kids get the sense of how reading stamina is like building a muscle. With practice they will get better at push-ups and extended test taking.

Turn and Talks

Keep the brain active for long-term reading by pausing and retelling with a friend.

Criteria Self-Assessment

Students design criteria for what active, focused reading looks like and then self-evaluate based on their own criteria.

Homeroom Challenge

Classes compete for the percentage that can successfully read the longest without looking up for a period/day/week.

Parent Night

Create a parents versus kids reading stamina competition.

IMMERSE STUDENTS IN THE TESTING
GENRE STARTING WEEK ONE

One of the components of an effective weekly reading test is to include a standardized test. I include this section of the test starting in week one. By including a standardized passage, I am getting real-time data as to how my kids would perform if the test were that day. I can analyze trends, note progress, and do O3 conferences based on that data.

I give each student a "secret number" and post the test scores. Each time students get 80% or higher on that section of the test, I write their number in green. If not, their number is in black. At first, there is a sea of black numbers. Over time, that chart grows green. It's pretty cool to look at with the whole class.

As mentioned, you will want to give your students several longer assessments to see how they do with a long standardized test in the same way that marathon runners do long runs before the real deal. Don't cluster them too closely or students will burn out. Most states offer past tests online.

RECOGNIZE LEVELED READING

What if your students can't read the standardized test because it's on their frustration level? When entering fifth grade, Sofia wasn't able to read (yet) a fifth grade level passage. Upon entering, she was on a first grade reading level; with Sofia's and our hard work, we wanted her on a fourth grade reading level by the end of the year. How is she going to apply the skills and test strategies I teach for standardized tests? This was a real concern when I taught fifth grade, as most of my students were far below reading level. And as you recall, I'm not a fan of giving kids texts on their frustration level. Therefore, we level our testing material by using state tests from lower grade levels. Although we don't have a 26 level gradient as we do in the A-Z continuum, we create three different levels. We use these levels on the standardized testing section that we include on our weekly tests. The grade kids receive on the differentiated test go into the gradebook. The closer we get to the test, the more we lift that scaffold so that students are applying the skills using grade level passages at least within two weeks of the test. Guided reading and shared reading also close the gap. During shared reading, students are exposed daily to grade-level or higher texts. Shared reading texts should be in a difficulty range similar to or greater than the state test.

DESIGN INTERVENTION GROUPS

Using data that you compile from test simulations, design a plan for how you are going to intervene with students. Groupings are based on what percentage of the class got an answer wrong, as shown in Table 12.1. They range from one-on-one work to reteaching the skill to the entire class.

Testing Skills

Identify which skills your students can do, and aren't doing yet, based on previous assessments. Then group students based on their needs. What skills do the tests teach? It depends by state, and even district, but the following are the most common:

1. Details
2. *All of the above* and *not* questions

Table 12.1 When to Reteach Based on How Many Students Mastered a Skill

Percentage of Students in Your Class That Got Strategy or Skill Wrong	What to Do
Less than 10% of your students get answer wrong	Conference during one-on-ones
11–20% of your students get answer wrong	Pull a small group during lunch
21–30% of your students get answer wrong	Spiral a couple times on do-nows next week and then retest following week
31–40% of your students get answer wrong	Spiral a couple times on do-nows, and include a homework solely dedicated to this skill
40+% get answer wrong	Reteach to the whole class with a new text

3. Sequencing

4. Author's purpose

5. Inference

6. Character

7. Cause and effect

8. Prediction

9. Fact and opinion

10. Main idea and summaries

11. Context clues

12. Author's craft

13. Figurative language

Instead of teaching each skill explicitly to the whole class during a test preparation unit, identify first which students need the explicit instruction. If 40% or more of your students aren't demonstrating mastery according to the sample tests you give, then teach it to the whole group. Otherwise, use the chart in Table 12.1 to determine how and when to teach which skills.

Skill Versus Strategy

If a student got a question wrong, don't assume that's because they can't do that skill. They could be struggling with stamina. Or they could be struggling by not using testing strategies such as reading all the answer choices before answering a question. In *A Teacher's Guide to Standardized Reading Tests*, Calkins, Montgomery, and Santman recommend meeting with students during a one-on-one and finding out why the students chose the answer.[92] Try these questions:

- Why did you choose this answer?
- Why didn't you choose this answer?
- Walk me through how you answered this question.
- What were you thinking when you wrote these answer choices?

DON'T WAIT 'TIL THE END

The highest predictor of reading achievement is extended independent reading. Therefore, avoid exclusively teaching to the test: it's definitely not kid-friendly, and it won't give you the results you, your kids, and their families want. However, I don't think you should wait to introduce reading test passages until a few weeks before the test. Just like with any genre, such as nonfiction, myths, poetry, and drama, students need multiple exposures. Here are ways I expose students to standardized passages throughout the year.

Include Standardized Tests Weekly

Instead of waiting until three weeks before the test to immerse your students in the genre of testing, incorporate a standardized test on each weekly test. If you include a passage on each weekly test, students will already have 20–30 passages with at least 10 or more hours of deliberate practice. Better yet, add daily do-nows for even more practice.

Do-Nows

Incorporate mini-standardized passages on do-nows. A do-now is an activity that students do right when they enter the room. Typically, do-nows should take five minutes with a few minutes for teachers to go over some answers. Don't take longer than a few minutes so you can maximize time for the lesson. Do-nows are an excellent way for you to reteach, remind, and reinforce throughout the year. Do-nows are a great tool for spiraling all sorts of things, as shown in Figure 12.1:

❑ Standardized test practice
❑ Routine reminders
❑ Vocabulary reinforcement
❑ Shout-outs to different students
❑ Reminders about upcoming binder checks
❑ Spiral review of strategies you taught from previous months

❏ Reinforcement of a strategy where 20–30% of students didn't demonstrate mastery

Do Now, Not Later

Directions: Answer each question in complete sentences when necessary. Use your neatest handwriting. Draw a heart above your last name. When you're done, take out your book and start reading.

Take That, and Rewind It Back

Write the letter of each literary device next to its example.
A. Simile   B. Personification   C. Metaphor
D. Allegory   E. Assonance

_____ Juan burned through his book like dry kindling in a campfire.

> Tracy was persistent last week and finished her 25th book!

Word to the Wise

Circle the word that is used incorrectly.

Reggie diligently plays the trumpet.
Jericho dilgented yesterday on his homework.

Write a nine-word sentence using the words aloof and assimilate.

Climb the Mountain, to College!

Contemplate your reading goals for the next week.

What's a genre that you are going to try during independent reading that you normally don't read?

_____

Where and when are you going to do most of your reading this weekend?

_____

Read the following excerpt from *Tangerine* by Edward Bloor and answer the question that follows. Underline the evidence in the passage that led you to your answer.

> I was standing at the back of a line of kids, waiting to board the bus for one of my first days at kindergarten. I would be accompanied by no one except Erik, my fifth-grade brother. But Erik did not accompany me for long. He was standing at the front of the school bus line with his fifth-grade friends when one of them turned, made a gesture, and called to me, "Hey, Eclipse Boy, how many fingers am I holding up?"

You can conclude that Erik's friends are doing what to the narrator? Use "because" in your answer.

Figure 12.1 Sample Do-Now

Teaching a reading test preparation follows the same *Reading Without Limits* guidelines, with a few tweaks. Be strategic, build stamina, and use data in order to intervene.

ADDITIONAL RESOURCES

1. Sample do-nows
2. Kid-friendly strategies for how to review do-nows
3. Ready-to-use test preparation unit plan

MILD, MEDIUM, SPICY NEXT-STEP SUGGESTIONS

	Mild	Medium	Spicy
Don't Change a Thing	Don't go crazy on test preparation. More practice doesn't equate to better test scores. Keep your test prep unit to one unit only.	Instead of giving kids standardized test practice for independent work, ask them to think like a test writer. Kids write their own standardized tests based on choice books they read. Then they put those tests with their finished choice books in a baggy back into the library. Then students who choose that book take their peer's test and if they do well on it, they get extra credit. My kids loved it.	Create a campaign like Think Blue or Got Pie where all staff participate. Put up incentivizing posters throughout the school to excite and motivate students.

	Mild	**Medium**	**Spicy**
Intervene	When starting an O3 conference based on test prep data, always ask your students why they chose the answer they did. It will provide a ton of insight into how they take tests.	There's a great resource called Hot Dots. It gives kids "magic pens" that light up when they get an answer right or buzz when they get an answer wrong. Great to use during O3 test preparation conferences.	Start pulling students during the first quarter based on data collected from the standardized test section of your weekly test. Pull kids who are in the minority that got a question wrong, i.e., five kids or fewer. If you can do that intervention as early as possible in the year, you will feel less stress as the test approaches.
Don't Wait 'til the End	Include weekly standardized tests (one passage) starting in the first quarter. Track the data.	Utilize do-nows by spiraling skills that 20–30% of your students didn't master based on weekly test data.	Using past state tests, give "real deal" simulations several times throughout the year to track stamina and progress.

FOR COACHES AND SCHOOL LEADERS

Schoolwide Incentive

During a staff professional development, split up your faculty in teams. It's their job to create a sell it campaign for test prep that they must present to the group. After each group presents, do a silent vote. The winning team gets a prize! This is how we came up with our Think Blue and Got Pie campaigns.

Buy Early

The materials that test preparation companies make are really helpful. Buy them early so teachers can use them for their weekly assessments. Avoid waiting until a month before the test to make purchases.

Read, Babies, Read

My favorite KIPP chant, written by Harriet Ball (Dave Levin's mentor):

> You gotta read baby read
>
> You gotta read baby read
>
> The more you read
>
> The more you know
>
> Knowledge is power
>
> And power is freedom
>
> And I want it!

The more your students read, the better they will do on the tests. Period. Research shows that the highest test performers read on average three hours a day. How much do your students read?

KEEPIN' IT REAL

Here are some problems that we faced when teaching standardized test preparation. Address the pitfalls in advance and I hope they won't happen to you!

Longer Units

We've played around a lot with the best, standardized test unit duration. For students new to the test, 15–20 class periods is ideal. For students who have done your fabulous unit before and are in an upper grade, do 10–12 lessons tops. Otherwise, students become less motivated.

Stress

The test is a stressful time for kids and for us. Remember that if you are stressed it will rub off on kids, as I've found from personal experience. Continue to stay positive and hopeful while still holding students accountable to grow goals. They are going to kick that test's butt!

TO SUM UP

- Teaching a standardized test unit is very similar to teaching any other unit. Follow the same principles.
- Build test-taking stamina.
- Recognize leveled reading.
- Start immersing students in the testing genre in week one. Do-nows are an effective way to immerse and spiral standardized tests. Incorporate standardized tests on your weekly assessments.
- It's essential that you create intervention groups, as there will be several students who need that small group support to master a skill that the rest of the class already mastered.

13

Testing 1, 2, 3 . . . Testing
Why We Don't Want Our Data, Like Our Laundry, to Pile Up

When I craft reading assessments, I follow a predictable structure that incorporates everything that I know I need to assess. This chapter shows in detail how to craft each of the following categories:

❑ Test this week's strategies with shared passage.
❑ Test this week's strategies with a passage students have never seen before.
❑ Spiral review content from the past month.
❑ Spiral review content from the past year.
❑ Incorporate standardized testing.
❑ Evaluate weekly vocabulary.
❑ End with a survey and self-assessment.

Also,

❑ Keep assessments kid-friendly.
❑ Don't let assessment logistics keep you from doing weekly assessments.

How often do you do your laundry? Do you let it go until it's overflowing or do you have a set weekly routine? My husband refuses to own more than seven pairs of socks. Maybe that's the reason why we do our laundry weekly! Our sock restriction keeps our laundry manageable. It's the same in our classrooms. Letting student knowledge pile up will be as laborious as letting your clothes pile up. The longer you wait to run the spin cycle, the longer it will be until you have fresh sheets, and the messier your hamper will be. Not testing frequently? Then your data, like your laundry, is piling up.

But it isn't just frequency that counts with assessments; as with laundry, we need to consider compartmentalizing as well. By compartmentalizing your assessments, you can track data overtime by category. Want to know how your students do on close reading strategies? Create a category on each assessment. Vocabulary? Category. Standardized testing? Category. You get the picture. Frequent assessments are essential in that they make teachers feel more powerful; knowledge is power, right? I will show that frequently assessing gives students more power as well. I remember a college class where I didn't receive any feedback until grades were due. Or I got grades every two months without feedback in between. I was leading myself blindly through the course. Without feedback, I didn't do as well as I could. Frequent assessment results are great feedback and therefore allow for powerful self-assessment.

TYPES OF READING ASSESSMENTS

Teachers constantly assess in their classrooms, and I've already introduced a few formative assessments that are essential in boosting reading achievement: checking for understanding, conferences, guided reading, and do-nows. This chapter will discuss summative weekly assessments.

Formative assessments are assessments *for* learning. They happen while learning is under way. Formative assessments include diagnostics (assessments that gauge what students know), all checks for understanding during lessons, and conferences. Formative assessments are not graded.

Table 13.1 Different *Reading Without Limits* Assessments

Formative (Not Graded)	Summative (Graded)
All classroom checks for understanding	Weekly assessment of week's objectives
Conferences	Assessing i-Think journals weekly or bi-weekly
Guided reading	Accountability for books read (end of book quizzes, reports, etcetera)
Do-nows	Running records

Summative assessments are assessments *of* learning. Summative assessments include quizzes, weekly tests, and standardized tests. They measure achievement status at a point in time, and sort students according to achievement for later intervention work; grades are later used for report card grading.

CRITERIA FOR A WEEKLY READING ASSESSMENT

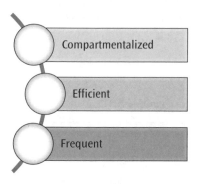

Figure 13.1 Criteria for a Weekly Assessment

When crafting summative assessments, there are three qualities I am looking for, as shown in Figure 13.1.

Compartmentalized

I want to have the same categories on my assessment so I can track a student's ability within that category over time. One essential component within a weekly assessment is assessing spiraled (or previously taught) material.

Efficient

Taking an assessment should be efficient and take one class period. I should be able to grade the assessments efficiently and consistently.

Frequent

Assessments should happen frequently. Both the students and I need to be on top of data in order to feel "powerful." It is for this reason that the best teachers assess at least every other Friday, if not every Friday.

I have just described the fundamental aspects of a *Reading Without Limits* assessment. Next I show how to put together a weekly (or bi-monthly) reading assessment that is compartmentalized, frequent, and efficient. Why test? Ultimately, you are helping students grow because you will be able to pinpoint exactly what they need. It also helps you revise your classroom instruction in order to address trends. Therefore, I believe you should keep tests simple and assess only the data you need. When I put together a weekly reading assessment, I include seven categories and no others. This is the data I need.

SHOW ME WHAT YOU KNOW (THIS WEEK'S STRATEGIES)

You've been collecting data all week: exit slips, listening to turn and talks, dipsticks, and reading conferences. It's essential to keep up summative checks for understanding because as the advocates of backwards planning, Grant Wiggins and Jay McTighe argue, the assessment of understanding is best done as a collection over time and not just one single event.[93] The end of week assessment is the icing on the cake. You get a snapshot of each student, have time to organize the data, and then can put a grade in your gradebook. For high school teachers with 200 students, you may not be able to analyze all students during the week. The end of week assessment allows you to get the data you need for every individual.

Use Shared Text

In order to assess whether or not students mastered what you taught, give them an excerpt from the shared text and have them apply the week's aims to that passage. Reading assessments should directly match your classroom's practice. Use an excerpt that you've shared before, ideally that week. That way, students who are below reading level will be able to access it. Keep the passage short—it should take the students less than a few minutes to read.

Assess Exactly What You Taught

After four or nine lessons, assess each of your daily objectives so you get frequent data. Write one test question per aim. You don't need to ask tons of questions—keep it efficient. Craft one question for each of your week's lessons, using that passage. Make use of different approaches in your questions, including graphic organizers, short responses, cloze, and matching. Mix it up to make testing less of a drag. Following is an abbreviated sample showing what I mean. The students were reading *The Watsons Go to Birmingham* while working on inferences derived from Common Core State Standard 1: *Read closely to determine what the text says explicitly and to make logical inferences from it; cite specific textual evidence when writing or speaking to support conclusions drawn from the text*. I included an excerpt at the beginning of the test. Then, I asked four questions (for the week's four aims), two of which are below.

1. **Read the two i-Think notes below. Why is the "Great Making More Inference" better than the "OK Making More Inference" (Tuesday's lesson)? Identify three reasons**.

   Great Making More Inference

   > Kenny is self-conscious about his wandering eye. He doesn't like to look at people head on so they won't see his eye. Also, he practices looking in the mirror trying to straighten his eye out. I think he's self-conscious because he feels different, and because his brother teases him.

   OK Making More Inference ☹:

   > I think that Kenny doesn't like his eye.

- _____
- _____
- _____

❏ Three *different* things are listed
❏ Reasons specifically reference Great Inference
❏ Reasons specifically reference OK Inference

2. **Reread the passage below. Draw a peace sign in the bottom right corner (I explain why I wrote that later in this chapter).**

Me and Joey cracked up, Byron kind of chuckled and Momma put her hand over her mouth. She did this whenever she was going to give a smile because she had a great big gap between her front teeth. If Momma thought something was funny, first you'd see her trying to keep her lips together to hide the gap, then, if the smile got to be too strong, you'd see the gap for a hot second before Momma's hand would come up to cover it, then she'd crack up too.

Using the criteria you listed in #2, create a *making more inference (Thursday's lesson).*
❏ Includes an inference that is not directly in the text
❏ Made more of the text by making a prediction
❏ Inference is supported by at least two details in the passage

Notice how

- I wrote down the day we did the lesson
- I asked a short answer question and a question that required students to make a list
- I included criteria for the answer

Criteria mean the exact elements that you believe make the skill exemplary. These criteria should be the exact same thing that you taught when you taught the lesson previously that week. See the next chapter for how to craft criteria.

I tested *exactly* what I taught the students that week using a text they've seen before. On Tuesday, we evaluated the difference between okay and great inferences. On Thursday students generated great inferences that had text support. If I test once a week, this first section includes four questions: one for each lesson. If I test bi-monthly, it includes nine questions: one for each lesson. I prefer the former; it's more efficient and effective.

For Struggling Readers: Create Specific Knowledge Goals and Provide Frequent, Specific Feedback

The two preceding indicators are key in raising achievement in struggling or disengaged learners. Design your assessment so that it is directly aligned to the knowledge goals (aims, learning objectives) that you taught in the week. Ensure that the knowledge goals are aligned to the same criteria that you taught. Then, using the criteria checklist, students will get immediate weekly feedback as to where they stand on the knowledge goals.

PLEASE, CAN I HAVE SOME MORE (THIS WEEK'S OBJECTIVES WITH AN UNFAMILIAR TEXT)

Use an Unfamiliar Text

Now that you have your students' data using a text they've seen before, you need to test them using an unfamiliar text to compare. Choose a passage that's leveled in the middle of your learners' abilities. For students who are far below the reading level, differentiate this part by inserting a different passage, but keep the questions and criteria the same. Finding short, leveled passages for this section of the assessment can be a pain. Consider going to www.greatleaps.com. This resource has a ton of short texts you can use.

Directions: Read the following excerpt from *Shiloh* by Phyllis Reynold Naylor. Shiloh, a small dog, has just arrived at the narrator's home.

> *"I looked that rabbit over good, Marty, and you won't find any buckshot in that thing," Dad says, buttering his bread. "I shot him in the neck."*
>
> *Somehow I wish he hadn't said that. I pushed the meat from one side of my plate to the other, through the sweet potatoes and back again.*
>
> *"Did it die right off?" I ask, knowing I can't eat at all unless it had.*
>
> *"Soon enough."*

1. **Circle the making more inference (Tuesday's lesson).**
   a. Marty and his father found bullets in the rabbit as they ate.
   b. Marty doesn't like eating rabbit.
   c. Marty feels guilty about eating the rabbit because he is worried that it may have suffered.
   ❏ A making more inference has textual evidence in at least two places

2. **Why won't the narrator eat until he finds out that the rabbit died instantly? (Thursday's lesson).**
   ❏ Includes an inference that is not directly in the text
   ❏ Made more of the text by making a prediction
   ❏ Inference is supported by at least two details in the passage

   Notice how

- My criteria for the making more inference in question 1 was the same criteria as the making more inference in question 2

- I assessed exactly what I taught on both Tuesday and Thursday (include a question for each day)
- I mixed up how I asked the questions by including multiple-choice so kids have variety. Mix it up for all grade levels!

After these two sections, students have the opportunity to show me whether or not they understood what I taught in two different ways: with a shared text and a new text. I stick to the data I need: to see whether or not students mastered what I taught this week. Don't be surprised if students don't do as well in Please, Can I Have Some More. By analyzing how they do in that section, you will know what you need to review or reteach.

REVIEW A FEW (SPIRALING CONTENT FROM LAST MONTH)

The weekly test also should include content that you taught in the past month. This content can include past objectives or vocabulary. Do not include a test of everything that you've taught in the past month. Choose two to three items.

In order to keep track of which content they are spiraling, great teachers make a tracking sheet. They list every strategy and literary term that they teach in the left-hand column. Then, each time it's reviewed on a do-now or test, they check it off. Remember the list of strategies in Chapter 2 that I recommended teaching in sequence? Create a tracking sheet listing those strategies and vocabulary that you teach at the beginning of the year (www.reading-without-limits.com has an example) and check away!

1. **Create a simile comparing our principal to one of the following (from the last unit):**

   A mountain   A river   A staircase

   ❑ Used simile comparison language
   ❑ Simile clearly shows what our principal and the thing shared in common

2. **Generate an open-ended question that you have about** *The Watsons Go to Birmingham* **(from four weeks ago):**
   ❑ Written in question format
   ❑ Question has potential for multiple answers

Notice how this section of the assessment is short. Spiral in a couple strategies or vocabulary terms that you taught in the past month. I like to copy and paste questions directly from do-nows or homework questions that I've already written. That saves me a ton of time.

TAKE THAT AND REWIND IT BACK (SPIRALING CONTENT FROM MONTHS OR EVEN YEARS BACK)

We have to review everything or we run the risk of forgetting. Test content from way back in the day, including from previous years. At KIPP Infinity, teachers exchanged jump drives that include all do-nows and assessments. That way, a sixth grade teacher has the fifth grade teacher's review work. She can copy and paste old questions into her do-nows or assessments keeping the knowledge fresh. Better Lesson is a great platform for sharing materials within a school or district. If you don't have the opportunity to do that, go back to the Common Core. Assess knowledge from a standard from one or two year's prior. Avoid randomly choosing strategies, vocabulary, or standards. Make sure to introduce the content during a do-now before you test it, so you have some sense of how kids are doing. After putting it on the weekly assessment, then you will know if kids need an old skill retaught.

1. **Draw the setting that you are currently in below:**

2. **Write a line of dialogue that a rat would say to a cat.**

I like to copy and paste a do-now from a previous year's class instead of rewriting the questions. That saves me a lot of time. Remember: keep it simple.

SOAR TO A FOUR (STANDARDIZED ASSESSMENTS)

In order to immerse students in standardized assessments, as the format is unlike the authentic learning that they are doing in *Reading Without Limits* reading, include one standardized passage with multiple-choice questions weekly starting the first week of school. It provides immediate data as to how students would perform on the standardized test if it were that week. Then chart their progress. One way is to purchase and download sample tests for the purpose of weekly reading assessments. Since there is such a high demand for test preparation, we are able to come by these materials cheaply and often get samples from the publishing companies. Include 10 minutes worth of standardized testing per assessment. The reason we don't include more than one passage is that we want the assessment to take one class period. We also want the assessment to be manageable to grade. There are times when students take longer standardized practice assessments, which I discuss in Chapter 12.

VOCABULARY

Don't forget to assess vocabulary! Chapter 10 shares the criteria for what to include in a weekly vocabulary assessment. Include this category in your larger general weekly assessment. Remember, when crafting a vocabulary assessment:

❑ **Start with Recall**: Ask questions that require students to identify a word's meaning.
❑ **Application**: Ask questions that push kids to apply each word's meaning.

316

❏ **Make It Kid-Friendly**: Instead of asking kids to simply write sentences, weave in opportunities to make it fun. For instance, *Write a sentence that includes the following words: bear, purse, diligent, and tree.*

❏ **Choice**: Instead of requiring students to answer all questions, give them places where they can choose which questions to answer.

❏ **Spiral**: Avoid including only this week's words.

SURVEY SAYS (SELF-ASSESSMENT)

This last section is a nice relief for kids once they turn to the final page. Last year I administered a test one-on-one to Jake each week. Jake was a fifth grader with a developmental disability who demonstrated high testing anxiety. We did the entire weekly test together one-on-one. Each week, as I sat watching him assess, when he turned to the last page, he smiled. Isn't that a nice way to end things? End the test with a survey, or self-assessment.

Including self-assessment where students reflect on their goals, what help they need, and what their next steps should be, makes a huge impact on student achievement. I can't stop pushing self-assessment, because the research is too strong. Research spanning decades concludes that strong achievement gains in student performance, according to standardized test data, occur when self-assessment is integral in your classroom. And very few interventions have the same level of impact on achievement as assessments for learning. According to John Hattie, who did meta-research on what factors lead to the greatest student achievement, using data from over a million students, the inclusion of self-assessment leads to the greatest amount of achievement. In fact, it was the number one indicator by a long shot. Self-assessment is so essential in our classrooms that I recommend including it on your weekly assessment.[94] Self-assessments do not count toward students' final grades.

Questions to ask on the survey so students can self-assess include

1. Star the question that you thought was the easiest. Circle the one that you thought was the most difficult.

2. (List week's learning aims) Which aim do you feel you most solidly mastered? For which do you need more help?

3. Write down your current conferencing goal. On a scale of 1–5, rate yourself on it.

4. What steps do you need to take (list three) in order to master your conference goal?

In addition, include general survey questions such as

1. What book are you dying to read next?

2. Did you get enough time to independently read in class this week?

3. How is at home reading going?

4. What's your current reading grow goal? On a scale of 1–5, do you think you met it?

5. What's one thing that you liked that I did this week? What's one thing that you wished I would stop doing?

Also, teachers like to include questions that build relationships, such as

1. What's one question that you want to know about me?

2. Who is your best friend? Why?

KEEP IT KID-FRIENDLY

We do the same format (all seven sections that I described above) once a week. It's important to also make assessments kid-friendly. Here are some ways that we like to spice it up.

Hidden Directives

Many kids don't read directions and that can be frustrating. Try putting hidden directives inside directions to see if kids are really reading directions. Did you notice the one I included on the sample test? "Include a peace sign in the bottom right hand corner." Another example is after the directions for a problem write, *Draw a heart above your last name*. These directions can be silly, like *Draw a picture of me in the right corner of this paper with a big hat*, or academic, like *Name three presidents from the twentieth century on the back of page two*.

Incorporate Choice

Want to really spice things up? Create two questions for each of your aims, and give kids the choice to choose which question they will answer. Make sure that the questions have similar difficulty level. Offering choice will maximize student comfort.

ASSESSMENT LOGISTICS TO CONSIDER

Assessments Take up Class Time

I am recommending that you administer tests once a week. For many of us, this represents 20% of total class time with students. But I recommend that students have more than one reading period a day with choice, guided, and shared reading. All too often teachers are harried trying to get through all the content that they have to teach. The approach of breadth over depth is harmful to lasting understanding, and the Common Core Standards, in response to breadth over depth, is slowing our curriculums down with 10 standards. Slow down your teaching by focusing on fewer reading strategies in order to address the 10 standards. By focusing on depth over breadth, dedicating 20% of your instructional time to assessments won't feel like a sacrifice; it will feel like the right step.

Grade the Tests Using Criteria for Success

Have you ever gone through a stack of 90 papers and as you near the bottom realized that you were grading harder with the first half of the papers? Oops. Or do you share grading with another teacher and sometimes question grading consistency? Including criteria for success will make grading consistent from beginning to end and teacher to teacher.

Track Data

As you grade the tests, keep a list of students who didn't achieve mastery for each of your skills. In the case of the truncated test above, the skills included

1. Making inferences
2. Supporting inferences with details
3. Simile
4. Open-ended question
5. Setting
6. Dialogue
7. Standardized test

Write down the names of kids who didn't demonstrate mastery for the skill and then create intervention groups based on the data as shown in Table 12.1. If the student got 80% of the questions related to that skill accurate, don't write down their name.

A template to track data that includes all suggested strategies and literary elements is available on www.reading-without-limits.com.

Sustainable Grading

Have 200 students? Teach five different content subjects? Can't imagine grading or creating a test with seven sections weekly? First, remember that each section is short. The test should take students about 45 minutes, or one class period, to complete. Also, the more frequently you test, the more targeted the test can be. Your tests won't have to be as complicated. Don't let your data, like your laundry, pile up. Still not possible? Here are some strategies that helped me:

❑ Start grading while the other classes are taking the test.
❑ If your school has clickers, have students click in their answers to multiple-choice questions. Clickers are an interactive tool that your school can purchase.
❑ Grade all of each section at once: grade all of section one, then section two, etcetera.

❏ For multiple choice questions, create an answer key on a transparency. Lay the transparency on top of the student's test. If the answers don't line up, they are wrong and you can quickly mark the test.

❏ Check out the mild suggestions below and apply them to your existing tests.

Then, after four (or nine) days, rinse and repeat by giving another assessment. If you do this each week, you will be meeting your kids' needs on so many different levels. You will be a data machine!

ADDITIONAL RESOURCES

1. Additional ideas to make your tests fun
2. Sample assessments for grades 3–10
3. Data tracking template with all strategies and literary elements aligned to Common Core Standards

MILD, MEDIUM, SPICY NEXT-STEP SUGGESTIONS

	Mild	Medium	Spicy
The Test	Start by adding hidden directives into your already existing tests. Make them funny with directions like, "Write your name backward and upside down in the heading."	Incorporate at least one test question that assesses each of the aims that you taught this week. In addition, lift a couple skills that you spiraled in do-nows for the week and include in your assessment.	Incorporate all seven sections and try to make it as kid-friendly as possible. Include growth mindset thought bubbles throughout the test like, "I am so proud of you for working hard!" Or "Your grit on this test is preparing you to become the best possible college student."

	Mild	**Medium**	**Spicy**
Grading	Worried about too much grading? Instead of administering weekly tests on your aims, give them twice a month. Then, on the other Fridays, give a multiple choice standardized or vocabulary assessment that can be automatically graded on scantrons or clickers. Eliminate the vocabulary and standardized test section from the other assessment.	Consider encouraging past students to help grade. They can earn "paychecks" where you take them out for frozen yogurt or allow time on your computer to go on Facebook.	Before grading the assessment, take it yourself, filling in an exemplary response for each answer. Use the criteria for success checklist to grade each answer. Compare student responses to your response.
Data Analysis	Keep a copy of a blank assessment. Each time a student gets a question wrong, jot their name down next to the question on the blank assessment.	Collect data on each skill using a tracking sheet. Create an action plan for how you will meet the needs of your kids through conferences, small groups, do-nows, homework, or reteaching.	Do this for homework. When you return the assessments, ask students to create a list of the different skills that they've mastered and the ones where they aren't there yet. Provide an exemplary, OK, and not great response for each assessment question. Ask students to self-assess which type of response they gave for each answer, then ask them to identify the criteria they needed to show in order to get the answer right. This will really boost evaluative self-assessment in your class.

KEEPIN' IT REAL

Here are some problems that we faced when doing weekly assessments. Address the pitfalls in advance and I hope they won't happen to you!

Include Criteria for Success on Tests

A common push back that I get from teachers is that by providing the criteria, I'm not truly assessing students' independent ability. In some ways that's true. At this point, I'm providing a scaffold for students because this is new knowledge and I want to know how they are doing at this point this week. I am assessing a grade level standard. By the following year, this same group of students will do much more sophisticated work with the same standard, and the criteria that I included on the test will be so ingrained in their memory that I won't need to include it. For instance, when we teach questioning first to our incoming group of fifth graders, we have to include putting a question mark at the end of the sentence as part of the criteria. By eighth grade, as students are questioning an author's intentions, that criteria would be silly. I include criteria for where my students are that week so I can measure that week's abilities. Including criteria for success shows students exactly how you will grade their response and it will allow consistent grading.

Grading

It's not easy to grade once a week. With weekly tests, you need to have a quick turnaround. If you wait too long, then you are testing soon after you returned your tests. The worst, and I've definitely been there, is when you have two week's worth of ungraded tests. If you find yourself in that situation, slow down weekly tests until you can get back into a grading routine. Ideally, tests given on Friday should be returned on Monday. I know, I know, teachers should definitely be paid more than we are!

Student Involvement

Do you want to get students to engage with their test grade? I often hear teachers get frustrated because they feel as if their students "don't care" about the low grades. That is probably due to fixed mindset. Try including a post-test reflection as part of your weekly homework. When you send home the weekly test to be signed by parents, ask students to make a goal for their next test, sharing what studying technique they will use. Post student progress in the classroom. Give each student a secret number and post weekly test scores in class.

Testing Overkill

Think testing once a week will make your kids hate school? It's just the opposite. Getting regular, bite-sized feedback is essential in building engagement. What kids don't like is not knowing how they are doing. They also don't like taking a super long unit test, and not getting the grade back for a couple weeks. Avoid overwhelming them with end of unit tests.

The Test Is Too Big

When you first try creating a test like I suggest, you might find that the test is too long to fit into one period. That's because you included too many questions in each section. Avoid overtesting the students. Only use data you need. The first and second sections should each have four questions. The sections that spiral content should only spiral a few content questions. Give one standardized test assessment to keep the test length fair. If vocabulary is making the test too long, try giving the vocabulary section as a quiz on a different day.

FOR COACHES AND SCHOOL LEADERS

Co-Grading

Offer to grade several tests as you meet with a reading teacher. If you find that grading is inconsistent, together rework the criteria for success so that it is specific, measurable, and clear.

Take the Test

Sit in on a reading test and take it. When the teacher posts the grades, she can put yours up on the bulletin board (if you score high points!) as well. Kids will get a kick out of it.

Analyze Data

Once a month, during a data meeting, co-analyze test results together.

FURTHER READING

Classroom Assessment for Student Learning by Richard Stiggins, Judith Arter, Jan Chappuis, and Stephen Chappuis

Driven by Data: A Practical Guide to Improve Instruction by Paul Bambrick-Santoyo[95]

TO SUM UP

- Assess once a week.
- Include questions for each objective that you taught, spiraled content, standardized immersion, vocabulary, and surveys.
- Make the assessment kid-friendly.
- Include criteria for success on your test to ensure consistent grading and expectations.
- When grading, perform trend analysis. Identify which skills you assessed, then determine how you will meet the needs of the students who didn't achieve mastery.
- Don't let assessment logistics keep you from doing weekly assessments.

PART 5

Putting It All Together

Planning a Lesson
Why Teaching Is Like Cooking

In this chapter I show that you get a lot of choices when cooking up a lesson plan. When writing a lesson plan

❑ Determine explicit criteria based on the aim.
❑ Follow the same predictable structure each day.
❑ Introduce the lesson by activating prior knowledge, sharing the purpose, and connecting to what students did yesterday.
❑ Teach with a read-aloud/think-aloud or close reading.
❑ Check for understanding throughout.
❑ Allow extended time for independent practice and reading (once it has been built).
❑ Don't forget to close out your lesson.

What's for dinner tonight? Something healthy? Comfort food? Something your five-year-old won't hate? To make dinner, you need a plan so you know what you're cooking. For instance, imagine tonight's **aim** or **objective** is to make a macrobiotic dinner. If I asked you to make a macrobiotic dinner, are you asking, "What the heck is macrobiotic?" Macrobiotic food's staple is whole grain with other supplements for balance. It has servings of beans, steamed vegetables, whole grains, and fermented soy or fish. It avoids processed food and most animal products. While you may think that sounds gross, our dinner **aim** is now clearer. That's because I provided the **criteria** (veggies, grain, and soy) for the macrobiotic dinner. My criteria for planning a lesson is to figure out the aim, set criteria, then make choices about the actual "ingredients" in the lesson.

Once you have the **aim** and **criteria** clear and precise, it's time to figure out what's going on the plate. Just like chefs determine which protein, vegetable, and starch they are serving, as teachers we also get tons of choices. Within the rest of the lesson template (**introduction, direct instruction, guided practice, independent practice, share, closing, and checks for understanding**)[96] there is *choice*. Scratch macrobiotic food. Our **aim** will be to make soul food instead! First, the **criteria**: include a meat dish (country fried steak, chicken, or fish), a side (black-eyed peas, sweet potatoes, or okra), greens (collard greens, turnip greens, or mustard greens), and bread (biscuits, cornbread, hushpuppies, or grits). Avoid eating only what's on your plate, as sharing is a big part of eating soul food. There are so many choices! We might have fried chicken with okra, collard greens, and grits, or fried oysters with black-eyed peas, mustard greens, and cornbread. Did I inspire any menus tonight? This chapter will show that you have a ton of choices when crafting a lesson plan, just as if you were putting together a soul food menu.

CREATE EXPLICIT CRITERIA BASED ON YOUR AIM

The first step in effective lesson planning is creating explicit criteria. After you've determined your aim, and before you write your lesson, first draft precise criteria.

Criteria

Remember the macrobiotic and soul food examples? Saphier, Gower, and Speca, authors of *The Skillful Teacher*, define criteria for success as "the qualities that must be present for performance and products to meet expectations and be deemed successful" (Saphier, Gower, and Speca, p. 278).[97] Macrobiotic food needs all of the components I described in order to be successful (whole grain, beans, steamed veggies, and fermented soy). No donuts. With that criteria, I can put together a macrobiotic dinner. Once your students know the criteria for your aim, they can start working to fulfill them.

Effective criteria . . .

- Describe the qualities of a successful product (i.e., what is a theme? character trait? important detail? What makes up macrobiotic food?)
- Shows what not to do (i.e., avoid processed food when eating macrobiotic)

Let's look at two examples in Table 14.1. One hits it right on, one doesn't.

The first example shows exactly what criteria should be: a clear description of the product that also includes what it isn't. The second example shows what criteria should not be. Spending time on the aim and criteria is really important. In fact, that's where I do most of my heavy lifting. First figure out what you want the kids to be able to do (the **aim**) and then define precisely what that is and isn't (the **criteria**).

> **For Struggling Readers: Create Specific Knowledge Goals**
>
> *Be specific as to what you want students to achieve by the end of the class period. Instead of asking your students to make inferences, say figure out what the author didn't say in the passage that led you to make an inference. Be specific, and struggling readers will know exactly what you want them to do.*

FOLLOW THE SAME PREDICTABLE STRUCTURE

As Lucy Calkins said in *The Art of Teaching Writing*, "the most creative environments in our society are not the kaleidoscopic environments in which everything is always changing and complex. They are, instead, the predictable and consistent ones—the scholar's library, the researcher's laboratory, the artist's studio. Each of these environments is deliberately

Table 14.1 Example and Non-Example of Criteria

	Aim	Criteria for the Aim
Yes	To determine themes	Themes: Arise from big ideas that you listed Are an author's statement about the world Are related to big ideas that span the book through the entire plot Include textual evidence from different parts of the book Do not include plot details. They are general statements. Are not one-word statements like "poverty" *Just by reading these criteria, you now know what to teach.*
No	To determine themes	1. Complete the sentence: ___ is/a theme in ___ because ___ 2. Answer includes a quote from the text 3. Answer explains how the quote proves your theme is accurate *What is the new information that the kids are learning? How to write a short answer? Using citations? How do they find a theme? What should they avoid? If we are unclear, the students will be unclear.*

kept *predictable* and *simple* because the work at hand and the changing interactions around that work are so predictable and complex" (Calkins, p. 32).[98] Predictable does not mean boring. By creating a predictable structure in your classroom, you are more likely going to get your readers into a state of flow.[99] Keep the routine from aim to share consistent so students can develop their own rhythms in your class.

To put together your lesson, follow a predictable routine. Below are the different categories within an effective lesson plan. www.reading-without-limits.com includes printable lesson plan templates for choice, shared, and guided reading that I hope you find helpful in your planning.

Introduce Your Lesson

The introduction takes one to two minutes and sets up your lesson. Here are different introduction strategies. I recommend choosing one or two per lesson.

Schema

Schema is information that you know about the world. For instance, do you know what a spanspek is? Spanspek has a minimal amount of calories and is in the same family as cucumber, squash, pumpkin, and gourd. Inside its rind there is a hollow cavity that contains seeds. Based on this definition, would spanspek make a good breakfast food? Not sure? Then look at an alternative definition. A spanspek is a rough-skinned cantaloupe native to South Africa. Now can you easily answer the question? By connecting to what you already know, or your schema, you are now able to answer the breakfast question: yes, spanspek makes a delicious breakfast food. Schema (what we know about the world, namely information about cantaloupe) taught us new information about spanspek. We know what cantaloupes are and we can envision a cantaloupe with a thick rind. Do the same thing in your lesson. Start with what your students know a lot about (kid and teenage stuff) and relate it to the new skill.[100]

Purpose of the Lesson

Summarize the lesson in one to two sentences. For instance, "Today we are going to build our playlist. Moving forward, we are going to spend time analyzing how the different texts relate to each other." Or "Today we are going to look at how themes take books from 'just a story' to something really deep and meaningful."

Connecting to What Students Did Yesterday

Lessons should include connections to past lessons. The purpose of the connection is to build academic schema. For instance, "Yesterday we were looking at character traits in dialogue. Today, we will be looking at character traits in another way. Authors leave lots of clues about traits and today we are going to find even more about our characters!" You can also ask students to remind you what you did yesterday in order to make it interactive.

Choose one or two introduction strategies and your lesson will be clearer and more meaningful. Avoid talking too much or your class will begin to snore. Keep your introduction to two minutes or less and remember to ask interactive questions.

Figure 14.1 Project the Text on the Board for Direct Instruction

Plan Direct Instruction (I Do/We Do)

Direct instruction is the part of the lesson where you are teaching new content. There are many ways to introduce new content in reading class. Here are some of my favorites that have been introduced in previous chapters:

❑ Read-aloud/think-aloud during choice or guided reading.
❑ Close reading during shared reading.
❑ Using scripts to show what to do and not to do for class discussions.

Check out sample lesson plans at www.reading-without-limits.com. Notice the back and forth interaction between the teacher and student, as passivity is something you really want to avoid.

GUIDED PRACTICE AND CHECKS FOR UNDERSTANDING (WE DO)

During direct instruction, you alone aren't doing all of the work. Stop several times to check for understanding. You are still guiding your readers during direct instruction. Then move into the next phase of the lesson, guided practice. During guided practice, you take more of a back seat and let your readers try the strategy in groups or alone while you give heavy guidance. Give students the opportunity to try the skill with you before launching to independent reading. Confer, ask questions, and fix misconceptions. Guided practice usually takes anywhere between two and ten minutes. During shared reading it can take much longer. Over the course of the book I've shared many different ways to check for student understanding during guided practice. A list of all the different types, from white boards to rotten tomatoes, are listed at www.reading-without-limits.com. Mix them up!

Time Check

So far we've covered the introduction, direct instruction, and guided practice. Don't forget timing. If you only get 60 minutes per class, then don't choose an extended introduction and guided practice. Keep the teaching part of your lesson short for lots of independent practice. In their book, *Switch*, Dan and Chip Heath explore the myriad ways small changes can make a big difference. In one instance they recount a famous cookie and radish study that backs up why checking the time is so important. In the study, two groups took part in a taste test. In the room was a plate of warm, gooey cookies and a bowl of radishes. Group one was told to eat the radishes and to not touch the cookies; group two was told to gobble up the cookies. Afterward, both groups were asked to solve a complicated puzzle, which unbeknownst to the participants was impossible. The purpose of the study was to measure how long people could persist in a difficult task. Those who had to resist the cookies lasted eight minutes on average before giving up. The cookie gobblers? Nineteen. Why did the cookie eaters last so much longer? We only get so much self-control reserve and self-control is exhaustible. The cookie abstainers used up all of their reserve while sadly nibbling radishes. The cookie eaters started their reserve during puzzle solving. If we use all of our students' reserves before independent practice either listening to a teacher drone on or doing arduous tasks for a long period of time, they won't have the stamina for extended independent reading. Next time you snap at your partner after a long day's work, let them know that you just ran out of self-control.[101]

INDEPENDENT READING (YOU DO)

It's our job to build lifelong readers. Lifelong readers *read*. Over time, build students' stamina so they can read their choice or assigned book for at least 30 minutes.

During independent reading, students are

❑ Deeply immersed in their books
❑ Following your stamina criteria or meeting assigned reading expectations
❑ Reading at a pace that meets their goal
❑ Following the magic ratio (not note-taking too little or too much unless they are doing close reading)
❑ Constantly reading *and* thinking in order to build deeper comprehension
❑ Demonstrating their thinking with i-Think notes, sticky notes, turn and talks, seminar, blogs, I Love Reading pages, or graphic organizers
❑ Getting immediate feedback from the teacher and implementing that feedback
❑ Talking about their book at designated times

During independent reading, you are

❑ Assessing that students mastered the aim by looking at their notes
❑ Conferencing with students one-on-one
❑ Doing halftime or racetrack conferences
❑ Checking that students are demonstrating proper stamina
❑ Responding to questions
❑ Looking for off-task behaviors like staring at a page, fidgeting, looking around, and helping students to refocus

Figure 14.2 Check in with
Students During
Independent Reading

- ❏ Praising effort
- ❏ Doing "the loop" to see that students are doing their assigned reading
- ❏ Recommending books
- ❏ Ensuring that students are following your reading routines

DON'T FORGET TO CLOSE OUT YOUR LESSONS

Closings

The closing is teacher centered and very quick. Studies show that people remember best what happens at the beginning and at the end of a lesson.[102] This is known as the serial position phenomenon. You need to capitalize on that, so do the following in your closing:

Two Sentence Summary

Summarize the lesson in two sentences or fewer. If you feel like you are adding new material at this point, that's a problem!

Challenge

While summing up, push kids to take action in their future. "Not only will you question the author, but question everything you see that has an author:

advertisements, movies, the Internet. Why did they write what they wrote? Don't be passive anymore. Be critical."

Repeat, Repeat, Repeat

Find a repetitive phrase and say it over and over. "When you don't understand, fix it. When you forget, fix it. When you get distracted, fix it."

Call and Response

Identify a closing one liner, say it, and then elicit it. "Visualize what you see by looking at all the details. Step into the scene each time there is a time shift and look at all the ____ (students respond "details"). Step into a scene each time there is a place shift and look at all the ____."

Share

Now it's time for kids to share all of the great thinking that they did! A share can happen with the whole group or in a turn and talk, or both. Sometimes I close first, sometimes I do the share first. Here are some share ideas. I like to mix it up.

Process Share

The process share checks how the process of learning went for the kids. Questions include

- What was tricky about today's aim?
- On a scale of 1–5, how did today's aim feel?
- What criteria were the easiest? What criteria were the most difficult?

Reflection Share

Reflection shares push kids to see how the aim helps them become better strategic readers. Questions include

- How can you use today's strategy in future reading?
- What did you learn about the text today due to today's strategy?

- How did today's strategy deepen your understanding?
- Of all the i-Think notes that you did today, which do you believe got you to the deepest level of thinking?
- How does today's aim help us love reading more? Improve our stamina?

Summarizers

Summarizers ask students to summarize the purpose of the aim. Summarizers include

- Draw a picture that represents today's aim.
- Write a haiku that represents today's aim.
- Summarize today's aim, starting with the letter O (the first letter of your crush's name, the last letter of your middle name, etcetera).
- Tweet a summary of today's aim in 140 characters.

Author's Chair

In this share, students share their i-Think notes. Then classmates give one piece of praise and one piece of feedback.

Awards

Students recommend something or someone from the text for an award like "Most Insidious Leader" (to develop vocabulary) or "Most Important Fact."[103]

Criteria for Success Evaluation

After the lesson is over, students exchange their i-Think journals with their partners. Using the criteria for success as a checklist, their partners grade their work.

Exit Slips

On a slip of paper, write a short text and ask students to demonstrate mastery of the day's aim using the text. Students can write another i-Think note, answer an open-ended question, or respond to multiple-choice questions. Collect, grade, and put in your grade book. Make sure to leave plenty of time for exit slips, at least five minutes.

Response Logs

Students at the end of class write down the key points they learned and the questions they still have. In addition, they self-assess their ability to do the lesson's aim. Then students identify what they still need to work on in order to meet the aim. Response logs are a great way to increase self-assessment in your classroom, and research shows self-assessment helps make profound gains in achievement.[104]

TO CONSIDER

As you plan, there are two things to consider on your back burner.

Pace Yourself

Find ways to trim time. For instance, if you are using media, have everything already cued up. Put papers on the desk before students enter the room. Have a student helper set up white boards and pens at the end of the previous class. If you cut down on transition time, that means more independent reading time!

Apply the Strategy Across Genres and Applications

After students have mastered a strategy, start teaching the same strategy with different genres. Ask them to try it using short and long texts. They can also apply the strategy they mastered in different situations, like partner books and book clubs. If you mix it up, it's more likely going to become a lifelong strategy.

ADDITIONAL RESOURCES

1. Ways to hook your students into the lesson
2. Lots of lesson plans
3. KIPP Infinity's 2010 reading scope and sequence of aims
4. Narrated think-aloud and close reading podcast that you can use in your classroom

MILD, MEDIUM, SPICY NEXT-STEP SUGGESTIONS

	Mild	**Medium**	**Spicy**
Criteria for Success (CFS)	Try incorporating CFS into one lesson plan a week as a start. Don't forget a non-example!	Have partners evaluate each other's work using CFS.	Incorporate CFS into daily lesson plans, post it on the board, and use it during assessments.
Pacing	In your lesson plans, preplan how long each section will take.	On your agenda, write out how long you want each part of your lesson to take so that the kids and you can see the pacing.	Assign a student with a stopwatch. Using the times that you put up on your agenda, teach them to hold up a sign when you only have one minute left.
Interactive	During your mini-lesson, allow students to turn and talk at least once. Listen in to partnerships and then share with the class one awesome thing you heard. Give students who need extra processing time the questions you want to ask in advance on a piece of paper.	Get a ball or stuffed animal and throw it to a student anytime you ask a question. Then, instead of you calling on students, they pass the ball to a raised hand.	Get Popsicle sticks and write the names of each student. During the lesson, pull sticks to ask questions. Try writing out the list of questions in advance. Give a student the list of questions that you plan to ask, and the student can be the teacher and ask the question.

KEEPIN' IT REAL

There are times when lesson planning didn't work for us. Here are some problems that have happened to us; now they won't happen to you!

Criteria

I've seen teachers list a dozen criteria for one lesson. If you have that many criteria, then your lesson is *too big*. Remember also that criteria are product based, meaning if you teach kids about theme, then the criteria are what make up a theme. See my example of ineffective criteria as an example of what not to do.

Introduction

Setting up the introduction of the lesson is very effective when it is quick, interactive, and engaging. Avoid sounding like the droning Charlie Brown teacher.

The Fine Line Between Direct and Guided Practice

Ensure that direct instruction is active instruction. That also means that you aren't blabbing during direct instruction but are purposefully and actively checking for understanding throughout. It's a common pitfall to overteach during direct instruction. That most likely means that your aim or criteria are too big and should be divided into separate lessons.

Pacing

Is your thirty minutes of independent reading looking more like three minutes? Then you need to rethink your recipe. You are making Beef Wellington, cassoulet, and a soufflé for your family—too complicated. For every soufflé that you make, the rest of the meal needs to be simple. If you have a pretty involved guided practice, then plan for the rest of the lesson to be short and sweet. Writing a lesson is a pacing negotiation, and you can't have each component be super complicated.

FOR COACHES AND SCHOOL LEADERS

Teacher to Student Talk Ratio

What is the ratio of teacher talk to student talk in your classrooms? How often are students participating? Do they participate in each part of the lesson? Brainstorm strategies with your team for how to make Q&A fun beyond just raising hands.

Pacing Help

For teachers who struggle with pacing, consider writing out how long each section of their lesson took. Then in the subsequent one on one, brainstorm together what parts could be taken out in order to increase independent reading.

TO SUM UP

- Spend time considering your criteria for success. Preplan exactly what you want your students to be able to do by the end of the lesson.
- Keep the routine of "I/We Do," "We Do," and "You Do" sacred and predictable each day. Model daily what you want your students to be able to do.
- Mix and match different introductions, guided practices, shares, and closings to keep your lessons fresh.
- Allow extended time for independent reading.
- Consider pacing and timing. If you have an intricately planned direct instruction, keep your guided practice simple.

15

Building the Reading Without Limits Program
Slow and Steady Wins the Race

All too often I see teachers trying to do too much, getting overwhelmed, and abandoning an approach all together. Instead, this chapter shows how you can intentionally incorporate all 12 *Reading Without Limits* elements into your program without becoming swamped. In order to do so, I will show that you should

❑ Start with the essentials and create predictable routines.
❑ Build when your class is ready.
❑ Spiral.

As a mother, I am reading many parenting books. One suggestion that holds true among all the books despite their differing philosophies is that mothers shouldn't try to be perfect. We shouldn't try to have perfectly prepared meals, perfectly clean kitchens, and perfect social lives. Just like teachers, parents have a lot of different things to juggle and it can get overwhelming pretty fast. The *Reading Without Limits* program also has many components to juggle. There are essential components that

I recommend introducing to your literacy program that will build lifelong readers. They include

1. Leveling students
2. Strategic reading
3. Choice reading
4. Shared reading
5. Guided reading
6. Targeted physical space
7. Intentional routines
8. Vocabulary
9. Conferences
10. Weekly assessments
11. Classroom discussion
12. Standardized test preparation

Teaching doesn't have to be a juggling act trying to squish in all 12 components at once perfectly in the same way parenting shouldn't be a juggling act. We would drop everything if that were the case, because if we try to do everything all at once perfectly it leads to things not being done well.

Instead, I recommend mindfully rolling out each of the essential program components into your classroom. We can choose when we roll out each of the elements into our classroom. Because we have that power, we can slowly and intentionally introduce new elements to our literacy program one at a time. I believe that slow and steady wins the race.

ROUTINIZE THE ESSENTIALS

In the beginning, prioritize routinizing what builds lifelong readers during choice and shared reading. It doesn't matter if that takes three weeks or an entire term. Your goal is to launch the *Reading Without Limits* program so that both you and students enter into a predictable routine. The question is: where should you start? I've divided the *Reading Without Limits* launch into three stages. Use the following as a checklist. Once all boxes are checked, it's time to move onto the next stage. Remember, there's no rush.

Stage One

The purpose of stage one is to introduce *Reading Without Limits* to your readers. You will launch choice reading, shared reading, vocabulary, and weekly assessments.

Stage One Choice Reading

First and foremost, assess your students' reading levels. I recommend using running records.

❑ Build a love of reading culture with an *intentional layout*. Set up a high-interest library. Get grow-goal and stamina charts up on the wall. Paint inspirational quotes. Send the message that your classroom is devoted to building lifelong readers.

❑ Launch choice reading. Explicitly teach *stamina habits*. Start building how many minutes the whole class and individual students can read. Revisit routines and expectations daily.

❑ Teach students how to strategically think as they read. Launch *read-aloud/think-alouds*. Start with whether or not books met their expectations, moving toward figuring it out and paraphrasing strategies. Launch a reading-is-thinking routine such as sticky notes or an i-Think journal. Try to launch only one thinking routine at this point.

In the beginning, a love of reading is probably the backbone of our class. My students feel a sense of ownership over their library. Throughout the year, they help me pick out books that they'd like for me to purchase for the library. We also do partner reading and make book recommendations for one another. We do cycles of reading in which partners will share a book and a next set of partners will share that book. This creates a buzz about a particular title and these books become part of a common language that we speak in class, a language that helps everyone develop a love for books and reading. If they don't love reading, they won't do reading that's slightly more difficult or dry. They need to love the idea of reading first and then teachers can pile on more difficult books and that love will get them through a book that maybe they didn't think they would enjoy at first.

—Sayuri

What's your goal? That students are reading for 30 minutes while in the flow. Don't rush it . . . they'll get there.

Stage One Shared Reading

Identify a text (short or long) that you want to use as a launch. I like starting with a short text. Make sure that you have a copy for each student.

Figure 15.1 Students Are in the Flow While Reading a Shared Text at KIPP NYC College Prep

❑ Teach shared text expectations including how to mark up the text and your expectations for questions and answers. Start building in active engagement activities like cold calling or Saphier's "The Envelope, Please."[105]

❑ Model strategic thinking, emphasizing figuring it out and paraphrasing.

What's your goal? When students are talking about the text they go back to the text, build off each others' thinking, and use figuring it out and paraphrasing strategies.

Stage One Vocabulary

❑ I recommend a vocabulary rotation that follows a Monday through Friday routine. Starting the first Monday, begin the rotation.

❑ After the launch, include intentional vocabulary homework extensions.

What's your goal? Vocabulary starts right away, and the routine itself doesn't build. Kids will be immersed in the routine starting day one, and the routine stays the same all year.

Stage One Assessments

Just like with vocabulary, start the routine of assessments the first week. Include all the different assessment categories I recommended.

❑ Teach students how to accurately self-assess using the student survey.

❑ Include a standardized assessment in the first test.

❑ After a couple weeks, determine your rhythm for grading and returning papers. Try not to hold on to their tests for more than four days.

What's your goal? You want to start the assessment routine. It's going to take students a couple weeks to get in the swing of the assessments and you might find that some students don't finish. Don't worry, they will in time. In the meantime, make sure that your assessments aren't too long.

BUILD WHEN YOU ARE READY

Once students and you are comfortable with stage one, then it's time to start adding components to your *Reading Without Limits* program. Notice that I don't suggest a particular amount of time for each stage—it completely depends on the needs of your individual classroom. Now that you are about to begin stage two, consider adding guided reading into your literacy program.

Stage Two

The purpose of stage two is to establish extended stamina and build in individualized feedback. Once that's established, you can integrate more components into the classroom.

Stage Two Choice Reading

- ❑ Once reading stamina is at 15 minutes, build in racetrack and halftime conferences.
- ❑ Set up comfortable reading spots.
- ❑ Review any and all routines.
- ❑ Launch at-home reading expectations.

What's your goal? Students are reading comfortably for 15 minutes, maintaining your expectations for reading routines, and you've started using real-time data to inform their daily reading.

Stage Two Shared Reading

- ❑ Apply the same strategies you taught with the first text with several new types of texts, which can include different genres or text lengths.
- ❑ Demonstrate cognitive empathy.
- ❑ Scaffold shared reading if it's on a student's frustration level.

Figure 15.2 Model Your Thinking with a Read-Aloud/Think-Aloud

- ❑ Incorporate "playing soccer" as you question students.

What's your goal? You want to show students that the strategies you teach apply to all types of texts. Students should be getting better at going back to the text and pushing each other's thinking. Now that all of your students are leveled, you are also mindful of differentiating shared reading when necessary.

Stage Two Guided Reading

❑ Once students are leveled, start guided reading.
❑ Keep to a consistent schedule where you meet with students during the same time and at the same place.
❑ Set up copies of guided reading texts for all levels before beginning.
❑ Show students how to read aloud without distracting others.
❑ Share the importance of growth over achievement.

What's your goal? Now that all students have been leveled, you can start guided reading. Make sure that all logistics are in place before you begin. Share the guided reading routine with students and the reason that guided reading is so important.

❑ Continue vocabulary and weekly assessments.

Stage Three

Stage three integrates all effective teaching strategies from *Reading Without Limits*. (I didn't list them all in the list that follows.) The point is that by this stage, *Reading Without Limits* has become routine, and now you can integrate the more sophisticated elements of the program.

Stage Three Choice Reading

❑ Incorporate a new type of reading-is-thinking routine like I Love Reading pages or blogs.

❑ Once students are reading for 30 minutes, start one-on-one conferences. Give each student their own grow goal. Build routines so grow goals are a real part of your classroom.

❑ Develop routines around partner reading, playlists, or book clubs.

❑ Continue teaching strategic reading, moving down the list of suggested strategies to teach.

Figure 15.3 Allow Students Choice for Independent Reading

What's your goal? By stage three, *Reading Without Limits* is in place. Your biggest goal is to continue modeling strategies that good readers use while also teaching stamina. At this point, reteach content that you taught at the beginning of the year throughout the latter half of the year to ensure that students apply the strategies independently once they leave your classroom and become lifelong readers.

Stage Three Strategic Reading

❑ Continue using a variety of text lengths and genres.

❑ Once students are reading for 30 minutes during choice reading, launch assigned reading (in class and at home) expectations.

❑ Try questioning hierarchy.

❑ Launch classroom discussions.

❑ As students become more comfortable figuring it out and paraphrasing, start pushing students to unpack implied meanings during close reading.

What's your goal? Students are applying close reading strategies with you, and independently during assigned reading. Texts become increasingly difficult as student levels increase. Since you've taught more strategies at this point, you are able to spiral all sorts of strategies as you question. Don't forget to incorporate a plenty of short, nonfiction texts.

Stage Three Guided Reading

❑ By now it's probably time to reassess and regroup. Reassess every six to eight weeks.
❑ Enlist the help of other teachers for guided reading and leveling readers.

Your biggest goal at this point is to be part of a sustainable routine so that guided reading is a reality. Doing guided reading all by yourself isn't something I recommend. Enlist the support of other teachers.

❑ Continue vocabulary and weekly assessments.

SPIRAL

Spiraling refers to reteaching, reviewing, and reinforcing. If we want our students to apply what we teach as lifelong habits, then we need to return to them again and again and again.

Do Now

I like to start each class with a do-now, which is essentially a brief, focused activity. You can spiral anything and everything in a do-now. Incorporate material that you covered last month, or even last year! Remember to keep it short. Kids shouldn't spend more than five minutes on a do-now.

Remind and Reteach

I can't get enough of this strategy from Roxeann Kriete's *The Morning Meeting Book*. It works as a spiraling tool for anything. I use the remind and reteach strategy as my go-to strategy for classroom management. I use it right when class starts ("Who can remind me what materials we need for class?"), in the middle ("Xavier, I noticed you are trying a different genre book.") to the end of class ("Who can remind me of our assigned reading expectations?").[106]

Use Scripts

Scripts are a great spiraling tool if you want to show students what you *do* want to see, and what you *don't* want to see. I love to share scripts when reinforcing a routine. They also work for reviewing classroom discussion expectations.

Rolling out *Reading Without Limits* is a fluid process. There are no necessary benchmarks to check off by the end of each month. Those curricular timetables ignore that we are all working with completely different student populations. If you find that your students are on stage one longer than your colleague's students next door, that doesn't mean that you are doing something wrong (it might mean you are doing something right!). What you are doing with your students is still incredibly rigorous and building critical thinking. In fact, if you follow the suggested goals, rigor should be starting *week one*. Avoid moving forward too quickly, and continue to impress upon your students the importance of building lifelong reading.

ADDITIONAL RESOURCES

1. Making-it-visible posters that you can use for each stage
2. Lessons for launching different routines, including i-Think journals and assigned reading
3. Self-assessments that both you and your students can use to see if the class is ready to move onto the next stage

MILD, MEDIUM, SPICY NEXT-STEP SUGGESTIONS

	Mild	**Medium**	**Spicy**
Stages One, Two, and Three	Give students self-assessments based on the criteria of the stage. Once your class has self-assessed that they are mastering the stage's goals, move to the next stage.	Create a predictable structure that you follow daily. For instance, Do-now Direct instruction Guided practice Independent reading Share Vocabulary	Ask a colleague to visit your classroom, looking for the stage's particular goals. Request critical feedback in ways you can work toward meeting the stage's goals.
Spiral	During shared reading, ask questions that spiral strategies you taught from the previous two weeks.	Include a do-now at the start of each class.	At the end of each term, spend a couple weeks reteaching the strategies that you taught that term.

KEEPIN' IT REAL

There are times when rolling out *Reading Without Limits* didn't work for us. Here are some problems that have happened to us; now they won't happen to you!

The Honeymoon Period

All too often I see teachers pushing kids' stamina during the "honeymoon period" (that first couple weeks of school). Then the teacher gets frustrated because bad habits start to break down great stamina. Avoid moving kids too quickly through routines just because they are being "well-behaved." Slow and steady wins the race.

Losing the Standards in the Process

One great thing about the Common Core is that they allow for flexibility and can be applied in many different ways. Take for instance the standard that students should always go back to the text with their thinking. That's a standard you should be assessing no matter what stage you are in: one, two, or three. Even if you are moving slowly through the stages, that doesn't mean that you are dropping the standards.

Too Much, Too Fast

The biggest pitfall I see is teachers trying too many innovations without realizing it. The best way to get a temperature check as to whether or not you are moving too quickly is to monitor your students. Are the routines in their muscle memories? Are they demonstrating mastery for most of your objectives? If the answer is no, you are probably moving too quickly.

FOR COACHES AND SCHOOL LEADERS

Moving Too Fast

As school administrators, we feel the burden of "getting through" the curriculum. Then we put teachers on a pacing calendar. Rigor doesn't equate to covering more content. The Common Core, in an effort to alleviate schools' emphasizing breadth over depth, has narrowed our reading standards down to 10. Within those standards, several standards overlap. One of the most common complaints I hear from teachers is that the curriculum asks them to move too quickly, and students (and teachers) are being left behind in the dust. Instead, prioritize maximizing student mastery of the Common Core Standards. By following the rollout of stages one through three of the *Reading Beyond Limits* program, you will be able to do just that.

TO SUM UP

- Start slowly by building choice and shared reading. Create predictable routines, and don't pile on too many components.
- Build when your class is ready. If your class isn't ready, then reteach routines.
- Even if your class is running like a well-oiled machine, continue to spiral your expectations so routines stay consistent for the entire school year.

Appendix A
List of Children's and Young Adult Texts Referenced and Recommended

Elementary
1. *Amber Brown Is Green with Envy* by Paula Danziger
2. *Amelia to Zora: 26 Women Who Changed the World* by Cynthia Chin-Lee
3. Bone Series by Jeff Smith
4. *Bud, Not Buddy* by Christopher Paul Curtis
5. *Chrysanthemum* by Kevin Henkes
6. *Dream: A Tale of Wonder, Wisdom & Wishes* by Susan V. Bosa
7. *Fast Sam, Cool Clyde and Stuff* by Walter Dean Myers
8. *Frindle* by Andrew Clements
9. Goosebumps Series by R. L. Stein
10. Harry Potter Series by J. K. Rowling
11. *Harvesting Hope: The Story of Cesar Chavez* by Kathleen Krull
12. *Hatchet* by Gary Paulsen
13. *Henry and Mudge* by Cynthia Rylant
14. *Holes* by Louis Sachar
15. *How Much Is a Million?* by David M. Schwartz

16. Junie B. Jones series by Barbara Park
17. *Maniac Magee* by Jerry Spinelli
18. Marvin Redpost series by Louis Sachar
19. *Matilda* by Roald Dahl
20. *My Name Is Maria Isabel* by Alma Flor Ada
21. *National Geographic for Kids* magazine
22. *Poop* by Nicola Davies
23. *Revolting Rhymes* by Roald Dahl
24. *Sadako and the Thousand Paper Cranes* by Eleanor Coer
25. Seymour Simon's books
26. *Seedfolks* by Paul Fleischman
27. *Tar Beach* by Faith Ringgold
28. *The Lightning Thief* by Rick Riordan
29. *Shiloh* by Phyllis Reynold Naylor
30. *The Sneetches and Other Stories* by Dr. Seuss
31. *The True Story of the Three Little Pigs* by Jon Scieszka
32. *The Watsons Go to Birmingham* by Christopher Paul Curtis
33. *Tiger Rising* by Kate DiCamillo

Middle

1. *Thirteen Stories That Capture the Agony and Ecstasy of Being Thirteen* by James Howe
2. *145th Street Stories* by Walter Dean Myers
3. "All Summer in One Day" by Ray Bradbury
4. *Anne Frank: The Diary of a Young Girl* by Anne Frank
5. *Are You There God? It's Me, Margaret* by Judy Blume
6. *A Wrinkle in Time* by Madeleine L'Engle
7. *Catcher in the Rye* by J. D. Salinger
8. *Chains* by Laurie Halse Anderson
9. *D'Aulaires' Book of Greek Myths* by Ingri d'Aulaire and Edgar Parin d'Aulaire
10. *Dragon's Blood* by Jane Yolen

11. DK Eye Witness Series

12. *First Crossing: Stories About Teen Immigrants* by Laila Lipski

13. *Hoops* by Walter Dean Myers

14. *Local News* by Gary Soto

15. *Lord of the Flies* by William Golding

16. *My Life in Dog Years* by Gary Paulsen

17. *My Sister's Keeper* by Jodi Picoult

18. *Naruto* by Masashi Kishimoto

19. "Priscilla and the Wimps" by Richard Peck

20. "Raymond's Run" by Toni Cade Bambara

21. *Roll of Thunder, Hear My Cry* by Mildred D. Taylor

22. *Shortcut* by Donald Crews

23. *Tangerine* by Edward Bloor

24. "Thank You, Ma'am" by Langston Hughes

25. *The Chronicles of Vladimir Tod* by Heather Brewer

26. *The Chocolate War* by Robert Cormier

27. *The Devil's Arithmetic* by Jane Yolen

28. *The Giver* by Lois Lowry

29. *The House on Mango Street* by Sandra Cisneros

30. *The Hunger Games* by Suzanne Collins

31. *The Laramie Project* by Moisés Kaufman

32. *The Outsiders* by S.E. Hinton

33. "The Road Not Taken" by Robert Frost

34. The Shadow Children Series by Margaret Peterson Haddix

35. *The Vampire Diaries* by L.J. Smith

36. *To Kill a Mockingbird* by Harper Lee

37. *Tomorrow, When the War Began* by John Marsden

38. *Twilight* by Stephenie Meyer

High

1. *Antigone* by Sophocles

2. *A Raisin in the Sun* by Lorraine Hansberry

3. "Because I Could Not Stop for Death" by Emily Dickinson
4. *Black Boy* by Richard Wright
5. *Brief Moment in the Life of Angus Bethune* by Chris Crutcher
6. *Collapse* by Jared M. Diamond
7. *Common Sense* by Thomas Paine
8. *Cool Salsa: Bilingual Poems on Growing Up Hispanic in the United States* edited by Lori Marie Carlson
9. *Destination Unexpected* by Donald Gallo
10. *Fahrenheit 451* by Ray Bradbury
11. *From the Notebooks of Melanin Sun* by Jacqueline Woodson
12. "Hope, Despair and Memory" by Elie Wiesel
13. *Interpreter of Maladies* by Jhumpa Lahiri
14. *Jane Eyre* by Charlotte Bronte
15. *King Lear* by William Shakespeare
16. *Letter from a Birmingham Jail* by Dr. Martin Luther King
17. *Macbeth* by William Shakespeare
18. Malcolm Gladwell's books
19. Maya Angelou's poetry and memoirs
20. *A Midsummer's Night Dream* by William Shakespeare
21. "Moonbeam Dawson and the Killer Bear" by Jean Davies Okimoto
22. *Narrative of the Life of Frederick Douglas, an American Slave* by Frederick Douglas
23. *Night* by Elie Wiesel
24. *Of Mice and Men* by John Steinbeck
25. *Pride and Prejudice* by Jane Austen
26. *Rising Voices: Writings of Young Native Americans* compiled by Arlene Hirschfelder
27. Tennessee Williams's plays
28. *The Autobiography of Malcolm X* by Malcolm X
29. The Gettysburg Address by Abraham Lincoln
30. "The Gift of the Magi" by O. Henry
31. *Their Eyes Were Watching God* by Zora Neale Hurston

32. "The Lottery" by Shirley Jackson
33. *The Joy Luck Club* by Amy Tan
34. "The Most Dangerous Game" by Richard Connell
35. *The Road* by Cormac McCarthy
36. *Things Fall Apart* by Chinua Achebe
37. Trial of Socrates by Plato
38. *Walden* by Henry David Thoreau
39. *Warriors Don't Cry: A Searing Memoir of the Battle to Integrate Little Rock's Central High* by Melba Pattillo Beals

References

ACT. "Reading Between the Lines: What the ACT Reveals About College Readiness in Reading." [www.act.org/research/policymakers/pdf/reading_report.pdf]. 2006.

Anderson, Jenny. "From Finland—an Interesting School-Reform Model." *New York Times*, December 12, 2011: 2.

Anderson, Richard C., and William E. Nagy. "The Vocabulary Conundrum." *American Educator* 16 (1992): 44–47.

Applebee, Arthur, Judith Langer, Martin Nystrand, and Andrew Gamoran. "Discussion-Based Approaches to Developing Understanding: Classroom Instruction and Student Performance in Middle School and High School English." *American Education Research Journal* 40, no. 3 (September 2003): 685–730.

Bambrick-Santoyo, Paul. *Driven by Data: A Practical Guide to Improve Instruction*. San Francisco, California: Jossey-Bass, 2010.

Barthes, R. *Image-Music-Text*. New York, New York: Hill and Wang, 1986.

Beck, Isabel L., and Margaret G. McKeown. *Conditions of Vocabulary Acquisition*. Vol. 2, in *Handbook of Reading Research,* by R. Barr, M. Kamil, P. Mosenthal, and P. D. Pearson, 789–814. New York, New York: Longman, 1991.

Beck, Isabel L., and Margaret G. McKeown. "Text Talk: Capturing the Benefits of Readaloud Experiences for Young Children." *The Reading Teacher*, no. 55 (2001): 10–20.

Beck, Isabel L., Margaret G. McKeown, and Linda Kucan. *Bringing Words to Life: Robust Vocabulary Instruction*. New York, New York: Guilford, 2002.

Beers, Kylene. *When Kids Can't Read: What Teachers Can Do*. Portsmouth, New Hampshire: Heinemann, 2003.

Black, Paul, and Wiliam, Dylan. "Inside the Black Box: Raising Standards Through Classroom Assessment." *Phi Delta Kappan* 80, no. 2 (1998): 139–148.

Bloom, Benjamin. "Taxonomy of Educational Objectives: The Classifications of Educational Goals." Edited by Green Longmans. *Handbook I Cognitive Domain*, 1956.

Bloom, Benjamin, "The Search for Methods of Group Instruction as Effective as One to One Tutoring." *Educational Leadership* 41, no. 8 (1984): 4–17.

Caine, Renate N., and Geoffrey Caine. *Education on the Edge of Possibility*. Alexandria, Virginia: ASCD, 1997.

Calkins, Lucy McCormick. *The Art of Teaching Writing*. Portsmouth, New Hampshire: Heinemann, 1986.

Calkins, Lucy McCormick. *The Art of Teaching Reading*. New York, New York: Addison-Wesley Educational Publishers, 2001.

Calkins, Lucy McCormick, Kate Montgomery, and Donna Santman. *A Teacher's Guide to Standardized Reading Tests: Knowledge Is Power*. Portsmouth, New Hampshire: Heinemann, 1998.

Chatzky, Jean. "Trick Yourself into Saving Money." *More Magazine*, June 28, 2011.

Clark, Ron. *The Essential 55: An Award-Winning Educator's Rules for Discovering the Successful Student in Every Child*. New York, New York: Hyperion, 2003.

Clay, Marie. *Becoming Literate: The Construction of Inner Control*. Portsmouth, New Hampshire: Heinemann, 1991.

Clay, Marie. *An Observation Survey of Early Literacy Achievement*. Portsmouth, New Hampshire: Heinemann, 1993.

Cohen, Gillian. "Why Is It Difficult to Put Names to Faces?" *The British Journal of Psychology*, vol. 81 (August 1990): 287–297.

Common Core State Standards for English Language Arts & History/ Social Studies, Science, and Technological Subjects. Standards, National Governors Association and the Council of Chief State School Officers, 2010.

Csikszentmihalyi, Mihaly. "Mihaly Csikszentmihalyi on Flow." Monterey, California: TED Talks, 2004.

Csikszentmihalyi, Mihaly. *Flow: The Psychology of Optimal Experience*. New York, New York: Harper Perennial Modern Classics, 2008.

Cunningham, Anne E., and Keith E. Stanovich. "What Reading Does for the Mind." *American Educator*, no. 22 (1998): 8–15.

Daniels, Harvey. *Literature Circles: Voice and Choice in the Student-Centered Classroom*. Vol. 1. Portland, Maine: Stenhouse, 1994.

Daniels, Harvey, and Stephanie Harvey. *Inquiry Circles in Action*. Portsmouth, New Hampshire: Heinemann, 2009.

Dweck, Carol. *Self Theories: Their Role in Personality, Motivation and Development*. Philadelphia, Pennsylvania: Psychology Press, 2001.

Ericsson, K. Anders, Ralf Th. Kramp, and Clemens Tesch-Romer. "The Role of Deliberate Practice in the Acquisition of Expert Performance." *Psychological Review*, no. 100 (1993): 363–406.

Fischer, Edmond H. "Edmond H. Fischer—Autobiography." *Nobelprize.org*. 1992. http://nobelprize.org/nobel_prizes/medicine/laureates/1992/fischer-autobio.html (accessed August 12, 2011).

Fisher, Douglas, and Nancy Frey. *Improving Adolescent Literacy: Strategies at Work*. Upper Saddle River, New Jersey: Pearson/Merrill/Prentice Hall, 2004.

Foer, Joshua. *Moonwalking with Einstein*. New York, New York: The Penguin Press, 2011.

Fram, Alan. "One in Four Read No Books Last Year." *The Washington Post*. August 21, 2007. http://www.washingtonpost.com/wp-dyn/content/article/2007/08/21/AR200708210 1045.html.

Fuchs, Lynn, Douglas Fuchs, and Pamela Burish. "Peer-Assisted Learning Strategies: An Evidence-Based Practice to Promote Reading Achievement." *Learning Disabilities Research and Practice* 15, no. 2 (2000): 85–91.

Gambrell, Linda, Barbara Kapinus, and Robert Wilson. "Using Mental Imagery and Summarization to Achieve Independence in Comprehension." *Journal of Reading*, no. 30 (1987): 638–642.

Gawande, Atul. "Should Everyone Have a Coach?" *The New Yorker*, October 3, 2011: 44–53.

Gee, James. *What Videogames Have to Teach Us About Learning and Literacy*. New York, New York: Palgrave Macmillan, 2003.

"Getting Started with Great Books in the Classroom," 2005, http://www.greatbooks.org /tutorial/index.html

Gunning, Thomas. *Building Literacy in the Content Areas*. Boston, Massachusetts: Pearson Education, 2003.

Gunning, Thomas. *Developing Higher-Level Literacy in All Students*. Boston, Massachusetts: Pearson, 2008.

Gunning, Thomas. *Creating Literacy Instruction For All Students in Grades 4–8*. Vol. 3. 3 vols. Boston, Massachusetts: Pearson Education Inc., 2012.

Guthrie, John T., and Marcia H. Davis. "Motivating Struggling Readers in Middle School Through an Engagement Model of Classroom Practice." *Reading and Writing Quarterly (Taylor & Francis)* 19 (2003): 59–85.

Hart, Betty, and Todd Risley. *Meaningful Experiences in the Everyday Experiences of Young American Children*. Baltimore: Brookes Publishing Company, 1995.

Hattie, John. *Visible Learning for Teachers: Maximizing Impact on Learning*. New York, New York: Routledge, 2012.

Heath, Chip, and Dan Heath. *Made to Stick: Why Some Ideas Survive and Others Die*. New York, New York: Random House, 2008.

Heath, Chip, and Dan Heath. *Switch: How to Change Things When Change Is Hard*. New York, New York: Random House, 2011.

Helstrup, Tore. "Serial Position Phenomenon: Memory for Acts, Contents and Spatial Position Patterns." *Scandinavian Journal of Psychology*, no. 25 (1984): 133–146.

Herman, Patricia A., Richard C. Anderson, P. David Pearson, and William E. Nagy. "Incidental Acquisition of Word Meanings from Expositions with Varied Text Features." *Reading Research Quarterly*, no. 23 (1987): 263–284.

Heward, William L., Ralph Gardner, Rodney A. Cavanaugh, Frances H. Courson, Teresa A. Grossi, and Patricia M. Barbetta. "Everyone Participates in This Class: Using Response Cards to Increase Active Student Response." *Teaching Exceptional Children* 28, no. 2 (1996): 4–10.

Higbee, Kenneth L. *Your Memory: How It Works and How to Improve It*. New York, New York: Marlowe & Company, 1977.

Hillocks, George. "Toward a Hierarchy of Skills in the Comprehension of Literature." *English Journal*, no. 69 (March 1980): 54–59.

Hotz, Robert Lee. "A Wandering Mind Heads Straight Toward Insight." *Wall Street Journal*, 2010.

Iyengar, Sheena, and Mark Lepper. "When Choice Is Demotivating: Can One Desire Too Much of a Good Thing?" *Journal of Personality and Social Psychology*. Vol. 79, No. 6 (2000): 995–1006.

Jago, Carol. *With Rigor for All: Meeting Common Core Standards for Reading Literature*. Portsmouth, New Hampshire: Heinemann, 2011.

Jensen, Eric. *Teaching with the Brain in Mind*. Alexandria, Virginia: ASCD, 1998.

Kamil, Michael. *Adolescents and Literacy Reading for the 21st Century*. Alliance for Excellent Education, 2003.

King, Martin Luther. "The Negro Is Your Brother." *The Atlantic Monthly* 212, no. 2 (August 1963): 78–88.

Krashen, Stephen. *Every Person a Reader: An Alternative to the California Task Force Report on Reading*. Culver City, California: Language Education Associates, 1996.

Krashen, Stephen. *The Power of Reading: Insights from Research*. Portsmouth, New Hampshire: Heinemann, 2004.

Kriete, Roxann. *The Morning Meeting Book*. Turners Halls, Massachusetts: Northeast Foundation for Children, 2002.

Lehr, Fran, Jean Osborn, and Elfrieda H. Hiebert. *A Focus on Vocabulary*. Pacific Resources for Education and Learning, Honolulu: Regional Educational Laboratory, 2004.

Lemov, Doug. *Teach Like a Champion: 49 Techniques That Put Students on the Path to College*. San Francisco, California: Jossey-Bass, 2010.

Lyman, Frank T. "The Responsive Classroom Discussion: The Inclusion of All Students." In *Mainstreaming Digest*, by A. Anderson, 109–113. College Park, Maryland: University of Maryland Press, 1981.

Marzano, Robert, and Debra Pickering. *Building Academic Vocabulary Teacher's Manual*. Alexandria, Virginia: ASCD, 2005.

Matz, Eddie. "Saviormetrics." *ESPN the Magazine*. March 2, 2012. http://espn.go.com /mlb/story/_/id/7602264/oakland-brandon-mccarthy-writing-moneyball-next-chapter -reinventing-analytics-espn-magazine (accessed March 2, 2012).

McWeeny, Kathyrn H., Andrew W. Young, Dennis Hay, and Andrew Ellis. "Putting Names to Faces." *British Journal of Psychology*, no. 78 (1987): 143–146.

Medina, John. *Brain Rules: 12 Principles for Surviving and Thriving at Work, Home and School*. Seattle, Washington: Pear Press, 2008.

Miller, Donalyn. *The Book Whisperer*. San Francisco, California: Jossey-Bass, 2009.

Miller, George, and Patricia Gildea. "How Children Learn Words." *Scientific American*, no. 27 (1987): 94–99.

Nash, Rose. *NTC's Dictionary of Spanish Cognates: Thematically Organized*. Lincolnwood, Illinois: NTC Publishing Group, 1997.

"Northern Ireland Curriculum," Belfast, Ireland: A PMB Publication, 2007. http://www.nicurriculum.org.uk/docs/key_stage_3/ALTM-KS3.pdf.

Patterson, James. "How to Get Your Kid to Be a Fanatic Reader." *CNN*. September 28, 2011. http://edition.cnn.com/2011/09/28/opinion/patterson-kids-reading/index.html.

Patterson, Kerry, Joseph Grenny, David Maxfield, Ron McMillan, and Al Switzler. *Influencer: The Power to Change Anything*. New York, New York: McGraw-Hill, 2008.

Pinnell, Gay Su, and Irene Fountas. *Word Matters: Teaching Phonics and Spelling in Reading/Writing Classrooms*. Portsmouth, New Hampshire: Heinemann, 1998.

Pinnell, Gay Su, and Irene Fountas. *Readers and Writers: Teaching Comprehension, Genre and Content Literacy*. Portsmouth, New Hampshire: Heinemann, 2001.

Pinnell, Gay Su, and Irene Fountas. Research Base for Guided Reading as an Instructional Support. Scholastic, 2010.

Resnick, L. B. "Making America Smarter." *Education Week* June 1999: 38–40.

Rivera, Diego. "The Flower Carrier," oil and tempura on Masonite, c. 1935 (Museum of Modern Art, San Francisco).

Robb, Laura. "Multiple Texts: Multiple Opportunities for Teaching and Learning." *Voices from the Middle* 9.4 (May 2002): 28–32.

Robb, Laura. *Teaching Reading in Social Studies, Science and Math*. New York, New York: Scholastic, 2003.

Rodriguez, Michael C. "The Role of Classroom Assessment in Student Performance on TIMSS." *Applied Measurement in Education* 17, no. 1 (2004): 1–24.

Rowe, Mary Budd. "Wait-Time as Rewards and Instructional Variables, Their Influence in Language, Logic and Fate Control." Paper presented at the National Association for Research in Science Teaching. Chicago, 1972.

Samuels, S. J., and Yi-Chen Wu. *How the Amount of Time Spent on Independent Reading Affects Reading Achievement*. Educational Psychology, University of Minnesota, Minneapolis:2003.

Santman, Donna. *Shades of Meaning: Comprehension and Interpretation in Middle School*. Portsmouth, New Hampshire: Heinemann, 2005.

Saphier, Jon, and Mary Ann Haley. *Activators*. Anton, Massachusetts: Research for Better Teaching, 1993.

Saphier, Jon, Mary Ann Haley Speca, and Robert Gower. *The Skillful Teacher,* 6th edition. Anton, Massachusetts: Research for Better Teaching, 2008.

Schwartz, Barry. *The Paradox of Choice: Why More Is Less*. New York, New York: Harper Collins, 2004.

Scott, J. A., and William E. Nagy. "Understanding the Definitions of Unfamiliar Words." *Reading Research Quarterly*, no. 32 (1997): 184–200.

Snow, Catherine E., Susan Burns, and Peg Griffin. *Preventing Reading Difficulties in Young Children*. Washington D.C.: National Academy Press, 1998.

Stahl, Steven A. *Vocabulary Development*. Cambridge, Massachusetts: Brookline Books, 1999.

Stiggins, Richard J., Judith A. Arter, Jan Chappuis, and Stephen Chappuis. *Classroom Assessment for Student Achievement: Doing It Right—Using It Well*. Portland, Oregon: Assessment Training Institute, Inc., 2004.

Taylor, Barbara, and Barbara Frye. "Time Spent Reading and Reading Growth." *American Educational Research Journal* 27, no. 2 (1990): 351–362.

"Test Your Awareness: You Do the Test," http://www.youtube.com/watch?v=Ahg69 cgoay4.

Tierney, Robert J., and John E. Readance. *Reading Strategies and Practices: A Compendium*. 5. Boston, Massachusetts: Allyn & Bacon, 2000.

Tovani, Cris. *I Read It, But I Don't Get It*. Portland, Maine: Stenhouse Publishers, 2000.

Tovani, Cris. *Do I Really Have to Teach Reading?* Portland, Maine: Stenhouse Publishers, 2004.

Vaughn, James E. "Review: Fine Structure of Synaptogenesis in the Vertebrate Central Nervous System." *Synapse*, no. 3 (1989): 255–285.

Vygotsky, Lev. *Thought and Language*. Edited by E. Hankmann and G. Vakar. Translated by E. Hanfmann and G. Vakar. Cambridge, Massachusetts: MIT Press, 1962.

Vygotsky, Lev. *The Development of Higher Psychological Processes*. Cambridge, Massachusetts: Harvard University Press, 1978.

Weick, Karl. "Small Wins: Redefining the Scale of Social Problems." *American Psychologist* 39, no. 1 (January 1984): 40–49.

White, Thomas G., Joanne Sowell, and Alice Yanagihara. "Teaching Elementary Students to Use Word-Part Clues." *The Reading Teacher*, no. 42 (1989): 302–309.

Wiggins, Grant P., and Jay McTighe. *Understanding by Design*. Alexandria, Virginia: Association for Supervision and Curriculum Development, 1998.

Wilhelm, Jeffrey. *Strategic Reading: Guiding Students to Lifelong Literacy 6–12*. Portsmouth, New Hampshire: Heinemann, 2001.

Wilhelm, Jeffrey. *Action Strategies for Deepening Comprehension: Role Plays, Text Structure Tableaux, Talking Statues, and Other Enrichment Techniques That Engage Students with Text*. New York, New York: Scholastic Professional Resources, 2002.

Wilhelm, Jeffrey. *You Gotta BE the Book*. New York, New York: Teachers College Press, 2008.

Wilhelm, Jeffrey, and Michael Smith. *Reading Don't Fix No Chevys: Literacy in the Lives of Young Men*. Portsmouth, New Hampshire: Heinemann, 2002.

Wong, Harry, and Rosemary T. Wong. *The First Days of School: How to Be an Effective Teacher*. Mountain View, California: Harry K. Wong Publications, 2009.

Zimmerman, Susan. "Bring the Joy Back to Reading." In *Comprehension Going Forward*, edited by Harvey "Smokey" Daniels, 34–45. Portsmouth, New Hampshire: Heinemann, 2011.

Notes

NOTES TO PREFACE

1. John T. Guthrie and Marcia H. Davis. "Motivating Struggling Readers in Middle School Through an Engagement Model of Classroom Practice." *Reading and Writing Quarterly* (Taylor & Francis) 19 (2003): 59–85; Renate N. Caine and Geoffrey Caine. *Education on the Edge of Possibility*. Alexandria, Virginia: ASCD, 1997; Eric Jensen. *Teaching with the Brain in Mind*. Alexandria, Virginia: ASCD, 1998.

NOTES TO INTRODUCTION

2. ACT. "Reading Between the Lines: What the ACT Reveals About College Readiness in Reading." (www.act.org/research/policymakers/pdf/reading_report.pdf, 2006); Jenny Anderson. "From Finland—an Interesting School-Reform Model." *New York Times*, December 12, 2011: 2; Catherine E. Snow, Susan Burns, and Peg Griffin. *Preventing Reading Difficulties in Young Children*. (Washington D.C.: National Academy Press, 1998).

3. Michael Kamil. *Adolescents and Literacy Reading for the 21st Century* (Alliance for Excellent Education, 2003); Catherine E. Snow, Susan Burns, and Peg Griffin, *Preventing Reading Difficulties in Young Children*.

4. S. J. Samuels and Yi-Chen Wu. *How the Amount of Time Spent on Independent Reading Affects Reading Achievement*. Educational Psychology, University of Minnesota,

Minneapolis: Minnesota (2003); Barbara Taylor and Barbara Frye. "Time Spent Reading and Reading Growth." *American Educational Research Journal* 27, no. 2 (1990): 351–362; Thomas Gunning. *Developing Higher-Level Literacy in All Students.* (Boston, Massachusetts: Pearson, 2008); Stephen Krashen. *The Power of Reading: Insights from Research.* (Portsmouth, New Hampshire: Heinemann, 2004).

5. James Patterson. "How to Get Your Kid to Be a Fanatic Reader." *CNN.* September 28, 2011. http://edition.cnn.com/2011/09/28/opinion/patterson-kids-reading/index.html.

6. Common Core State Standards for English Language Arts & History/Social Studies, Science, and Technological Subjects, Appendix A: Research Supporting Key Elements of the Standards. Standards, National Governors Association and the Council of Chief State School Officers, 2010.

7. Arthur Applebee, Judith Langer, Martin Nystrand, and Andrew Gamoran. "Discussion-Based Approaches to Developing Understanding: Classroom Instruction and Student Performance in Middle School and High School English." *American Education Research Journal* 40, no. 3 (September 2003): 685–730.

8. Gay Su Pinnell, and Irene Fountas. *Research Base for Guided Reading as an Instructional Support.* (Scholastic, 2010).

9. K. Anders Ericcson, Ralf Th. Kramp, and Clemens Tesch-Romer. "The Role of Deliberate Practice in the Acquisition of Expert Performance." *Psychological Review*, no. 100 (1993): 363–406.

10. K. Anders Ericcson, Ralf Th. Kramp, and Clemens Tesch-Romer. "The Role of Deliberate Practice in the Acquisition of Expert Performance."

CHAPTER 1

11. Thomas Gunning. *Creating Literacy Instruction for All Students in Grades 4–8.* (Vol. 3. Boston, Massachusetts: Pearson Education Inc, 2012).

12. Lev Vygotsky. *The Development of Higher Psychological Processes.* Cambridge, Massachusetts: Harvard University Press, 1978.

13. Marie Clay. *An Observation Survey of Early Literacy Achievement.* (Portsmouth, New Hampshire: Heinemann, 1993).

14. Carol Dweck. *Self Theories: Their Role in Personality, Motivation and Development.* (Philadelphia, Pennsylvania: Psychology Press, 2001).

15. Marie Clay. *Becoming Literate: The Construction of Inner Control.* (Portsmouth, New Hampshire: Heinemann, 1991).

CHAPTER 2

16. James Gee. *What Videogames Have to Teach Us About Learning and Literacy.* (New York, New York: Palgrave Macmillan, 2003).

17. Susan Zimmerman. "Bring the Joy Back to Reading." In *Comprehension Going Forward*, edited by Harvey "Smokey" Daniels, 34–45. (Portsmouth, New Hampshire: Heinemann, 2011).

18. James E Vaugn. "Review: Fine Structure of Synaptogenesis in the Vertebrate Central Nervous System." *Synapse*, no. 3 (1989): 255–285.

19. Harvey Daniels and Stephanie Harvey. *Inquiry Circles in Action.* (Portsmouth, New Hampshire: Heinemann, 2009).

20. Jeffrey Wilhelm. *You Gotta BE the Book.* (New York, New York: Teachers College Press, 2008).

21. Kerry Patterson, Joseph Grenny, David Maxfield, Ron McMillan, and Al Switzler. *Influencer: The Power to Change Anything*. (New York, New York: McGraw-Hill, 2008).

22. Jon Saphier, Mary-Ann Haley Speca, and Robert Gower. *The Skillful Teacher*, 6th ed. (Anton, Massachusetts: Research for Better Teaching, 2008).

23. Mary Budd Rowe. "Wait-Time as Rewards and Instructional Variables, Their Influence in Language, Logic and Fate Control." *Paper presented at the National Association for Research in Science Teaching.* Chicago (1972).

24. Doug Lemov. *Teach Like a Champion: 49 Techniques That Put Students on the Path to College.* (San Francisco, California: Jossey-Bass, 2010).

25. William L. Heward, Ralph Gardner, Rodney A. Cavanaugh, Frances H. Courson, Teresa A. Grossi, and Patricia M. Barbetta "Everyone Participates in This Class: Using Response Cards to Increase Active Student Response." *Teaching Exceptional Children* 28, no. 2 (1996): 4–10.

26. Jon Saphier, Mary-Ann Haley Speca, and Robert Gower, *The Skillful Teacher*.

27. Gillian Cohen. "Why Is It Difficult to Put Names to Faces?" *The British Journal of Psychology*, vol. 81 (August 1990): 287–297.

28. Kathyrn H. McWeeney, Andrew W. Young, Dennis Hay, and Andrew Ellis. "Putting Names to Faces." *British Journal of Psychology*, no. 78 (1987): 143–146.

CHAPTER 3

29. Stephen Krashen. *The Power of Reading: Insights from Research.*

30. K. Anders Ericcson, Ralf Th. Kramp, and Clemens Tesch-Romer, "The Role of Deliberate Practice in the Acquisition of Expert Performance."

31. Benjamin Bloom. "The Search for Methods of Group Instruction as Effective as One to One Tutoring." *Educational Leadership* 41, no. 8 (1984): 4–17; Paul Black and Wiliam Dylan. "Inside the Black Box: Raising Standards Through Classroom Assessment." *Phi Delta Kappan* 80, no. 2 (1998): 139–148; Michael C. Rodriguez. "The Role of Classroom Assessment in Student Performance on TIMSS." *Applied Measurement in Education* 17, no. 1 (2004): 1–24.

32. Roxann Kriete. *The Morning Meeting Book.* (Turners Halls, Massachusetts: Northeast Foundation for Children, 2002).

33. Lucy McCormick Calkins. *The Art of Teaching Reading.* (New York, New York: Addison-Wesley Educational Publishers, 2001).

34. Jean Chatzky. "Trick Yourself into Saving Money." *More Magazine*, June 28, 2011.

35. Alan Fram. "One in Four Read No Books Last Year." *The Washington Post.* August 21, 2007; Carol Dweck. *Self Theories: Their Role in Personality, Motivation and Development.*

36. Jeffrey Wilhelm and Michael Smith. *Reading Don't Fix No Chevys: Literacy in the Lives of Young Men.* (Portsmouth, New Hampshire: Heinemann, 2002).

37. Schwartz, Barry. *The Paradox of Choice: Why More Is Less.* New York, New York: Harper Collins, 2004; Sheena Iyengar and Mark Lepper. "When Choice is Demotivating: Can One Desire Too Much of a Good Thing?" *Journal of Personality and Social Psychology.* Vol. 79, No. 6 (2000): 995–1006

38. Donalyn Miller. *The Book Whisperer.* (San Francisco, California: Jossey-Bass, 2009).

39. Mihaly Csikszentmihalyi. *Flow: The Psychology of Optimal Experience.* (New York, New York: Harper Perennial Modern Classics, 2008).

40. Laura Robb. "Multiple Texts: Multiple Opportunities for Teaching and Learning." *Voices from the Middle 9.4*, (May 2002): 28–32.

41. Lynn Fuchs, Douglas Fuchs, and Pamela Burish. "Peer-Assisted Learning Strategies: An Evidence-Based Practice to Promote Reading Achievement." *Learning Disabilities Research and Practice* 15, no. 2 (2000): 85–91.

42. Lucy McCormick Calkins, *The Art of Teaching Reading*.

43. Joshua Foer. *Moonwalking with Einstein*. (New York, New York: The Penguin Press, 2011).

44. Cris Tovani. *Do I Really Have to Teach Reading?* (Portland, Maine: Stenhouse Publishers, 2004).

45. John Medina, *Brain Rules: 12 Principles for Surviving and Thriving at Work, Home and School*. (Seattle, Washington: Pear Press, 2008).

46. Tovani, Cris. *I Read It, But I Don't Get It*. (Portland, Maine: Stenhouse, 2000).

CHAPTER 4

47. Lev Vygotsky. *Thought and Language*. Edited by E. Hankmann and G. Vakar. Translated by E. Hanfmann and G. Vakar. (Cambridge, Massachusetts: MIT Press, 1962); Carol Jago, *With Rigor for All: Meeting Common Core Standards for Reading Literature*. (Portsmouth, New Hampshire: Heinemann, 2011); ACT. "Reading Between the Lines: What the ACT Reveals About College Readiness in Reading."

48. George Hillocks. "Toward a Hierarchy of Skills in the Comprehension of Literature." *English Journal*, no. 69 (March 1980): 54–59; Benjamin Bloom, "Taxonomy of Educational Objectives: The Classifications of Educational Goals." Edited by Green Longmans. *Handbook I: Cognitive Domain*, (1956).

49. Martin Luther King. "The Negro Is Your Brother." *The Atlantic Monthly* 212, no. 2 (August 1963): 78–88.

50. Thomas Gunning, *Developing Higher-Level Literacy in All Students*. (Boston, Massachusetts: Pearson, 2008); George Hillocks. "Toward a Hierarchy of Skills in the Comprehension of Literature." *English Journal*, no. 69 (March 1980): 54–59.

51. Lauren Resnick. "Making America Smarter." *Education Week* (June 1999): 38–40.

52. Donna Santman. *Shades of Meaning: Comprehension and Interpretation in Middle School*. (Portsmouth, New Hampshire: Heinemann, 2005).

53. Carol Jago. *With Rigor for All: Meeting Common Core Standards for Reading Literature*.

54. Kylene Beers. *When Kids Can't Read: What Teachers Can Do*. (Portsmouth, New Hampshire: Heinemann, 2003).

CHAPTER 5

55. K. Anders Ericsson, Ralf Th. Kramp, and Clemens Tesch-Romer. "The Role of Deliberate Practice in the Acquisition of Expert Performance."

56. Lev Vygotsky, *Thought and Language.*

57. Irene Fountas, and Gay Su Pinnell. *Word Matters: Teaching Phonics and Spelling in the Reading/Writing Classroom.* (Portsmouth, New Hampshire: Heinemann, 1998).

58. Roxann Kriette, *The Morning Meeting Book.*

CHAPTER 7

59. John Medina, *Brain Rules: 12 Principles for Surviving and Thriving at Work, Home and School.*

60. Atul Gawande. "Should Everyone Have a Coach?" *The New Yorker*, October 3, 2011: 44–53.

61. Kenneth L. Higbee. *Your Memory: How it Works and How to Improve It.* (New York, New York: Marlowe & Company, 1977).

62. Roxann Kriete, *The Morning Meeting Book*; John Medina, *Brain Rules: 12 Principles for Surviving and Thriving at Work, Home and School.*

63. Lucy McCormick Calkins, *The Art of Teaching Reading.*

64. Frank T. Lyman. "The Responsive Classroom Discussion: The Inclusion of All Students." In *Mainstreaming Digest*, by A. Anderson, 109–113. (College Park, Maryland: University of Maryland Press, 1981).

65. Harry Wong and Rosemary T. Wong. *The First Days of School: How to Be an Effective Teacher.* (Mountain View, California: Harry K. Wong Publications, 2009).

66. Ron Clark. *The Essential 55: An Award-Winning Educator's Rules for Discovering the Successful Student in Every Child.* (New York, New York: Hyperion, 2003).

CHAPTER 8

67. Eddie Matz. "Saviormetrics." *ESPN the Magazine.* March 2, 2012.

CHAPTER 9

68. Robert Lee Hotz. "A Wandering Mind Heads Straight Toward Insight." *Wall Street Journal*, 2010; Edmond H. Fischer, "Edmond H. Fischer—Autobiography." Nobelprize.org. 1992.

69. Karl Weick. "Small Wins: Redefining the Scale of Social Problems." *American Psychologist* 39, no. 1 (January 1984): 40–49.

70. Chip Heath and Dan Heath. *Made to Stick: Why Some Ideas Survive and Others Die.* (New York, New York: Random House, 2008).

CHAPTER 10

71. Betty Hart and Todd Risley. *Meaningful Experiences in the Everyday Experiences of Young American Children.* (Baltimore, Maryland: Brookes Publishing Company, 1995)

72. Patricia A. Herman, Richard C. Anderson, P. David. Pearson, and William E. Nagy. "Incidental Acquisition of Word Meanings from Expositions with Varied Text Features." Reading Research Quarterly, no. 23 (1987): 263–284; George Miller and Patricia Gildea. "How Children Learn Words." *Scientific American*, no. 27 (1987): 94–99; Anne Cunningham and Keith E. Stanovich. "What Reading Does for the Mind." *American Educator*, no. 22 (1998): 8–15; Richard C. Anderson and William E. Nagy. "The Vocabulary Conundrum." *American Educator* 16 (1992): 44–47; Isabel L. Beck and Margaret G. McKeown. "Conditions of Vocabulary Acquisition." Vol. 2, in *Handbook of Reading Research*, by R. Barr, M. Kamil, P. Mosenthal, and P. D. Pearson, 789–814. (New York, New York: Longman, 1991); Fran Lehr, Jean Osborn, and Elfrieda H. Hiebert. *A Focus on Vocabulary. Pacific Resources for Education and Learning.* (Honolulu: Regional Educational Laboratory, 2004).

73. Fran Lehr, Jean Osborn, and Elfrieda H. Hiebert. *A Focus on Vocabulary.*

74. Robert Marzano and Debra Pickering. *Building Academic Vocabulary Teacher's Manual.* (Alexandria, Virginia: ASCD, 2005).

75. Isabel L. Beck, Margaret G. McKeown, and Linda Kucan. *Bringing Words to Life: Robust Vocabulary Instruction.* (New York, New York: Guilford, 2002).

76. Thomas G. White, Joanne Sowell, and Alice Yanagihara. "Teaching Elementary Students to Use Word-Part Clues." *The Reading Teacher*, no. 42 (1989): 302–309.

77. Fran Lehr, Jean Osborn, and Elfrieda H. Hiebert. *A Focus on Vocabulary;* Thomas G. White, Joanne Sowell, and Alice Yanagihara. "Teaching Elementary Students to Use Word-Part Clues." *The Reading Teacher*, no. 42 (1989): 302–309; Steven A. Stahl. *Vocabulary Development.* (Cambridge, Massachusetts: Brookline Books, 1999).

78. Isabel L. Beck, Margaret G. McKeown, and Linda Kucan. *Bringing Words to Life: Robust Vocabulary Instruction;* Robert Marzano and Debra Pickering. *Building Academic Vocabulary Teacher's Manual.*

79. Robert Marzano and Debra Pickering, *Building Academic Vocabulary Teacher's Manual.*

80. Rose Nash. *NTC's Dictionary of Spanish Cognates: Thematically Organized.* Lincolnwood, Illinois: NTC Publishing Group, 1997; Fran Lehr, Jean Osborn, and Elfrieda H. Hiebert, *A Focus on Vocabulary.*

81. Fran Lehr, Jean Osborn, and Elfrieda H. Hiebert. *A Focus on Vocabulary.*

82. J. A. Scott and William E. Nagy. "Understanding the Definitions of Unfamiliar Words." *Reading Research Quarterly*, no. 32 (1997): 184–200; Fran Lehr, Jean Osborn, and Elfrieda H. Hiebert, *A Focus on Vocabulary.*

83. Isabel L. Beck and Margaret G. McKeown. "Text Talk: Capturing the Benefits of Readaloud Experiences for Young Children." *The Reading Teacher*, no. 55 (2001): 10–20.

CHAPTER 11

84. "Getting Started with Great Books in the Classroom." 2005, http://www.greatbooks.org/tutorial/index.html

85. Harvey Daniels. *Literature Circles: Voice and Choice in the Student-Centered Classroom.* Vol. 1. (Portland, Maine: Stenhouse, 1994).

86. Donna Santman. *Shades of Meaning: Comprehension and Interpretation in Middle School.*

87. "Northern Ireland Curriculum. "A PMB Publication, 2007. http://www.nicurriculum.org.uk/docs/key_stage_3/ALTM-KS3.pdf

CHAPTER 12

88. Stephen Krashen. *The Power of Reading: Insights from Research*.

89. Stephen Krashen. *Every Person a Reader: An Alternative to the California Task Force Report on Reading*. (Culver City, California: Language Education Associates, 1996).

90. Lucy McCormick Calkins, Kate Montgomery, and Donna Santman. *A Teacher's Guide to Standardized Reading Tests: Knowledge Is Power*. (Portsmouth, New Hampshire: Heinemann, 1998).

91. Lucy McCormick Calkins, Kate Montgomery, and Donna Santman, *A Teacher's Guide to Standardized Reading Tests: Knowledge Is Power*.

92. Lucy McCormick Calkins, Kate Montgomery, and Donna Santman, *A Teacher's Guide to Standardized Reading Tests: Knowledge Is Power*.

CHAPTER 13

93. Grant P. Wiggins and Jay McTighe. *Understanding By Design*. (Alexandria, Virginia: Association for Supervision and Curriculum Development, 1998).

94. Benjamin Bloom. "The Search for Methods of Group Instruction as Effective as One to One Tutoring." *Educational Leadership* 41, no. 8 (1984): 4–17; Richard J. Stiggins, Judith A. Arter, Jan Chappuis, and Stephen Chappuis. *Classroom Assessment for Student Achievement: Doing It Right — Using It Well*. (Portland, Oregon: Assessment Training Institute, Inc., 2004); John Hattie. *Visible Learning for Teachers: Maximizing Impact on Learning*. (New York, New York: Routledge, 2012).

95. Richard J. Stiggins, Judith A. Arter, Jan Chappuis, and Stephen Chappuis. *Classroom Assessment for Student Achievement: Doing it Right — Using It Well;* Paul Bambrick-Santoyo. *Driven By Data: A Practical Guide to Improve Instruction*. (San Francisco, California: John Wiley & Sons, 2010).

CHAPTER 14

96. Jon Saphier, Mary-Ann Haley Speca, and Robert Gower, *The Skillful Teacher*.

97. Jon Saphier, Mary-Ann Haley Speca, and Robert Gower, *The Skillful Teacher*.

98. Lucy McCormick Calkins. *The Art of Teaching Writing*. (Portsmouth, New Hampshire: Heinemann, 1986).

99. Mihaly Csikszentmihalyi, *Flow: The Psychology of Optimal Experience*.

100. Chip Heath and Dan Heath. *Made to Stick: Why Some Ideas Survive and Others Die*.

101. Chip Heath and Dan Heath. *Switch: How to Change Things When Change Is Hard*. (New York, New York: Random House, 2011).

102. Tore Helstrup. "Serial Position Phenomenon: Memory for Acts, Contents and Spatial Position Patterns." *Scandinavian Journal of Psychology*, no. 25 (1984): 133–146.

103. Douglas Fisher and Nancy Frey. *Improving Adolescent Literacy: Strategies at Work*. (Upper Saddle River, New Jersey: Pearson/Merrill/Prentice Hall, 2004).

104. Richard J. Stiggins, Judith A. Arter, Jan Chappuis, and Stephen Chappuis, *Classroom Assessment for Student Achievement: Doing It Right — Using It Well*; Benjamin Bloom, "The Search for Methods of Group Instruction as Effective as One to One Tutoring"; Paul Black and Wiliam Dylan. "Inside the Black Box: Raising Standards Through Classroom Assessment." *Phi Delta Kappan* 80, no. 2 (1998): 139–148.

CHAPTER 15

105. Jon Saphier, and Mary Ann Haley. *Activators*. (Anton, Massachusetts: Research for Better Teaching, 1993).

106. Roxann Kriete, *The Morning Meeting Book*.

Index